# A Jewish Guide in the Holy Land

# A Jewish Guide in the Holy Land

*How Christian Pilgrims Made Me Israeli*

JACKIE FELDMAN

INDIANA UNIVERSITY PRESS

*Bloomington and Indianapolis*

This book is a publication of

INDIANA UNIVERSITY PRESS
Office of Scholarly Publishing
Herman B Wells Library 350
1320 East 10th Street
Bloomington, Indiana 47405 USA

iupress.indiana.edu

*Manufactured in the United States of America*

*Library of Congress Cataloging-in-Publication Data*

Names: Feldman, Jackie, author.
Title: A Jewish guide in the Holy Land : how Christian
    pilgrims made me Israeli / Jackie Feldman.
Description: Bloomington ; Indianapolis : Indiana University
    Press, [2016] | Includes bibliographical references and index.
Identifiers: LCCN 2015036094| ISBN 9780253021250 (cloth : alk. paper) |
    ISBN 9780253021373 (pbk. : alk. paper) | ISBN 9780253021489 (ebook)
Subjects: LCSH: Tourism—Israel. | Tourism—West Bank. | Christian
    pilgrims and pilgrimages—Israel. | Christian pilgrims and pilgrimages—
    West Bank. | Feldman, Jackie. | Tour guides (Persons)—Israel—Biography.
Classification: LCC G155.I78 F45 2016 | DDC 915.69404/54092—
    dc23 LC record available at http://lccn.loc.gov/2015036094

1 2 3 4 5   21 20 19 18 17 16

*To my beloved late grandparents, Max and Pola Lipschutz;*
*my father, Henri (Chaim) Feldman;*
*and my mother Ruth Feldman (may she live).*
*To my wife Rachel and my children Elika and Shaya.*
*And in tribute to my late professor and mentor, R. J. Zwi Werblowsky,*
*who introduced me to the passion of comparative religious study.*

# CONTENTS

# FOREWORD

It was a great pleasure for me to write a foreword to Jackie Feldman's book. I have been following Jackie's personal and academic careers—which have been, as this book shows, virtually inseparable—for well over thirty years. Our acquaintance began when Jackie was writing his MA thesis on Second Temple pilgrimages and consulted with me about sociological approaches to pilgrimage. It was a rare occasion in the Hebrew University for a student of the Department of Jewish Thought, in the Faculty of Humanities, to "cross lines" and approach someone in the Social Sciences Faculty for advice—most scholars in Jewish studies at that time kept away from a sociological perspective in their historical or religious studies. But it was a characteristic step for Jackie; as this book witnesses, he has specialized in crossing lines in his work as a Jewish guide of Christian pilgrims. Our early encounter also constituted an unintended beginning of his gradual transition from Jewish studies to social anthropology, which eventually became the discipline on which he based his academic career.

Jackie's doctoral dissertation, which he eventually turned into a book on the journeys of Israeli-Jewish youths to the Nazi extermination camps in Poland, was still a conventional anthropological study in which the author's voice is that of the participant-observer describing and analyzing the ideological background and the complexities of these pilgrimages to sites of death. However, save for stating his personal engagement with the topic, he did not dwell on his own role in those trips and kept himself in the background. In sharp contrast, this book is a hybrid work that straddles the boundaries between personal biography, autoethnography, and anthropology, in which the author entertains a double position, constituting as much a part of the *explanans* as of the *explanandum*.

Being multifaceted, Jackie's book can be read according to different scripts: I believe that the most significant one is the autobiographic—that of the unique, perhaps idiosyncratic way in which Jackie, an immigrant to Israel, escaped the stultified atmosphere of Orthodox Judaism in the United States and formed his Jewish identity and his relationship to Judaism and Israel in the course of his work as a Jew guiding Christians in the Holy Land. He achieved that not by confronting Christianity but rather by engaging with it deeply and sympathetically, without identifying with it. The descriptions of his rhetoric performances, in which he takes a Christian religious perspective while at the same time establishing a border between himself as a Jew and the Evangelical Christian pilgrims, are among the most interesting and entertaining features of the book. But his gambit could succeed, as Jackie himself recognizes, only in the spatially and temporarily isolated context of the pilgrimage situation.

A second script touches upon the role of Jackie's encounter with the Christian pilgrims in the formation of his attitude to Israel. Notably, he invokes Ahad Ha'am's vision of Jewish autonomy, as a precondition for Jewish cultural flourishing, rather than Herzl's vision of Jewish independence in a national state. Jackie is not a political Zionist, and he hardly mentions Zionism in the book. Indeed, Jackie's encounter with the harsh but petty realities of Israeli daily life, in which he found himself, as an "Anglo-Saxon" immigrant, an outsider, led him to choose guiding as an opportunity to present the Holy Land to pilgrims on a grander scale, unencumbered by those distractions. At the same time, his encounters with Arab coworkers in the course of his work made him aware of the plight of the Palestinians under Israeli rule, turning him into an increasingly more critical citizen of his adopted country.

Finally, the book is an exceptionally perceptive and insightful piece of anthropological research that could have been written only by a researcher with a long and varied experience with different denominations of Christian pilgrims and their distinctive perspectives and interests. And only an anthropologist with an experienced guide's rhetorical abilities could have given us such a lively and often amusing insider's story of how Christian pilgrimages to the Holy Land are performed.

Jackie believes that the Holy Land, despite different readings of the symbols inscribed on its landscape, provides a common ground on which Jewish guides and Christian pilgrims could meet. The book's message is one of Jewish-Christian mutual understanding, if not of total reconciliation of their divergent interpretations of that landscape. But this is achievable only due to the suspension of the pilgrimage situation from the realities of ordinary life. Implicit in Jackie's presentation is the realization that a similar mutual understanding between Israeli Jews and Palestinian Arabs is not so easily achievable, because their encounter cannot be suspended from those realities. But he still believes that there is space enough in the Holy Land for both these people to coexist.

*Erik Cohen*
*Bangkok, February 2015*

# ACKNOWLEDGMENTS

ONE SUMMER, A couple of years after I had become a licensed Israeli tour guide, I was sitting in my grandfather's office in New York. He took me downstairs to the diamond bourse to show me off. An old acquaintance of his, a diamond dealer from Antwerp like himself, came by, and he boasted of his grown grandchildren: "There's Ronnie, he's in Peace Studies at Berkeley. And David, he's in quantum mechanics; Jongy, he went into the Business. And Jackie," he turned to me, "he lives in Israel."

My grandfather, of blessed memory, reckoned that nothing good, or at least nothing very respectable, could come out of tour guiding. In part, I wrote this book to prove him wrong.

This research would not have been possible without the help and support of my colleagues. I thank my friends at Ben Gurion University of the Negev who read and commented on drafts of the book and related articles: Fran Markowitz, Nir Avieli, Andre Levy, Lev Grinberg, and the late Shmuel Ben-Dor, as well as other members of the Department of Sociology and Anthropology. Thanks also to Yoram Bilu, Virginia Dominguez, Kirsten Endres, Harvey Goldberg, Moshe David Herr, Michael Herzfeld, Steve Langfur, Chaim Noy, Amnon Raz-Karakotzkin, Amos Ron, David Satran, Adoram Schneidleder, Keren-Or Schlesinger, and Detleva Tochova and to my research assistants Smadar Farkas, Michal Padeh, Josh Schmidt, Matan Shapiro, and Michele Syen, as well as the anonymous readers of the publications that reviewed the manuscript and previous articles. Special thanks to Yael Guter for material from tourguide interviews and to my fellow guide and professor Amos Ron for the innumerable conversations in the tour guide course hotel dining rooms, cafeterias, community colleges, cars, desert jeeps, seminars, each other's houses, coffee shops, and every other place we have schmoozed in over the last thirty-five years.

Thanks to my mentors Don Handelman and the late Zwi Werblowsky and to Erik Cohen, who not only stimulated my thinking through his critical reading and conversation but also graciously agreed to write a foreword for this book. I am grateful to Burkhard Schnepel and the Martin Luther University, Halle, Germany, and to the Katz Center at the University of Pennsylvania for their support and the excellent conditions they provided for writing and thinking on my sabbatical in 2012. Research was supported by two grants from the Israel Science Foundation: "Christian Pilgrim, Jewish Guide, Holy Land: Negotiations of Religious Identity (77/03)," and "Guide My Sheep: Catholic Pilgrim Guides in Historical and Ethnographic Perspective (291/13)" (with Yvonne Friedman).

Without the gracious and open conversations with Hani and Sami Abu-Dayyeh of Near East Tours, as well as with the many drivers and guides who have worked with them and with me over the years, this research would not have been possible.

Finally, to my wife Rachel and children Elika and Shaya, who have had to put up with my guide stories and mental absence twice—once when guiding and once again when reliving the experiences for the book: I couldn't have done it without you.

The material in this book draws on my previous articles and book chapters, though this material is expanded and considerably revised. These publications include "How Guiding Christians Made me Israeli," in *Ethnographic Encounters in Israel*, edited by Fran Markowitz, 23–39 (Bloomington: Indiana University Press, 2013); "Contested Narratives of Storied Places—The Holy Lands,"*Religion and Society* 5 (2014): 106–127; Amos Ron and Jackie Feldman, "From Spots to Themed Sites—The Evolution of the Protestant Holy Land,"*Journal of Heritage Tourism* 4, no. 3 (2009): 201–216; "Constructing a Shared Bible Land: Jewish-Israeli Guiding Performances for Protestant Pilgrims,"*American Ethnologist* 34, no. 2 (2007): 349–372; "Abraham the Settler, Jesus the Refugee: Contemporary Conflict and Christianity on the Road to Bethlehem,"*History and Memory* 23, no. 1 (2011): 62–96; "Changing Colors of Money: Tips, Commissions, and Ritual in Christian Pilgrimage to the Holy Land,"*Religion and Society* 5 (2014): 143–56; "Vehicles of Values: Souvenirs and the Moralities of Exchange in Christian Holy Land Pilgrimage," in *Towards an Anthropology of Nation Building and Unbuilding in Israel: Essays in Honor of Alex Weingrod*, edited by Fran Markowitz, Stephen Sharot, and Moshe Shokeid, 259–273 (Lincoln: University of Nebraska Press, 2014); and "The Seductions of Guiding Pilgrims," in *The Seductions of Pilgrimage: On and Off the Roads to the Sacred*, edited by Michael diGiovini and David Picard (New York: Palgrave, 2016).

As the reader will see, I've put a lot of myself into this book. Even when I depict other guides' experiences, they resonate with my own. For this reason, I have used "he" rather than "she" as the default pronoun. I believe that most of the dynamics I discuss applies equally to women guides, although the sexual and gender tensions between female guides, on the one hand, and male pastors and drivers, on the other, still await description.

# A Jewish Guide in the Holy Land

# 1 HOW GUIDING CHRISTIANS MADE ME ISRAELI

IT'S ALMOST 6 o'clock and still over 90 degrees outside. I'm guiding a British charismatic ministry through the sites of Jesus's ministry around the Sea of Galilee. The packed tour bus jiggles and bounces over the patched road on its way back to the hotel. I take the microphone and turn to the group: "Ladies and gentlemen, if you have any questions, about anything whatsoever that I might have explained today, please feel free to ask."

A middle-aged Salvation Army guy with an Irish brogue pipes up: "Why don't you Jews accept Jesus Christ as your true Lord and Savior?" I launch into a five-minute explanation on conflicting messianic expectations, varying interpretations of Isaiah, the plurality of Jewish sects in Jesus's day, and how the contingencies of history formed deniers and followers of Jesus into Jews and Christians. After five minutes, I put down the microphone. Dead silence. Fifty-five people crammed into the bus and not a sound but the drone of the motor.

A sweet woman in the fifth row tries to help out. "I once heard the Chief Rabbi of England say that when the Jews' messiah arrives, he wouldn't at all be surprised if indeed he were Jesus." Well, I guessed at what the Chief Rabbi might have meant. And I knew that none of the group would understand it that way. For them, the Chief Rabbi had admitted that "the Jews got it wrong first time, but they'll do better next time around." In most circumstances, I would have put down the microphone and continued to the hotel in silence. I don't have to answer. But this time, I am tired. Very tired. So I take the mike and say, "You know, ladies and gentlemen, the Chief Rabbi of England is right. I wouldn't at all be surprised. But you would!" The group's pastor grabs the mike and harrumphs, "Well, let's all look at *tomorrow's* program."

At age 22, I, a once-Orthodox Jew from New York City, came on *aliya* to Israel to study Jewish philosophy and see if I could make my future in a Jewish homeland far away from the Jewish home I grew up in. Three years later, I had become a licensed tour guide, working for Palestinian tour agents specializing in Christian tours to the Holy Land. For reasons I only gradually learned to understand, I had chosen to make my living as a *rebbe far di goyim*, a rabbi for the Gentiles, presenting and representing Israel, Judaism, and Christianity to a variety of Christian groups from Northern Europe and the United States. I encountered people I probably would never have met otherwise and played a variety of roles, which I came to see as dynamic performances not only for pilgrims but for myself as well. By presenting the land, Judaism, sacred texts, and myself to Christians, I came to appreciate and interrogate my own relations to Judaism, Israeli belonging, voyages of memory, Israeli-Palestinian politics, and religious truths in new ways.

When I first arrived in Israel, guiding seemed a natural choice. My chances of financial survival as an MA student of Jewish philosophy were slim. The tour guide course offered a chance to learn the lay of the land, spend time with Israelis, connect my Jewish textbook knowledge with the realia of mountains, streams, and buried stones – and have fun doing it. Tour guiding offered (or so I thought) a flexible schedule that would enable me to earn a decent living without disrupting my studies. I loved to travel and spoke several European languages, and I enjoyed telling jokes and being on stage. I knew Jewish history and the Bible, had studied Second Temple Jewish thought, and had taken courses in early Christianity and New Testament Greek. I even kind of liked Jesus, especially when he acted like an *apikores*, a heretic in face of authority. I found some of the moralizing and coming-of-the-kingdom apocalypticism a bit heavy, but in his encounters with the Pharisees, Jesus told them what I'd have liked to say to my high school rabbis but didn't dare. After all, straining out gnats and swallowing camels (Matthew 23:24) was a common pastime of quite a few of them. And anyone who overturned the tables of the money-changers in the temple couldn't be bad.

So, after finishing the tour guide course, leading lethargic Jewish teenagers on long hikes in the summer heat, and presenting my face and business card to an endless array of Israeli and Palestinian travel agents ("We'll call if we need you"), I was offered a real job working for a Palestinian tour company, guiding British Protestants, and later German Catholics, Dutch Reformed, and American Evangelicals. Why Palestinians? Because they offered me work. Why Christians? Probably because I feared that working with Jewish visitors, most of them American, might remind me too much of where I came from. The enclave diaspora mentality that I'd come to Israel to escape might provoke allergies. Also, I thought I knew enough about Jews and wanted to meet someone else. As for nonreligious visitors, many are "post-tourists" who delight in rapid shifts from cynical distance to serious contemplation to hedonistic enjoyment. They enjoy the play of surfaces and the inauthenticity of tourist attractions as a mark of their own connoisseurship and "coolness."[1] Pilgrims, on the other hand, often come in search of a "hotter" authenticity, a more profound sense of self.[2] They want to learn and experience rather than merely relax and be entertained.[3] As a student and sometimes practitioner of religion, I thought they'd be more interested – and more interesting.

Guiding pilgrims also meshed with my own religious search: I had come to Israel out of a strong sense of Jewish commitment, mixed with a deep dissatisfaction with the Orthodox Jewish milieu I was raised in. I was convinced that the rabbis who had educated me had hidden something from me. There must have been more to Judaism than what they fed me in Washington Heights: obedience to the Law, obsession with halakhic detail, preparation for upward mobility, and defense of the borders of the enclave against the ogres of anti-Semitism and assimilation. I registered for a masters' degree in Jewish Thought at Hebrew University, hoping to study the history of heresy. I sought fellow travelers. I began reading Dead Sea Scrolls and the New Testament in Aramaic and Koiné Greek. I sought an ur-period of unity, before exile and defensiveness, before the Talmudic hair-splitting and the bourgeois conformity my New York rabbis worshipped.

When I began guiding, I was working on a thesis on Second Temple pilgrimage. On opening the authoritative work at the time, Shmuel Safrai's *Pilgrimage to the Second Temple*, I was dismayed to find the long first chapter devoted to "the commandment of pilgrimage."[4] Impossible, I thought. Are my rabbis here too? Did Jewish pilgrims 2,000 years ago carry miniature law books in their pockets and call their rabbis to ask, "am I or am I not required to go to Jerusalem this year?" What interested me was the pilgrims' experience. What did pilgrimage provide them that made them undergo sacrifice and hardship to come to Zion? In Victor and Edith Turner's writing, I found, not the concern with following the rules, but the transformative search for liminality, for a break from structure and transformation through sensory experience.[5] I sought evidence of this experience in the texts of Josephus, the Apocrypha, Philo, and the Mishnah. And I imagined I would find it among the Christian pilgrims I guided. They too might be fellow travelers.

Working with British Protestants (both Church of England and "nonconformist") was indeed a learning experience. In time, I would learn to decipher their cultural codes: distasteful food was "interesting," a breathtaking sight was "lovely, isn't it?," and complaints were to be addressed by letter to the travel agent two weeks following return home. More challenging were the religious encounters. Pilgrims' attitudes to Judaism and Israel were shaped not so much by contemporary Israeli-Palestinian politics as by Christian theological views on Judaism that were incorporated into Western cultural understandings – even if pilgrims were not aware of them. While many interactions were determined by the institutional framework of the guided tour, the structure was flexible enough to allow guides like me to relate a variety of narratives and present myself in several different roles.

## PERFORMING JEWISHNESS FOR CHRISTIAN PILGRIMS

The groups I was assigned to guide came, for the most part, on 8–15-day tours, along with their pastor or priest. Whereas in other institutionalized group excursions, "the principal expectation of mass tourists from Professional Guides is that they provide information and interpretation," in pilgrim groups, the pastoral leader often plays a major interpretative role through his readings and sermons.[6] The knowledge pilgrims request most is knowledge that augments their faith experience. The "head" of the leader and guide is valued as a tool for reaching the "heart."

The groups' itineraries focused on sites of significance to Christian faith and history, and were frequently advertised as "a walk in the footsteps of Jesus." They regularly conducted Christian worship, read Bible passages, and sang hymns in the course of their visit. The pilgrims inhabit an environmental bubble, which intensifies interaction within the group while protecting the group from most direct contact with the surrounding environment.[7] Thus, the tour guide (and sometimes, the driver) is often the only local person they converse with in the course of their visit.

Besides being a "native," as a Jew, I was marked by pilgrims in certain emotionally charged ways. Jews were seen as people of the Book, as bearers of the longest memory and as older natives of the land, who possess geographical and scriptural knowledge. They became witnesses and authenticators of Christian sites and truths, often in spite of themselves.[8] Whatever Christian pilgrims' views of Israel and Jews, they are rarely indifferent.

As is frequently the case in intercultural encounters in commodified tourism, the visitors' images of the country and its inhabitants, which are at variance with the daily realities on the ground, often create pressure on the part of "native" guides and service workers to comply with touristic images.[9] Thus, both the structure of the roles on the guided tour and the spiritually charged nature of biblical knowledge may place the Jewish guide in the position of mediator between Christian pilgrims and their sacra – the Bible, Jesus, and the holy places. I should add that in this encounter, not only are these sacra charged with a history of painful (Christian-Jewish) power relations, but some of those sacred symbols are shared by Jews and Christians, who interpret them in very different but partially overlapping ways.

Many guides deal with these sources of tension (which they discover only gradually, usually by trial and error) by employing subtle strategies to distinguish between themselves and the spiritual leader and mark role distance without offending the pilgrims on whom they rely for their livelihood. I chose another path.

On my very first job guiding a Christian group headed by a booming-voiced evangelist from Cornwall, we approached the Catholic Church of the Beatitudes. At the time, the area around the perimeter of the church had been excavated, and workmen were injecting concrete around the foundations to protect the church from structural damage caused by settling.

"Why are they doing that?" inquired Pastor Don.

I answered, "To prevent the floor from cracking. You see, the church is built on sand."

"Oho!" he exclaimed. "There's my next sermon!"

From my successful initiation into guiding Christian groups, I deduced that the planting of emotionally resonant and frequently multivocal symbols was often more important than the train of historical causation or the details of specific cultural meanings. Even Scripture has a wide penumbra that may include commentaries, expositions, and even other texts intoned to sound like Scripture.[10] The evocation of resonant symbols and key words was frequently commended by the group's pastor and applauded by the group members. Yet my playful attempts at seduction were sometimes misunderstood as the profession of a shared faith or as the first step toward a relationship of commitment and conversion. This issue became most acute in my work with Evangelical or Fundamentalist Protestant groups. For many, the world was divided into Christians and heathens, and perhaps also biblical Hebrews who haven't yet seen the light. What's more, many came from "seeker churches," whose membership included many who had grown up in a variety of other denominations or even religions. For them, I was often a prime target for conversion. My "strategy of seduction" complicated matters, insofar as I spoke sympathetically of Jesus, recited by heart passages of the New Testament, or neglected to add the distancing phrase "according to tradition" before each mention of, say, Jesus's miracles at a particular site. After all, I thought, Jesus was Jewish, and my job was to bring the Bible to life throughout the land – not to expound my personal religious or political views – right?

Repeatedly, I found my position misconstrued. Even if I took care to stand to the side during their prayers and not speak of Jesus as "messiah," "our Lord," or "savior," groups would ask, "So when did you discover Jesus?" Theological explanations on Jewish messianic beliefs rarely made a difference; the same questions and testifying would continue. To borrow Evangelical terminology, for them, if I wasn't born again yet, by talking the talk, I had demonstrated that I had "come under conviction."[11]

Next, I tried ritual. On the day of our visits to the Western Wall, I packed my *tallit* (prayer shawl) and *tefillin* (phylacteries) in my backpack. When we arrived at the plaza in front of the wall, I wrapped myself in the tallit, recited the blessings in Hebrew, wound the tefillin around my arm, and translated the accompanying prayer text to them. As the group photographed me, while looking at the similarly attired worshippers at the wall, I sensed the coin dropping. "Ah, he's not one of us." Even for Evangelicals, ritual did the trick; it marked the border. Afterwards, they would ask me, "So what do you Jews think of Jesus?" That was an improvement.

After a year or so of these tallit and tefillin performances at the Western Wall, I reconsidered. At age 16, my father gave me hell for not putting on tefillin for prayer each morning. "Your father put on tefillin, your grandfather wore tefillin! Your cousins all wear tefillin! Only you – no. No-good family!" I refused to wear the phylacteries to please my father. Was I now going to put them on for show to please the *goyim*?

The religious context of the performance (at the Western Wall, at prayer time, like that done by the worshippers at the wall) left little room for role distance. Was I not then saying – to them and ultimately to myself – that this is what real Jews do? How then would I explain, if asked, why I did not put on tefillin every day without appearing totally irreligious and irreverent?

This interaction was a precarious tango with religious symbols across religious lines. The ritual worked in defining an effective border between myself-as-Jew and them-as-Christians because the context was perceived as religious and worthy of respect, especially since the prayer text I recited over the tallit and translated for them referred to verses that are part of the Christian Bible as well. Because donning the tallit and tefillin and reciting the prayer could be seen as an act of commitment (which, in certain ways, it was), they might then expect me to behave as Orthodox do in order to be authentically Jewish in their eyes.[12]

Thus, the tourist/pilgrim gaze on the religious symbols changes their nature for myself as performer as well.[13] As the group's gaze moves from the leather straps on my arm to those worn by the Hasidim praying closer to the wall, what do they see? Do they reclassify me as an outsider? Have the Hasidim now become less strange? Or, perhaps, do the onlookers come to appreciate that their Jesus wore straps much like these, and was, in fact, far more Jewish than they had imagined previously? As in the case of many natives' representations of their culture to outsiders, the tourists'/pilgrims' interpretation of symbols can never be fully controlled by the performers.

In retrospect, I wonder, why didn't I take the safer path of role distance and separation, letting the pastor do the "religious stuff"? First, because it's less fun. If I'm on stage, why not get a good role? I saw my challenge as not just providing information but as crafting an itinerary partly determined by geography and economics into the path of the pilgrims' progress. In this project, I was aided by many pastors, especially Evangelical ones. Catholic pilgrimages during Holy Week are structured around liturgy so that following the events of the Passion may become a leitmotif for the entire journey. Thus, the "native" liturgy of the group performs the work of structuring time and space, syncopating the rhythm of pilgrimage. For most Protestants, whose pilgrimages are less in tune with calendrical cycles of ritual, the pastor may employ ritual and sermons to structure time and tune expectations. As one pastor I worked with summed up his sermon at the Sea of Galilee:

> We haven't come here to take pictures, though we will take pictures. We haven't come here to be world travelers, though you are all now world travelers. We haven't come here to be educated, though we've all learned much. We've come to seek our God and dedicate ourselves to Him. . . . The purpose of this trip is not travel, education and enjoyment, but to have ourselves drawn nearer to our Creator. . . . So, when you come back, you can tell your friends that the plane ride was terrible. Or you can tell them how the spirit of God touched you.

The rhetoric and feeling tone create a performative repetition that helps orient the religious tourists away from the rhythms and (dis)comforts of mass tourism and toward the spiritual goals designated by the pastors. And many of these rhetorical devices and feeling tones are accessible to non-Evangelical guides. Their successful adoption gives rise to appreciation, applause, and often, a larger tip (or "love-offering") at the end of the voyage.[14]

Second, my willingness to take some risks allowed me a safe space for play. The liminal frame of pilgrimage allows not only for communitas but also for religious flirtation in a time-space that is safe because it is well demarcated: "this is (only) a pilgrimage." The timeframe of the guided pilgrimage is limited: even the worst group leaves in ten days. I don't have to answer to them when they're gone, or even once they check into the hotel at night. My citations of the New Testament in front of the group will not have the same effect as reading the text out loud for my family at home. When my daughter was a child, and I was at the beginning of my guiding career, I would recite to her biblical (First Testament) stories each night before bedtime. One day, when I could not think of a new story, I began telling her a story about Jesus. After ten minutes I stopped and decided never to tell her a New Testament story at bedtime again. Let the New Testament stories, if she reads them as an adult, be just stories, while the Hebrew Bible stories remain "Daddy's stories," imbued with the emotional warmth of bedtime storytelling.

Within the setting of the tour and within the constraints/permission of professional conduct as guide, I could read, appreciate, and perform the New Testament without being suspected (or at least, without necessarily being suspected) of having converted to Christianity. My friend and veteran tour guide Steve Langfur formulated it as follows:

> Like a picture-frame or a cinema film, or a book, or a ceremony . . . the role of the frame is that you leave your disordered life, which is the "real" life. . . . When you're in the frame, for the time of the frame you leave your defenses behind. . . . Nothing can harm me as long as I'm inside the frame. . . . The group stands together as one to listen to you at the site. In the tour, you move from frame to frame, and in each frame, everyone feels at ease. Some of our defenses can be relinquished, so we feel more open. The frame includes the distance. I and they are inside this frame, so I don't need to establish additional distance from the group (Interview, June 2004).

Perhaps it was that same frame that made things safe enough for me to proclaim a connection to my tefillin-wearing father without worrying about crossing the lines into Orthodoxy. Perhaps through guiding I obtained recognition as a Jew in the liminal capacity of rabbi-for-the-Gentiles without having to work through all the ambivalences and making the commitments entailed in being a Jew-among-the-Jews in Israeli social space.

Guides frequently become authorities on Israel and the Bible as well as objects of adulation on the part of pilgrims, who depend on their guides' historical and geographical knowledge to provide material "proofs" for their Christian faith. Some guides succumb to the (frequently expressed) admiration and come to believe that they're as smart as their pilgrims say they are. I found that the well-defined frame of the guided tour, supplemented by minirituals of decompression at the end of the day (like moving my hand down across my face to "peel away" the frozen smile), facilitated transition from the role of exemplary Jew to the quotidian responsibilities of father and husband. Thus, while I felt the role strains of accommodating pilgrims' expectations, I did not reach the stage of questioning my own authenticity in daily life, as described in the case of stewardesses who could no longer distinguish their real feelings from their professional presentations of self.[15]

As a knowledgeable, Hebrew-speaking "older brother" and guardian of the Book, I could even venture onto the pilgrims' holy ground, incorporating Jesus into a chain of Jewish tradition, though not always without contestation: "The Chief Rabbi of England is right. I wouldn't at all be surprised. But you would!"

## BECOMING A NATIVE THROUGH GUIDING

When, before I left New York, I told my friends I had decided to come on aliya to Israel, I spoke of leaving the moribund swamp of America to live where the Jewish future would be made. While I was certainly influenced by the communitas of New York rallies for Israel and for Soviet Jewry, and the safety and freedom of movement I experienced on my summer visits to Israel, I had also been impressed by the writings of Zionist thinker Ahad Ha'am. According to Ahad Ha'am, only Israel could become a center for spiritual renewal for the Jewish world, because Judaism could only thrive as a viable modern culture under physical and political conditions that granted it a measure of autonomy. In exile, he wrote, the practice of Judaism could not be sheltered from the power of the omnipresent Gentile gaze. Hence it would either fashion itself as a walled enclave or accommodate itself to the Gentile gaze and assimilate.[16] The State of Israel was to be a place of freedom from other majority cultures.

This attracted me. The Judaism I grew up with, in a high-crime mixed Jewish-Irish-Dominican neighborhood of New York, was the Judaism of side streets and interiors. "Remember Hitler and the other goyim who want you dead." Jews were inside – in the homes, schools, synagogues; goyim were on the streets, in the street. My grandmother would remind me, "Don't park your car on the wrong side of Broadway. . . . Always carry a quarter for the muggers. . . . Come home right after school and study for your exams. . . . You wanna grow up to be a *sheigitz* [non-Jewish man]?"[17]

The Land of Israel that attracted me at age 22 was a land of open spaces without danger, a land of being in the majority, a place where one didn't need to be religious to be Jewish. The street was Jewish and – at least in Tel Aviv – it had sand that got into your sandals, and it ended at the beach. And it was far away from my Orthodox home.

The Israel I found when I moved here was not the Israel of my dreams. I spent hours waiting in the wrong lines in banks, post offices, government ministries; I lacked *protekzia*, the connections that might ease my way through bureaucracies. I struggled with the far more impersonal university system. Though I spoke Hebrew well, for years merchants and people on the street would address me in English. The wide-open Jewish country fragmented into territories of Arabs and Jews, Palestinians and Israelis, Orthodox and secular, Mizrahim and Ashkenazim. If in New York I was a Jew, in Israel I became an American, or most bizarrely, an "Anglo-Saxon." My new friends were mostly recent immigrants from the West, and the religious communities that might have been options for affiliation turned out to be – to my horror – entirely populated by Americans!

The tour guide course I entered a year after my arrival was, for me, an initiation into Israeliness. While hiking was an integral part of Israeli *sabra* culture, the links made between the land and the biblical text resounded with my New York yeshiva day school education.[18] Hiking uniquely tied the desire for physicality and open space with a familiar Jewish grounding. It linked the small place of mountains and valleys with the big place of historical Israel.[19] It took Judaism out of the classroom and into the valleys and fields in ways that made sense to me.

By being the guide to the Land of Israel I could overcome the cognitive dissonance of my own aliya to Israel. One of the ways of overcoming cognitive dissonance, write Festinger et al., is by missionizing, bringing the outside world into accord with one's own beliefs.[20] In this case, it was the belief and practice of "preaching" Israel as the "big place" of Jewish/Biblical history and destiny, rather than the "small place" of local daily life. By "making souls" for the land, showing how a geographic understanding of the land and a knowledge of Jewish history could enrich pilgrims' own faith and their link to Israel, I could acquire a role as an exemplary Israeli that was denied me as a new immigrant in Israeli society. Given that status, and the distribution of power between Jewish-Israeli guide and Christian-foreign pilgrim, I could also let Jesus be Jewish without worrying that my Hanukkah menorah would be obscured by the shadow of an enormous Christmas tree. Ahad Ha'am was right.

So, my turn to tour guiding was a way of being in Israel without being with Israelis, being home while spending my time away from home. The enthusiasm displayed by pilgrims in many of the sites and vistas of the land (and my assigned task of stimulating it) also recharged the emotional connection to the land that had originally brought me here but that had weakened with time and routine. And of course, it provided me with a livelihood that enabled me to build a home and a family in Israel. What's more, it endowed me with an honorary status – as Israeli, knowledgeable Jew, and for some Evangelicals, agent of the divine plan. As several pilgrims asked me in the later days of their voyage, "Don't you feel privileged to come back home?" In part thanks to the pilgrims, I did.

## TOUR GUIDING AND POLITICAL AWARENESS

The two-year-long tour guide course was my initiation into Israeliness. I spent twelve class hours each week studying archaeology, history, flora and fauna (quite new to a Manhattan boy), religions, and more. Once a week over the course of two years, the fifty participants would travel by bus to hike, take notes, and mark up our 1:50,000 contour maps at sites throughout the country. The courses were sponsored by the Ministry of Tourism, and placed emphasis on the Jewish and Zionist heritage of the country. Occasionally we were reminded that we were Israel's best ambassadors. After graduating from the course, when I first stepped on a tour bus of Christian pilgrims, the link between the Jewish people, the Land of Israel, and the State of Israel seemed to me to be natural and self-evident.

As it turned out, my first and principal employers were Palestinian travel agents located in East Jerusalem. Making the rounds of travel agents on Ez-Zahara Street, entering their offices to be interviewed over Arab coffee, was a crossing of borders, even if it was only two miles from my home. At times I would frequent more shops and meet more people on the main street of Arab East Jerusalem than in the center of Jewish West Jerusalem. I developed a taste for Turkish coffee. These travel agencies, owned by Palestinian Christians and staffed by both Christians and Muslims, worked primarily with Christian pilgrims. They used Palestinian-owned bus companies and employed Palestinian drivers and, frequently, Israeli guides. At one point, after the establishment of the Palestinian Authority, my chief employer explained, "We've come under pressure from the Arab Tourist Agency to use only Arab guides. I tell them, *t'faddalu* [please], you give me licensed Arab guides who know the tourists' language well enough and are knowledgeable enough in Bible and history and I'll hire them. Until then, I can't afford to lose the business." I also learned from him of the difficulties in competing with Jewish-owned hotels that received tax benefits from the state, the delays and searches at the airport and at the Allenby Bridge when he left or reentered the country, and his virtuosity in using his leadership skills during a nine-month term for tax evasion in an Israeli prison to enhance his standing in Palestinian society.

The Palestinian bus drivers I worked with also provided new and often unexpected insights, primarily into the realities of life in East Jerusalem under Israeli rule during the first *Intifada* (uprising) – building permits denied, schools closed for months, older sons rounded up and taken out of their houses at night, and the concern of fathers to provide life skills for their children and keep them out of trouble and prison. Above all, I became aware of the precariousness of their employment situations and how essential extended family networks were to their survival. If no tourism work was available – and sometimes tourism would cease for months or even years at a time, as during the second Intifada – drivers were frequently laid off. Even more than Israeli tour guides, Palestinian drivers had very few alternative income opportunities. To survive hard times, they often invested in the networks of their extended families, lending each other money for a wedding, house building, or the purchase of tour buses and taxis. This precariousness often made drivers extremely hungry for the tourist dollars available, and some would pressure guides to arrange more controlled shopping time so as to increase their commissions. When a pastor I worked with took his pilgrim group to the shop of a "friend of his" on the group's free day (when the driver was assigned to another group and could not survey the group's purchases), the driver was indignant. "Who does he think he is? He comes here to take the bread out of the mouth of our children!"

As I continued to work with the same bus companies, I saw that within the tight network of Palestinian society and the still smaller one of Palestinian bus drivers, conversation and gossip served to build frameworks of confidence or suspicion. When I boarded a bus with a Palestinian driver and company I had never worked with before, more often than not the driver had received a report about me from his fellow drivers. A display of honesty and trust toward one driver would bring immediate dividends in the relationship with the next.

We rarely engaged in extended political discussions, although we did speak of the latest current events as they unfolded: Lebanon War, Oslo accords, Intifada. I listened to drivers' hope and subsequent disappointment with the peace process. I heard them curse Arafat and his Tunis cronies, saying even Israeli rule was better than the Palestinian Authority. "The main thing is that the tourists should come and we can make a living." At the beginning of the Intifada, one driver "rescued" me from the suspicious gaze of a Palestinian Authority policeman when, contrary to regulations, I tried to sneak into Bethlehem under cover of my American passport. I found myself stunned by the conspiracy theories some developed to explain the Six Day War, and moved by the generosity others displayed toward me. Once, when I was walking down the street near my house with my arm in a sling after a bicycle accident, a bus driver stopped the bus in the middle of the thoroughfare to ask how I was doing and offer me money to help while I was out of work.

None of these encounters made me a political activist. They did encourage suspicion toward some of the official Israeli terms I had previously accepted at face value: security risk, illegal construction, preventive detention. More importantly, they provided a human face with which to counter the stereotypes and generalizations of politicians and press, which surfaced in conversations among friends. To my friends' talk of the murderous hatred of the Palestinians (especially during the second Intifada, when four major suicide bombings took place within a half-mile of my home), I countered with the life stories of the drivers who sought the same future for their children that we sought for ours.

My basic Arabic improved, enriched with words for tour company, schedule, lunch, prayer, museum, priest, and percentage. There was even some tour bus code, often used to discuss money issues on the bus without alerting the pilgrims. Occasionally, religious discussions would arise. I remember one that made me reflect on my own religious orientations. Khalil and I were parked outside the Garden Tomb, waiting for the group to exit after their service. I turned to Khalil, who looked tired from fasting through the hot summer's day.

"So when will Ramadan end?"

"*Inshallah* [God willing], tomorrow," he answered. "If they don't sight the moon, then the day after." He then added, "You know, I heard that you Jews have the true calendar. You know exactly when the moon will appear." I smiled and told him that early Judaism had preferred the evidence of eyewitnesses (as in Islam), rather than calculation, and that the calculated date for the new moon was instituted only after the Byzantine rulers forbade the publicizing of the new moon by the *Sanhedrin*(the Jewish high court in the Second Temple and Roman-Byzantine periods). I then told him a *Midrash* (a corpus of interpretations, folk stories, and law linked to biblical texts) in which God sets up the chairs in the celestial court for the New Year and prepares the judgment books. At the very last moment, He is obliged to fold up the chairs and put everything away, because the Sanhedrin has announced that the new month will be postponed for a day. God then smiles and says, "My children, you have defeated me." Khalil was crestfallen. "But then that is the decision of men, not of God!" "Yes! Yes!" I exulted. "Once the Torah was given, it is up to human beings to interpret it."

Sitting in a bus outside the Garden Tomb, a Jewish tour guide and a Muslim bus driver conducted a discussion on revelation, tradition, and divine agency. This was more than I imagined when I decided to make my living as a tour guide.

In June 2000, I received my doctoral diploma. This was a record year for pilgrimage to the Holy Land. Until September, that is. Then the second Intifada broke out and tourism plummeted for four years. I diverted my energies to writing and searching for an academic position. I probably owe my academic career, in part, to the shortsightedness of Arafat and Barak. Had the peace process continued, I might have remained a tour guide for too long.

In the following years, with my immersion in academia and my distance from the daily practice of guiding, I reflected more on those practices and the political implications of tourism. When tourism and pilgrimage picked up again several years ago, the field had changed, and so had I.

In the 1980s, before cellphones and the internet, guides could improvise their schedules more and were essential in providing the interpretation of sites. Today, many sites are thoroughly institutionalized and must be booked in advance. This applies not only to Catholic masses but also to admission to Yad Vashem, City of David, the Herzl Museum, and the Western Wall tunnels, to mention only several sites in Jerusalem. Many of these sites offer multimedia presentations that provide the ideologically tinged interpretations of the site managers, making the guide's narrative on the site secondary, if not superfluous. Thus, the ideological content of tourist sites, which is present through their naming, framing, and elevation, has become far more intrusive than it was in the past, particularly for group tourists.[21] The guide has less freedom to place them within a temporal sequence and sociopolitical context of his choosing than he did in the past. If he does, he must compete with the audiovisuals.

Twenty years ago, the City of David was a half-reconstructed, lightly marked, sometimes garbage-strewn archaeological site open to the public all day and night. At its base was an ancient water tunnel (Hezekiah's Tunnel), shared by tourist/pilgrims, Arab children of Silwan who went there to play, and Hasidim who came to immerse in the water for purification. Guides provided candles and photocopies of the Siloam inscription for the tourists/pilgrims in their charge or had visitors purchase them from local Palestinian vendors. Today, reservations must be made in advance by Internet or phone at the visitors center. Many agents will book the high-tech three-dimensional presentation on the "eternal City of David," which portrays it as the heart of Israel ("here it all began") and creates a seamless narrative linking the biblical inhabitants with the Jewish settlers of today while ignoring the historical Palestinian and Muslim presence completely. The narrative, also presented in a state-of-the-art website, is further reinforced by selective excavation and reconstruction, pathmarking, signposting, and in-house narration (as documented for the Jewish Quarter in Abu el-Haj, 1998). The digs done by the Israel Archaeological Society in the middle of the Palestinian neighborhood of Silwan adjoining

Jerusalem's Old City walls are funded by the settlers' organization, El-Ad (an acronym for "to the City of David"). These excavations reveal "Jewish heritage," which must then be fenced off and protected. The system of excavated tunnels, marked paths, and signposts bypasses the Palestinian houses, while the declaration of the tunnel as a national heritage site (with paid admission) has effectively placed it off limits for the Palestinians of Silwan. El-Ad works with the Israel Defense Forces to make the site a required visit for all soldiers, with the Jerusalem Municipality to secure territories and enforce eviction orders against Palestinian residents of the area, and with the police to restrict movement of Palestinians through areas of their village during their guided tours.[22]

Otherwise put, when I began guiding, the political issues involved in tourism were invisible to me because I took for granted a new immigrant's image of Israel as the Promised Land and the consensual views of the tour guide course. As a result of changes in my political understanding, the critical eye on representation, the politics of memory fostered by anthropological discipline, and the more intrusive display of ideologies through multimedia presentations, I now find the site problematic. Pilgrimage involves the poetics of faith, rather than a hermeneutic of suspicion.[23] Most pilgrims have come to confirm their faith rather than challenge it. They want to see the place where David was, not receive a lesson in the politics of tourism. How, then, is one now to guide in such a place? It's hard to speak back to power without raising your voice.

## A RABBI FOR THE GENTILES

It's been more than thirty years since I first took the microphone on a tour bus. Over time, I learned to step back and shut up when hearing things I didn't like and felt I couldn't change. I also learned where and when I could introduce a grain of doubt into the shell of the tour and get away with it.

By now, I've spent most of my life in Israel; English is my children's third language (after Hebrew and my wife's French), and merchants will address me in Hebrew, even when I dress like a tourist. I no longer need the pilgrims to feel Israeli. My flirtation with Christianity has become less emotionally charged as I grow older and define myself in other situations, as opposed to other others – mainly Jewish-Israelis whose religious or political orientations I disagree with. In working with Christian groups, I sometimes marshal tried-and-tested answers to parry confrontations before they are voiced. Many of the religious questions I struggled with as a 22-year-old new immigrant, with his *kippa* (skullcap) no longer on his head but still in his pocket, have lost much of their urgency.

Yet I still guide Christian groups when I can find the time. I miss the enthusiasm and the applause, the escape from the office to the open air of the sites, the changing colors of the flowers in the Galilee, and the lively curiosity of visitors for whom the sites really matter. Perhaps, too, I miss the living presence of Christianity as the whetstone on which to sharpen my Jewish-Israeli identity.

The Jewish-Israeli/Christian encounter through pilgrimage continues to fascinate me – in spite of my occasional cynicism. The shared yet differing attachments to the Land of Israel and the Bible of differing groups of Jews and Christians made me aware of the role of imagination in understanding the Holy Land. It reminded me of how differing religious and cultural understandings can render familiar sites and texts strange and contingent.

Guiding Christian pilgrims for a Palestinian company also provided moments in which my own story, those of the Christian pilgrims I guided, and the Palestinian bus drivers that accompanied me intersected in ways that surprised me. While it can become an escape from the conflicts of daily life, the environmental bubble of pilgrimage may provide guides, as well as pilgrims, with the confidence and security that facilitate self-exploration and intimacy. At its best, it engenders moments in which an emotional and spiritual charge jumped the synapses of conflicting faiths and histories, to envelop us in communitas and – dare I say it? – hope. It reminded me, even through the course of two Intifadas, that the land, small as it is, is wide enough to accommodate more than one people, more than one truth. This is the story I will try to tell in the course of this book.

# 2 GUIDED HOLY LAND PILGRIMAGE: SHARING THE ROAD

THE HOLY LAND exerts tremendous force on the Christian imagination. In 2010, of the approximately 3.5 million tourists to Israel, about half were Christian pilgrims. Whether they refer to it as the Holy Land, the Bible Land, Palestine, Israel, or Zion, more and more Christians are coming to visit the sites where Jesus walked, preached, died on the cross, and was resurrected from the dead. Post-Soviet pilgrims now crowd the Holy Sepulchre. Three popes have come on pilgrimage in the course of fifteen years, encouraging flocks of Catholic faithful to follow. For Evangelicals – from the United States but also from Brazil and Nigeria – a voyage to the Holy Land is becoming an integral part of Christian practice and discourse. Most of these pilgrims come in organized groups and are guided by government-licensed Jewish-Israeli tour guides.

I have been a licensed guide for more than three decades; for more than twenty years, such groups provided me with my daily bread. The pilgrims I guided and studied came with their Bibles, their hymnals, and their faith but also with the images of conflict and violence broadcast on the evening news. Thus, at the outset, Israel/Palestine is not only the "cradle of civilization" and birthplace of Christianity but also the bloody battleground of Israelis and Palestinians, Jews and Muslims, and, for some, the church and the forces of the Antichrist. The guided group pilgrimage provides an environmental bubble that shelters pilgrims from the inconveniences and many of the conflicted quotidian realities of Israel/Palestine.[1] While it "keeps their eyes on Jesus," this protective bubble encloses not only the Christian pilgrim and his pastor but also the Jewish-Israeli guide, and the Palestinian (Muslim or Christian) driver. It creates a hothouse effect in which, over the course of an eight- to twelve-day tour, charged identity issues of participants and their guides ripen and ferment.

In the *Encyclopedia of Religion*, Edith Turner provides the following definition of pilgrimage:

A religious believer in any culture may sometimes look beyond the local temple, church or shrine. Feel the call of some distant holy place renowned for miracles and the revivification of faith and resolve to journey there.[2]

This definition, by the coauthor of what is probably the most influential anthropological book written on pilgrimage, *Image and Pilgrimage in Christian Culture* (1978), is significantly off-center: not "pilgrimage is" but "a religious believer . . . may sometimes look beyond . . . feel the call of some distant holy place." Not a condition but a process. Not a practice conforming to the logic of a social structure, but something sensed, heard, felt, seen, that attracts the seeker to resolve to transcend the horizon of his daily experience, the well-marked boundaries of his social world.

Eade and Sallnow, in their major critique of Victor Turner's universalist model, characterized pilgrimage as a realm of contested discourse – a conjunction of person, text, and place in which a variety of culturally and historically specific agents exercise power and shape discourse.[3] Simon Coleman suggested that this latter definition, though opposing Turner, essentially applies Turner's work on the multivocality of dominant symbols to pilgrimage itself.[4] A single place may "shape and express polysemic meanings of place for different users," what some scholars of pilgrimage refer to as confluence.[5] If a symbol's meaning is far more than its "legitimate" interpretation, then actors with widely divergent understandings of pilgrimage determine its meanings through their differing relations and actions in the shared pilgrimage sphere.[6]

In this spirit, I extend the frame of analysis of Christian pilgrimage to include the Jewish guide and the Christian pilgrims as performers of an interreligious phenomena – generators of a field of sometimes contested but often overlapping meanings. While such meanings are certainly produced by family and religious networks, traditional texts, and images consumed by pilgrims (and their guides) in the process of their socialization, something new happens in the performance of the pilgrimage. As Victor Turner emphasized, "The action situation of ritual, with its social excitement and direct physiological stimuli . . . effects an interchange of qualities between its poles of meaning.[7] Norms and values on the one hand, become saturated with emotion, while the gross and basic emotions become ennobled through contact with social values."

This analytic frame builds on several recent tendencies in research on pilgrimage and tourism. If the anthropology of tourism was dominated by the paradigm of "hosts and guests," I will accentuate the role of guides as mediators of cultural and religious experience; such mediators are neither completely "of the place" nor "of the (pilgrim) group."[8] While I will not ignore the differences between the roles, aims, and performances of Jewish-Israeli guide and those of foreign Christian pilgrim, I see pilgrimage as a contact zone in which the guide-as-native leaves his home to interact in a fluid, international, and inter-religious space.[9]

As I will demonstrate in the course of this book, for both guide and pilgrim, the land, as viewed, explained, and performed in pilgrimage, can never be fused entirely with the quotidian life-world. Thus, the guided tour is a liminal space for both guide and pilgrim. Even when players attempt to assume a well-defined role – Christian pilgrim or Jewish guide – the action mode of bodily performance and the significance sedimented in land and Bible pull toward a unity-in-difference. Even profound theological, national, and political differences between the performers that may surface in pilgrimage are a function of the guide's and group's ability to inhabit a shared space of significance and performance.

This perspective heightens the performative dimension of pilgrimage as a ritual whose meanings, in spite of millennia of ecclesiastic institutionalization, are largely generated through creative interactions in which participants may be caught up, in spite of themselves.[10] Of course, what pilgrims get out of their voyage depends greatly on what they bring with them and on the continuities of the experiences of pilgrimage in their home religious life on their return. Indeed, Hillary Kaell has recently authored a book that takes this approach, following American Christian women before, during, and after their voyage to the Holy Land/Bible Land. I find that both pilgrims and guides recognize the gap between pilgrimage and daily life outside.[11] I chose to follow here the emphases of my mentor, Don Handelman, who criticizes the hermeneutic approach to rituals as overemphasizing the interface between ritual and daily life. "The ease of slippage between the mundane and the ritual," writes Handelman, "makes all ritual (so it seems) comprehensible in terms of social and cultural order."[12] Ritual thus becomes understood "primarily as a didactic mold especially good for agents of socialization and indoctrination," rather than something that should first be analyzed "in and of itself."[13] By focusing on the significance of activities taking place within the pilgrimage frame, I recognize the potential that pilgrimage may have for transforming quotidian reality or for representing alternative realities. This perspective, following Turner on pilgrimage and as applied by Edward Bruner and others to tourism, recognizes that culture is not merely expressed through performances but is also constituted through them.[14]

Through the ritual of pilgrimage, quotidian reality can be examined and questioned. Because of the symbolically charged nature of the pilgrimage space, as well as the differing objectives of Jewish guide and Christian pilgrim, the Jewish-Christian interfaith encounter will often be more varied and more visceral than say, in organized interfaith dialogues. The pilgrim has come to understand his own faith commitment and finds that Judaism intrudes in shaping it. The guide's presentation of Israel, the Bible, current politics, and his own life story both confirm and question pilgrims' initial religious and political views. The Jewish guide initially seeks to satisfy his Christian customer and do his job well. But in presenting his (native or adopted) country, he finds a Christian map of significance covering it. The pilgrims' perspectives and their expectation that the guide engage them, may lead guides to reaffirm or question their relation to the land as Jews and Israelis. It is because of the "selfishness" of the motives of pilgrims and guides that concealed feelings can be expressed and self-understandings can be altered.

One might say that in the guided tour, Judaism, Christianity, and the land form a triangle in which the third term mediates the relation between every pair. Thus, the pilgrim's relation to the land as birthplace of his faith and concretization of sacred history is mediated through the Jewish relation to the homeland and the biblical past. The relation of Christianity and Judaism to each other is mediated by their shared attachment to the land, as well as their differences in their sense of belonging; furthermore, the changed power relations between Jews and Christians in Israel make the taken-for-granted relations in the diaspora more contingent. Finally, the Jewish-Zionist relation to the land is both reaffirmed and contested through Christians' sense of belonging. While undoubtedly Palestinians, Islam, and the Israeli-Arab conflict are important mediating factors and will be discussed, Judaism, Christianity, and the land are the most prominent in this book, insofar as they draw heavily on my own experience as guide.

The issues I raise in this book arise directly from my own subject positions as committed Jew, American immigrant, critical Israeli citizen, tour guide, and academic anthropologist. Guiding made familiar places strange, even as I tried to make them familiar to Christians. Thus, guide and pilgrim are both on a voyage in which each learns about his own world through dynamic encounter with the other, as mediated by the land and the biblical text.

## NARRATIVES OF ABUNDANT SITES – THE HOLY LAND

In Edith Turner's definition, the pilgrim is drawn to "some distant holy place renowned for miracles and the revivification of faith."[15] The space of pilgrimage is a place sedimented with meaning, a storied place; like Mount Moriah of

Isaac's sacrifice, it is "one of the mountains I shall tell thee of" (Genesis 22:2 – King James translation), a space beyond the horizon that becomes a focus of vision and imagination, a place that calls people to take to the road to journey there.[16] It is a place that creates desire and sometimes, transformation.

I consider the Holy Land an "abundant site," drawing on Robert Orsi's definition of "abundant events": events that "cannot be completely accounted for by social and cultural codes, that go beyond authorized limits . . . a cultural experience of . . . uncanny awareness of something outside us and independent of us, yet still familiar to us.[17] Abundant events are saturated by memory, desire, need, fear, terror, hope or denial, or some inchoate combination of these."[18]

The two aspects delineated by Orsi – sociocultural codes and what lies beyond – have elective affinities to two major approaches in the study of religion and space as identified by Kim Knott: One is "a social constructivist approach . . . interested in the production, practice, and representation of space, and its relationship with knowledge and power." The second, phenomenologically oriented, deals with place as a "fundamental form of embodied experience – the site of a powerful fusion of self, space, and time."[19] While phenomenological approaches do not necessarily include the uncanny, they tend to be more receptive to the nonverbal, less reductionist of the sacred.

Both approaches are crucial in understanding the authority and the immediacy of the pilgrimage experience. The revelatory founding events, the accretion of new stories around the original ones; the transmission of those narratives in text, ritual, and iconography through the generations, beyond borders, all contribute to the spiritual charge or "magnetism" of the place; but the interactions that take place among participants and between participants and transcendent forces may spiral out of the control of the pilgrims and their guide, making the Holy Land an abundant site of performance.[20]

I will outline some of the social and cultural codes that have been generated by the Holy Land in the course of history and that form the background for many pilgrims' images and expectations, and then I will describe the training program for guides and their employment trajectory and place it within the historicized practices of Israeli hiking and touring. Subsequently, I detail the logistic frame of the group pilgrimages analyzed in this book and question the distinction between pilgrims and tourists. I conclude the chapter with reflection on the pilgrims' impact on the space of the Holy Land and a brief sketch of their relation to the Israeli-Palestinian conflict before outlining my methodology. In subsequent chapters, I will show how these images and expectations of the Holy Land are reflected and transcended through touring performances.

## THE SOCIAL CONSTRUCTION OF THE STORIED SPACE OF THE HOLY LAND

### *1. The Christian Pilgrim's Space*

As part of his pioneering work on collective memory, Maurice Halbwachs devoted an entire book to "The Sacred Topography of the Gospels," treating the Christian Holy Land as an exemplary model for how the sedimentation of memory in space is socially constructed. In describing Peter's denial of Jesus at the house of Caiaphas, he writes that Peter needed to distance himself from Jesus in order to become a witness.[21] "Sacred places. . ." he writes, "commemorate not facts certified by contemporary witnesses but rather beliefs born perhaps not far from these places and strengthened by taking root in this environment."[22] People "*need to establish distance* [emphasis mine] in order to preserve a collective memory."[23]

At sacred places, the disciplinary power of sacred texts mediate the experience of pilgrims in ways different from those experienced by the prototypical "native" at home. Moreover, the itinerary and the frame of the group tour foster a semiotic mode of looking. Even vernacular landscapes and cultures are constantly scanned for signs of difference from the home world or typicality.[24] Moreover, if "dwelling involves a lack of distance between people and things, a lack of casual curiosity, an engagement which is neither conceptualized nor articulated, and which arises through *using* the world rather than through scrutiny," sacred places have an evocativeness that often challenges daily routines and calls for the symbolic processing of experience.[25] Though it is not the pilgrims' home, the life-world of their homes or the idealized "home" of religious visions may infuse the unfamiliar with an uncanny sense of familiarity. Alternatively, it may lead to disappointment or even rage, when the imagined "home" and the actual world at the site of pilgrimage do not properly align.

The distinction between pilgrim space and home space was already noted by the philosopher Philo of Alexandria, a pilgrim to the Temple in Jerusalem two thousand years ago: The Jews dispersed throughout Europe and Asia, he writes, "consider the Holy City as their mother city (*metropolis*), because in it is the holy Temple of God Most High. The villages that they have inherited from their ancestors of preceding generations they consider their homeland (*patris*), for there they were born and raised."[26] While the *patris* is the daily life-world of home, the *metropolis* is the mythical place of origin, akin to long-time Greek colonists' attachment to their motherland, Hellas.[27]

We know very little about Christian pilgrimage in the first three centuries of the Common Era. Scholars have sought its origins in the adoption of Jewish popular pilgrimages to prophets' tombs, in tourism customs of Roman elites, and in the transposition of the cult of martyrdom onto the Gospel sites of the Holy Land.[28] According to Markus, in the fourth century, Christian holy places were marked out in accordance with Christian sacred narrative and liturgical practice.[29] Here, dogma and Byzantine liturgy (selectively consecrating and forgetting specific past events, choosing and elevating selected texts) precede sacred place and continue to reshape places in their image. Beginning in the fourth century, imperial or ecclesiastical power was imposed on the "center out there," which in turn radiated legitimacy back to ecclesiastical structure and the empire, transforming the landscape from Aelia Capitolina into Hagia Polis Ierusalem, from Roman Palestine into Terra Sancta.[30] Thus, pilgrim itineraries and stories often serve as predecessors to the construction of "facts on the ground." Hence, pilgrimage is a form of political power that partitions space in ways that make it possible for noncritical thought to accept the resultant reality at face value – in this case, as marking the Christian Holy Land.[31]

From the late fourth century on, pilgrims' itineraria provide descriptions of holy places.[32] Numbers of pilgrims varied widely throughout history, mostly as a function of the safety and ease of access to the Holy Land. From the late thirteenth century on, the mendicant orders led in supplying guides, monopolizing both the choice of the route ("The Holy Circuit") and its religious interpretation. In 1335, the Franciscans became the custodians of the holy places, placing new emphasis on the Via Dolorosa. They structured the routes of pilgrimage through their lists of indulgences and altered the religious experience by quantifying the holy.[33] They provided spiritual interpretations enacted through ritual, looked after the pilgrims' technical, touristic needs, and also insulated the pilgrims from the alien environment, minimizing the influence of the ruling Muslim powers.

The Christian pilgrim's gaze on the Holy Land has been materialized through changes in the landscape – through constructing buildings, streets, and churches, and through acts of preservation, excavation, restoration, display, or destruction, signposting, gating, and ordinance and access regulations. The sites objectify our experience of social interaction, structure subsequent movements, and assume dramatic qualities that make the words into a "scene," "an opened text, whose narrative we read even as we interact."[34]

Furthermore, as the panorama became a dominant way of seeing and exhibiting visual mastery in the West and over the rest, Protestant pilgrim itineraries in the Holy Land structured movement and positioned the viewer in imitation of Holy Land panoramas exposed in Western locales.[35] Since the nineteenth century, Western Christianity has been strongly involved in colonial projects in Israel/Palestine.[36] In the nineteenth century, colonial forces (Britain, France, Germany, and Russia) erected churches in Jerusalem and throughout the country to impose their power on the disintegrating Ottoman Empire and assert Western claims to the Holy Land, creating "facts on the ground."[37]

Over the past century, new Christian religious sites have been created. If Antonio Barluzzi built over a dozen Catholic pilgrimage shrines between 1919 and 1955 to create a recognizably Catholic (and Italian) Holy Land, Protestants have founded new sites, such as the Garden Tomb and the Jordan River baptismal site, fashioned with natural or (pseudo-)archaeological features that conform to Protestant sensibilities.[38] Quite recently, a series of new Christian sites (such as Nazareth Village and Biblical Resources) has been constructed by the Israeli government, by local churches or by private entrepreneurs, some providing multimedia entertainment and simulations, thus blurring the lines between heritage, theme parks, and holy sites.[39]

## 2. The Jewish-Israeli Guide's Space

Zali Gurevitch argues that, given the paradigms of biblical history, as reinforced in the long exilic experience, Jewish Israelis can never become "natives": "Nativity is . . . founded on the identification of voice (self) and place (world). It is being-in-place as dwelling – the self and the world cosmologized in the place."[40] Of the Holy Land, on the other hand, he writes, "the book that tells the place's story . . . also resists the place as a totality that harmonizes the relation between humans and their immediate earthly abode. . . . The Judaic story of place subverts the settled idea of nativity."[41] Yehuda Amichai, reflecting on the dual suffix – *ayim* – of the Hebrew word *Yerushalayim* (Jerusalem) writes: "Why is Jerusalem always two? The Jerusalem above and the Jerusalem below. And I want to be in a middle Jerusalem, without bumping my head above or bruising my leg below."[42]

At sacred sites in Israel, this gap between dwelling and place is widened by the power of the pilgrim's gaze and the nonquotidian nature of pilgrim practices. At the pilgrim's "center out there," the "local" may be subject to the often denaturing power brought by the pilgrim and her host society or religion. In speaking of pilgrimage to the Second Temple, the Midrash proclaims: "One does not rent out houses in Jerusalem, because one does not own them."[43] Ideally, the House of God attenuates and challenges human possession; thus the ideal future Temple in Ezekiel belongs to no tribe but as "an offering to God," is intertribal and exterritorial.[44] Jerusalem residents were obliged to open their houses to pilgrims, the guests of the Master of the House. While the sacredness of the city may bring both financial benefit and status to its permanent inhabitants, residence in places of pilgrimage often imposes surveillance of the moral state and the daily lives of the "local" inhabitants, including the urban fabric of the city.[45]

While the dual nature of the land – the biblically textualized Holy Land versus the in-dwelling life-world – may be more pronounced in my own case, as a product of an Orthodox Jewish diaspora education and as an anthropologist, it nonetheless infuses much of Jewish-Israeli life, especially that of immigrants, who make up a substantial portion of pilgrim guides. As I will demonstrate in chapter 3, this view is reinforced by the Protestant influence on Zionist historiography, which in turn shaped Israeli hiking practices as well as tour-guide training. The Christian pilgrims' view of the land confirms this basic duality.

## THE MAKING OF A JEWISH-ISRAELI PILGRIM GUIDE

All tour groups traveling in Israel, including pilgrim groups, are required to be accompanied by a licensed guide. While some (mainly Catholic) groups use the services of religious guides who have "green cards" issued by the Christian Information Center in Jerusalem, most Protestants and many (perhaps most) Catholics are guided by (mainly Jewish) graduates of the government-approved Israeli tour guide course.[46] The course is intensive – two years, 12 hours a week, with major emphases placed on biblical history, archaeology, and Christianity. In addition to attending lectures and passing exams, guides participate in 75 full-day tours throughout the country, led by a veteran tour guide who serves as a cultural role model for the novice guides. His guiding techniques are grounded in the cultural praxis of "knowledge of the land" hikes, which were an integral part both of Israeli school and army education, as well as of the tour guide course.[47] Such hikes cultivate national sentiment and attachment to the land by "mobiliz[ing] the Bible as a source of cultural meaning and linguistic practice."[48] During those trips "information and interpretations were selected primarily in order to arouse feelings of belonging to the place," and timetables were contracted to dramatize stories and "give the . . . audience the feeling of witnessing scenes and heroes of the past, as if they were taking place here and now."[49]

Jewish Israelis take the guide course and decide to work as tour guides for a variety of reasons: to travel, to broaden their knowledge, to make (what they perceive of at first as) easy money, to work outdoors in nature, to meet a variety of people, and to represent Israel and Judaism to foreigners. The Ministry of Tourism coordinator of the tour guide course, Haim Carel, said, "the guide is the ambassador of the state. . . . What happens in the tourism industry should not be determined only by financial considerations, but by national ones" (interview, September 2004). More recently, the Ministry of Tourism's website proclaims: "The Ministry of Tourism sees tour guides in Israel as the spearhead of the tourism industry and as the ambassadors of Israel in face of its critics."[50] Nevertheless, the guide course falls far short of political indoctrination, and guide narratives reflect a range of political positions.[51] Following their certification, guides who choose to work with incoming tourists seek work among Jewish-Israeli and Palestinian Christian travel agencies, guiding groups in the languages they master.[52] Although few guides begin the course with the express aim of guiding Christian pilgrims, many find themselves doing so, as Christian pilgrims are such a substantial sector of the group tourism market. While agents or group leaders may ask for the services of a specific guide, or request guides of particular faiths, genders, or ethnicities, most do not. The quality of guiding, so say most agents, is a crucial element for the success of the pilgrimage tour.[53] Consequently, good local tour agents know their guides and invest time in building a varied supply of expert guides and in matching guides with their groups. Committed guides, in turn, often invest considerable effort in pleasing their group leaders, as this may garner future requests for work.

Guides accompany the groups for the full length of their stay and are responsible for carrying out the itinerary and providing explanations. They direct the bus driver, pay entrance fees, arrange lunch stops, hand out hotel keys, and are responsible for the safety of their group members. The sites (though not all) may be fixed in the itinerary, but the amount of time spent there, the places and objects pointed out, and the story told about them are up to the guide, working together with the group's spiritual leader. Erik Cohen developed a typology, characterizing the four essential tour guide roles as path-finding, mediating, facilitating social interaction, and communicating.[54] In the case of Christian group pilgrimages, many of the mediative and social functions are performed by the pastor/priest who accompanies the group from abroad.[55] Although the communicative function is undoubtedly the most essential of the four, I will show (chap. 3) how the guide performs an additional spiritual function, forming the diverse sites of the tour into a spiritual path.[56] In doing so, the use of appropriate feeling tones, the selective creation of empathy with key figures of the past, and imaginative and personalizing descriptions of historical events are often more important than virtuoso displays of knowledge of facts and figures.[57]

In assuming the spiritual role, the guide must enter into tacit or (sometimes) explicit negotiation with the group leader and the pilgrims on the interpretation of Scripture and the land.

## THE GUIDED PILGRIMAGE TOURING FRAME

Most contemporary Christian pilgrims to the Holy Land come on group bus tours. These groups are often organized by a Christian church body or travel agent catering to a Christian market. Such groups may hold orientation sessions prior to departure and regularly conduct Christian worship, read Bible passages, and sing hymns in the course of their visit.[58] During their 8–14-day stay in the Holy Land, their hotels, meals, buses, guides, and services are organized by a local Israeli or Palestinian company. Their itineraries focus on sites of significance to Christian faith and history, and are frequently advertised as "a walk in the footsteps of Jesus." The trip itinerary, between 1 and 66(!) pages in length, is often printed on glossy paper and posted on church websites. It is a complex document negotiated by pastoral group leaders, travel agents in the pilgrims' home country, and local Israeli or Palestinian tour agents. It is a contract (both legal and spiritual), list of travel tips, advertisement, schedule, mission statement, and platform for devotional preaching, all rolled into one. While some groups rarely refer to the itinerary, others employ it as a kind of "bible" or contract, calling guides to account for any deviation from the printed schedule. It is also frequently consulted by tour guides to decipher the orientation of their groups prior to their arrival.

The technologies and infrastructures of travel – like the hotel, jet plane, tour bus, access roads, and electronic communications – create conditions that may shape pilgrims experience even more than theologies do.[59] The lifestyle of many Westerners dictates fast and familiar food, air-conditioning, and a minimum of walking. The structure of working life in the West, with its limited time for vacation and emphasis on quantification of time and money, often generate packed, rushed itineraries. The result is more "type A" tours, covering more sites in a shorter duration.[60] Touring hours are long, and pilgrims have little, if any, free time to explore on their own in the course of the day. The itineraries and infrastructure of the tourist industry – which is shared by pilgrims – facilitates the preservation of the environmental bubble of the group tour, a bubble that most guides and drivers are eager to maintain for political or economic reasons.[61] Religious language may assign the bubble moral value: "we" pilgrims as opposed to "those tourists"; we "people of God" (or "mystical body of Christ") as opposed to "they" who have not come here to seek or have not yet found the Lord.[62] This bubble also increases the intensity of interaction of fellow worshippers in the abundant storied sites, and they often share their concerns and desires with other group members.[63]

Unquestionably, there are important differences between Catholics, Protestants, and Orthodox in their Holy Land/Bible Land discourse, preferred sites, and practices, and these differences are reflected in the language of itineraries as well.[64] Thus, certain Catholic churches are frequented almost exclusively by Catholics, whereas Greek Orthodox have their own sites nearby, commemorating the same events with their own icons and aesthetics (Annunciation, birth of the Virgin Mary, Wedding at Cana, Transfiguration at Mount Tabor, and more). Most Protestants mark the resurrection of Jesus at the Garden Tomb, rather than the Holy Sepulchre, and the Mormons have designated their own Shepherds' Field at a Bedouin encampment several kilometers away from the traditional Catholic and Orthodox sites. Many Protestant groups prefer to visit and worship in nature areas and archaeological sites rather than churches, especially if those are Catholic or Orthodox churches, whose iconography and Oriental decor repel many Protestants. Protestants frequently clutch printed words and diagrams – Bibles, programs, hymnals, and maps; Catholics don't. Protestants may organize their tour based on a geographical logic; Catholics often follow the events of the Holy Week and Jesus's life-career.[65]

In addition to the biblical sites, most pilgrim tours include visits to several Israeli tourist sites (Masada, Dead Sea, Yad Vashem), shopping, and sometimes a minimal amount of free time. Being at "original" or "authentic" sites, however such authority is conferred, is important for both Evangelicals and Catholics, as is the potential tension between the desire to see and touch and the worship of a God that transcends place.[66] The sacred sites and paths of the Holy Land/ Bible Land are in themselves "strong texts" – "frequently repeated narratives, in which geographical features of the landscape act as mnemonic pegs on which moral teachings hang."[67] The stage on which guide/group interactions take place is precharged with expectations and spiritual meaning.

### PILGRIMS OR TOURISTS?

I have often visited the Holy Sepulchre with groups of British or American Evangelicals who witness the practices of the Russian Orthodox pilgrims as they prostrate themselves, weep, and embrace the Stone of Unction, before emptying their shopping bags of souvenirs on it, so that each item may receive blessing from contact with the slab. The Evangelicals' somewhat disgusted reaction is "thank God we're not pilgrims!" When asked however, "Are you tourists then?" they hem and haw in their efforts to find a formulation they can live with.

Those who prostrate themselves with tear-filled devotion at the Stone of Unction may spend the next day smearing mud on their bodies at the Dead Sea or shopping in the marketplace, only to return to the Holy Sepulchre for vespers. Between their two prayers, do they cease to be pilgrims? As Simon Coleman reminds us in describing pilgrimage to Walsingham, "Cultural and material spaces can prompt engagement from visitors, be they casual tourists, or pious and experienced pilgrims. Even ironic pilgrims may find themselves caught up in a more emotionally powerful experience than they might have expected."[68]

The self-classification of pilgrims, like that of ethnic identity is situational.[69] As Paul Basu writes with respect to "roots-pilgrims," "For the majority of my informants, pilgrimage . . . is popularly understood as *representing* a 'sacred other' to secular practices associated with tourism."[70] Pilgrims, even when highly influenced by mobility and change, often assert stasis, purity, and fidelity to an unchanging past.[71]

Scholars' attempts to draw rigid distinctions are no more fruitful – Catholic scholars may wish to classify Protestants as merely "religious tourists."[72] The distinction may also be employed by the church "to turn the tourist's presence at religious sites and events into an occasion for a religious experience or act of worship."[73] Government tourist industries and ecclesiastical authorities may use such classifications as a way of selectively allocating finances and resources ("true pilgrims" may not need trained Israeli guides in their language or as much investment in tourism infrastructure).[74] Devotional magazines and manuals may sharpen the distinction between pilgrim and tourists in order to bring pilgrim/tourist behavior in accordance with Catholic norms for solemnity or to flatter well-behaved pilgrims.[75] Some scholars of pilgrimage, implicitly reinforcing particular Catholic understandings of the approach to the sacred (such as penitential practices or the quest for miracles, pardon, merit, mystical experience, or supernatural assistance – few of them traditionally at the center of Holy Land pilgrimage), may feel uncomfortable having the ("superficial," "curiosity seeking") tourists in their midst.[76] Historians may find the tourist/pilgrim divide a comfortable way of highlighting certain distinctions between premodern and modern phenomena or even between modern and postmodern ones, often by essentializing one or the other. Ellen Badone[77] suggests that the desire to separate tourists from pilgrims reflects structures of Judeo-Christian and classical culture that oppose serious pilgrimage to frivolous tourism as follows:

| *Tourism* | *Pilgrimage* |
|---|---|
| Money | Asceticism |
| Consumption | Poverty |
| Evil | Good |
| Low | High |
| Materialism | Spiritual |

Other scholars have highlighted the continuities between the pilgrim and the tourist or the deeply motivated visitor to secular or political sites.[78] Erik Cohen's studies on pilgrimage and tourism are useful in this regard.[79] By classifying five tourist/pilgrim experiences ranging from the diversionary to the existential, he reminds us to look not at types of visitors but at structures, motivations, and cosmologies of travel that distinguish between modes of tourist and pilgrim experiences.[80]

Alan Morinis chose to define pilgrimage as "a journey undertaken by a person in a quest of a place or state that he or she believes to embody a valued ideal."[81] Unlike the centrality of penance and the search for healing and miracles that characterize many pilgrimages to Catholic shrines, in the case of the Holy Land, pilgrimage has traditionally been undertaken to reenact religious history, reaffirm basic tenets of faith, and assert belonging to the larger community of the faithful.[82] These emphases make the borders between pilgrimage, religious tourism, heritage tourism, and political tourism particularly fluid in Holy Land travel.

This fluidity is well illustrated through an experience I had while guiding an American group. At the end of a long day of touring around the Sea of Galilee, the Evangelical pastor I accompanied gathered his flock at the Mount of Beatitudes for a sermon paraphrasing Jesus's Sermon on the Mount:

> You have heard it said: "imprint many images on your digital memory cards";
> but I say: "imprint the image of your father on your heart and mind."
> You have heard it said: "this is the trip of a lifetime";
> but I say: "I am your God for all time."
> You have heard it said: "the historical perspective is highly educational";
> but I say: "learn of Me."
> You have heard it said: "carry your snacks, water, hats, coats, suntan lotion";
> but I say: "eat of me and I am your covering."
> You have heard it said: "the water level has changed, the natural borders have changed, the rainfall has changed";
> but I say: "I never change."[83]

The effectiveness of the sermon relies on the listeners' ability to identify and identify with the voice of the guide as well as the structure of the Gospel text. While summoning the listeners to subordinate the "tourist" to the "pilgrim" mode, it reminds them that they are both pilgrims and tourists.

## HOLY LAND PILGRIMAGE AND POLITICAL AND ECONOMIC CONFLICT

> History is compressed in these places. They are intensely located in the present, but the past impresses them, and they bleed into the future. . . . Our genealogies and thus our identities are realized in space and place.[84]

In the Holy Land, narratives have been especially important in claiming and shaping space and practices of movement – precisely because these are spaces of nondwelling: the elements of distance, desire, impermanence, and textualization typify the pilgrim's experience. These elements make stories count for more, as does the power held by distant agents to shape the sacred landscape in their own image. The cultural diffusion of mythic or authoritative stories of places and the practice of communal rites or ceremonies transforms many of these marked places not only into "legitimate theatre[s] for practical actions" but into consciously designated sites of memory, *lieux de mémoire*, privileged venues for religious or commemorative practices.[85] Possession of a holy site, the display of symbols, and the performance of pilgrimage there stake a claim not only to the territory but to the superior truth/power of the world religion and the political entity that displays its colors, icons, and symbols at the site.

While this applies to the Holy Land as a whole, it is particularly true of Jerusalem, the Holy City. Consider the conquest of the town of Jebus by King David and its establishment as capital of the twelve tribes of Israel, the construction of the First Temple, its destruction and rebuilding, the destruction of the Second Temple by the Romans, Constantine's foundation of the Holy Sepulchre, the building of the Dome of the Rock by Omar, the Crusaders, Mamelukes, Ottomans, British, Jordanians, Palestinians, and Israelis – in each era, sacred pilgrimage sites both establish a center for the privileged community and advance a polemic claim against other communities who (previously or concurrently) lay claim to the site.[86] The desire to experience the transcendent in place generates a surfeit of historical markers, sacred places, plaques, buildings, flags, testaments, tokens of desire, initials carved into stone, foundation stones of past glories and future visions. And this desire is often jealous, exclusive, a rage for possession of the beloved site or object. As poet Yehuda Amichai wrote: "The air over Jerusalem is saturated with prayers and dreams like the air over industrial cities. It's hard to breathe.[87]

Thus, the amazing success of the Holy Land's "career" sows the seeds of conflict. For centuries, it has been a point of contestation between conflicting claims of locals, visitors, and empires; laity and hierarchy; Israelis and Palestinians; and Jews, Christians, and Muslims. Christian pilgrimage, however much pilgrims would prefer to ignore it, both reflects these conflicts and plays a role in them. For example, in the itineraria of the Crusader period, the "invention" of holy places strengthened the political claims to them, as at the Temple Mount or in the Cave of Machpelah in Hebron. In the fifteenth century, the contention between the Jews and the Franciscans over Mount Zion became an international issue.[88] In certain periods, the presence of Catholic pilgrims in the Holy Land and at places like the Holy Sepulchre and the performance of rituals in public space manifested the Catholic Church's political claim to territory and antiquity.

Active conflict at religious sites in the Holy Land has been exacerbated by modern nationalism. Given the totalization, rigidity, and abstraction of nationalist practices as a whole, spaces sacred to the nation tend to be preoccupied with the marking of territorial and group boundaries.[89] If religion often renders territorial conflicts more violent, when nationalisms become involved in religious sites, it leads to a hardening of lines, purification, and conflict, especially when the fault lines between religions and those between national or ethnic groups coincide.[90] In the nineteenth century, the accommodation and hosting of Christian pilgrims spurred (and provided an excuse for) the construction of embassies, hospitals, hospices, and churches which staked the claim of the Western powers to Jerusalem in their battle against the "sick man of Europe," the Ottoman Empire.[91]

Contemporary Christian pilgrimage takes place in a context profoundly shaped by religion.[92] Sacred sites, especially in Jerusalem, were critical to forming the national identity of Israelis and Palestinians, and both the Islamic Movement and the Temple Mount Faithful have orchestrated pilgrimage as a manifestation of presence, a reclamation of territory and legitimacy from the impure national-religious other.[93] Some Holy Land pilgrims and their guides are intensely focused on the Israeli-Palestinian struggle and evoke sacred texts or morally loaded religious language in support of one of the parties to the political conflict.[94] For most (though not all) pilgrims, conflict is inimical to the spirit of the pilgrimage, which for many, is about "putting it all together." It's less about fostering doubt, challenging faith, or confronting complexity, than about reinforcing the hope, strength, and belief that can help pilgrims through their tribulations back home. So, narratives and itineraries will often ignore potential causes of discord, unless all participants are committed to a common political view.[95] How Christian presence at holy sites is enmeshed in the *longue dureé* struggle to lay claims to territory and antiquity remains beyond the ken of all but the most knowledgeable and politically aware.[96]

Pastors, guides, tour itineraries, and group rituals (or their absence) can often create the environmental bubble that shields the group from the ferocity of the conflict.[97] For example, during the first Intifada, in order to facilitate safe passage, the Palestinian driver and I regularly switched the display of the Hebrew newspaper and the Arabic *kefiyya* (headdress) in the bus window as we moved from Israeli security checkpoints to Palestinian neighborhoods. This remained unnoticed by the passengers.

Holy Land pilgrimage also has significant economic impact on its Israeli/Palestinian surrounding, particularly in Jerusalem and Bethlehem. Souvenir shopping supports Palestinian or Israeli shopkeepers, and is often framed as an act of charity or political support. Furthermore, the commissions obtained from group shopping are the object of economic struggle as well as cooperation between guides and drivers on the one hand, and group leaders, on the other. The material objects purchased may also serve as conveyors of messages to friends and families of pilgrims back home.[98] The meanings attributed to money and material objects purchased are religious and social, even for groups that disparage materiality on theological grounds.[99] These aspects will be discussed in chapter 5, while the political expressions of spending money in West Jerusalem/West Bank will be discussed briefly in chapter 4.

While the larger political and economic conflict is not the subject of this book, aspects of the Israeli-Palestinian struggle inevitably infiltrate the tour bubble. Pilgrimage is one of the few areas of everyday contact between Israelis and Palestinians in which a wide variety of power relations obtain. In my own experience as tour guide, I worked intensively for two decades with Palestinian bus drivers but also as an employee of Palestinian tour agents and, occasionally, as a coworker with Palestinian guides on multibus groups. The charged political events affected our relations even as we worked to maintain an atmosphere of peaceful cooperation. The practice of cooperation, on the other hand, and the maintenance of mutual respect and trust tempered the tensions and hostilities, especially during the years of the first Intifada.

## METHODOLOGY

This book is based primarily on my experiences working as a tour guide for Christian pilgrims for more than thirty years; from 1981 to 2000, as I pursued graduate studies and raised a family, it was the primary source of my livelihood. As the center of my life-world moved from the tour bus into academia and my guiding work became more sporadic, I continued to reflect on the nature of the guide-group-land encounter that I had helped orchestrate for twenty years. During the first years of the second Intifada, from 2002 to 2004, along with a research partner (and fellow tour guide), Yael Guter, I carried out a series of two- to nine-hour-long semistructured interviews with approximately 25 (mostly) then unemployed veteran guides of Christian groups. We also interviewed pastoral leaders, Ministry of Tourism officials, and travel agents. In the case of tour guides, we asked them to reflect on their practices and positions, and relate some of their favorite experiences in the field. Our familiarity with the guiding world, including our knowledge of travel agent–guide relationships, interactions between Jewish guides and Palestinian drivers, and practices of tipping and shop commissions, enabled us to zero in on potential conflicts and tactics of improvisation. I also sent two research assistants, Smadar Farkash and Matan Shapiro, to accompany groups on day tours and interview guides and pilgrims. More recently, I conducted participant-observation while accompanying several Spanish-speaking Catholic groups.

My own position minimizes some aspects of contemporary Christian Holy Land pilgrimage – notably the dynamics of pilgrimages led by Christian priest-guides, the tours led by Palestinian guides, and the reception of the guide's performance and its integration into the pilgrim's long-term goals and understandings.[100] It is also skewed in favor of the national groups whose languages I guided in (English, German, Dutch, and French), and in favor of my primary experience with American Protestants (though many of the German and some of the French groups were Catholic). The guides interviewed included some working in various other languages (Spanish, Portuguese, Japanese, Russian, Indonesian) and denominations (Catholic, Orthodox, Mormons, Makuya), as well as several Christian and/or Palestinian guides. Although some of the differences between Holy Land pilgrims and their guides were noted previously, very little ethnography has been published to date, and I hope that this book will encourage others to plow adjacent plots and broaden the field. Some research has been done or is currently underway – on Mormons, Greek Orthodox, on Palestinian guides, and on seminars for Catholic religious.[101] Yvonne Friedman and I are currently researching Catholic priest-guides. There are also several articles documenting politically oriented tours in which Christian backgrounds or Scriptural knowledge play a role.[102]

As for the pilgrims' reception, though I have done my best to record the questions of the pilgrim sitting in the tenth row, this book is primarily a view from the front of the bus. Recently, Hillary Kaell and Donna Young have provided two poignant views from the back of the tour bus. Kaell has recently provided an ethnography of elderly American women on Holy Land pilgrimage, which voices their concerns and desires – for health, their children's welfare, their proper Christian burial by family members, and so on, providing a commentary often quite different from the discourse of the guide and pastoral group leader.[103] Donna Young provides a similar perspective from the point for view of middle-aged Anglophone Catholic religious and educators, many of whom have taken a break from their lives to cope with crises of faith.[104] I believe, however, that my own conflicted choices and life circumstances and my experience guiding groups of many nationalities and denominations will reveal things along the road that might otherwise escape the sight of the pilgrim, even one who has been to the Holy Land several times.

### DESIDERATUM – SHARING THE ROAD

In his discussion of Jerusalem's contested and shared sacred sites, Glenn Bowman reminds us: "Ethnographic knowledge is by its nature perspectival, and profoundly partial; the wider theoretical and anthropological knowledge the anthropologist carries . . . cannot produce an image of the 'real' city all of these groups share. This is because, at least in the experiential sense, there is no 'real' Jerusalem which can be caught in any single representation; Jerusalem is the compound setting of the life worlds of the peoples that cohabit in it whilst engaging it, and each other, differently."[105]

I suggest that Jewish-guided Christian pilgrimage can help us understand the limits of our knowledge, the perspectives of our positioned selves and our separate historical paths better, even as it creates places in which we can share the road.

### OUTLINE OF THE BOOK

Chapter 3 examines how the Bible Land is coproduced by Jewish guides and Protestant pastors and how Zionist, Protestant, and American understandings of place and history are evoked and confirmed through guiding performances. Chapter 4 shows how political understandings of the Israeli-Palestinian conflict are made self-evident through Christian religious language in itineraries, brochures, and guides' discourses and practices, while competing understandings are silenced. Chapter 5 turns to money and souvenirs, showing how religious and political values are expressed through the material transactions of pilgrimage. Chapter 6 shifts focus, analyzing how a loosely-tied community of Jewish-Israeli guides struggles with the seductions of Christianity and of their own performances in the course of shepherding pilgrims through the land. The seventh and final chapter returns to the questions posed at the outset and explores the implications of the study, especially as regards the mechanisms of identity construction through performance.

# 3 OPENING THEIR EYES: PERFORMANCE OF A SHARED PROTESTANT-ISRAELI BIBLE LAND

EARLY IN THE morning of their first day in Jerusalem, the guide Galia takes her Protestant pilgrims to view the panorama from atop the Mount of Olives. Choosing a spot overlooking the Muslim Dome of the Rock, Arab East Jerusalem, and the Old City but out of earshot of the Palestinian vendors of postcards and camel rides, she begins her orientation to the city. In an interview, she explained her approach: "I start with Abraham and Melchizedek and go through the Six-Day War. . . . I deal with the view, the Temple, what you see there – the Valley of Jehosaphat and the Gate of Mercy. . . . For me, this is a mission. I aim to open their eyes, so they ask questions. Nothing is the way it seems" (interview, June 2001).

How do Jewish guides enable Protestant pilgrims to see the Bible Land? What is effaced from view? What makes these ways of seeing natural and comfortable for all participants? In this chapter, I will show how Jewish-Israeli tour guides and Protestant pastors and pilgrims become coproducers of a mutually satisfying performance that transforms the often-contested terrain of Israel-Palestine into Bible Land. Through listening to guides' narrations of biblical sites as they view them and move through them, visitors are constituted as pilgrims and assert a claim to the landscape, and the guide is granted place-making authority as biblical witness, native, and professional.

I begin by surveying the Protestant gaze on the Holy Land and the ways that gaze has been materialized in Protestant construction of holy sites and their narratives. I then provide examples of shared Zionist-Protestant practices through orientation narratives in four spaces with different distributions of power: the panoramic view of the Old City of Jerusalem, the tour bus at Ben Gurion Airport, the excavations of the Southern Wall of the Temple Mount, and the beginning of the Via Dolorosa. Each of these spaces offers its own

*37*

opportunities and challenges and evokes other strategies on the part of the guide. In each case, I will demonstrate how the guides' narratives draw on historically embedded, shared Protestant-Zionist social-memory practices, and how those practices enable Jewish-Israeli guides and Protestant pilgrims to strengthen their commonality and sacralize the landscape. I also illustrate how the isolating environmental bubble of the guided tour encourages both guides and pilgrims to affirm a common sense of belonging and suspend skepticism – sometimes by marginalizing Palestinians and Muslims from the shared Bible Land.

Most of the material will be based on *shtick* – tricks of the trade – formalized, often comic routines, mainly my own.[1] Each is performed at the threshold to a particular area to orient and introduce pilgrims to a particular geographical-biblical unit. While these performances depict my experiences as a US Jewish immigrant to Israel, working with US Protestant pilgrims, mostly Evangelicals, the tactics and performances I describe – if not the specific details of the performance – are widespread. In fact, some of these routines are adapted – or stolen – from other guides' performances.[2]

## THE MAKING OF PROTESTANT PILGRIM GAZES AND SPACES: COMMANDING HEIGHTS, UNTOUCHED NATURE, REVEALED ARCHAEOLOGY

The spaces of the Holy Land are not an empty stage for pilgrim performance of the biblical text. The ability of a given site to support certain readings and evoke the sense of simultaneity with a particular past may be site-specific, influenced by culturally and religiously transmitted aesthetic expectations. As was the case with early Christianity, Protestantism too inscribed its own understandings on the well-marked palimpsest of the Holy Land in the attempt to produce a textualized sacred landscape in its own image.[3]

Protestants were initially ambivalent toward Holy Land pilgrimage. John Calvin dismissed the veneration of relics through pilgrimage as "vain speculation."[4] Pilgrimage was linked with the Catholic cult of the saints, with popular folk beliefs, and with the medieval system of penance and indulgences – as opposed to the Protestant affirmation of *sola scriptura*, that the only way to God is through the Word, rather than through the mediation of a priesthood and ritual objects. Furthermore, pilgrimage is a practice involving all the senses – "praying with one's feet," rather than strictly through the intellect and a heart moved by listening to the Word. Consequently, Protestants were relative

For Protestants, the landscape calls forth words, not as heard but as seen, as if lettered across the view. Pastor Carley Kendrick references the Biblical story of David and Goliath at the overlook of the Elah Valley. © *Salem Bible College and Thiessen Photography. Used by permission.*

latecomers to the pilgrimage scene and today still display ambivalence toward words like "pilgrim" and "Holy Land."[5]

Beginning in the nineteenth century, however, Protestants of various denominations began to come in increasing numbers, to test and confirm the topographical truths of scripture. The increasing ease and safety of travel to the Holy Land, the rise in disposable income, and the greater familiarity of the Protestant faithful with the accounts of returning pilgrims led to an upsurge in Protestant pilgrimage. The encouragement and accommodation of pilgrims was inseparable from the colonial project of dismantling the Ottoman Empire in the Middle East.[6] This was manifested in the establishment of churches, modern hotels, hostels, and hospices to serve the needs of pilgrims of colonial powers. Over the past few decades, Bible Land pilgrimage has become integrated into much American Evangelical practice, and the spread of Charismatic Evangelicism has led to an upsurge of Protestant pilgrims from places such as Nigeria, the Philippines, and Brazil.[7]

Although Protestants take exception to "holy sites" in the sense of places whose sanctity was transferred to them through physical contact with the divine, they have increasingly been drawn to the land as the physical illustration of significant places of their faith.[8] Protestant pilgrimage to the Holy Land has become "a powerful catalyst for the cultivation of spiritually powerful experiences rooted in the interaction between believer and Bible."[9] For Protestants, the landscape calls forth words, not as heard but as seen, as if lettered across the view. Their outward sight should call forth in inward vision the words of remembered prayers and scriptural passages.[10]

Protestant pilgrimage itineraries are replete with vistas, panoramic views, and open spaces. A Protestant-oriented itinerary begins:

> "Go up to the top of Pisga, and lift up your eyes Westward and Northward and Southward and Eastward and behold it with your eyes" (Deut. 3:27). A land was chosen by God where he could reveal himself to mankind. . . . [This] Land God chose to come into direct contact with his creation, the [*sic*] humanity.
>
> A careful reading of the Old and New Testament shows an intrinsic relation between God, man and land. . . . [11]

One tour guide explained, "It's all linked to mountains: Carmel, the Mount of Beatitudes, Mount Sinai, Mt. Tabor – and, if you like, Golgotha."[12] The Holy Land acquires prestige among Protestants because it contains those landscapes in which Jesus, gazing over valleys and hills toward the distant horizon, would have experienced the sublime. Rather than bow down and touch or kiss wood and stone (Orthodox icons or Catholic statues and relics), nineteenth-century Protestant pilgrims remained vertical: upright in their saddles, seeking the most extensive pictorial vista, the largest possible view.[13] The distance from the site is also a distance from immersion in the Orient. Thus, the outlook, embodying a gaze that combines diffuse sanctity with distance and control is a practice constituting the Protestant pilgrim as Western. Almost every Protestant pilgrimage to Jerusalem (in contrast to, say, Greek Orthodox pilgrimage) begins with an outlook from the Mount of Olives, and many prayer and meditation sites are mountaintop vistas.

Protestants also have a preference for nature sites. For Catholics, holiness arises from the sense of being part of a long history during which the will of Jesus has been enacted in the world through the agency of the Church.[14] One Catholic monk, pilgrim guide, and member of the Brotherhood of the Holy Sepulchre, Father Peter Vasko, said to me, "The views are beautiful, but they're homed in on the shrines" (interview, May 2005). The shrines derive their authority through their visual marking with recognizably Catholic iconography and through the sanction of the church.

For Protestants, on the other hand, a holy place "covered over" with Orthodox or Catholic churches is, in effect, a site that commemorates institutional domination rather than the truth that, in their view, the ecclesiastical institution has usurped and distorted. In Lock's words, "The Protestant task is always to return to that first simplicity which so exactly matches the Protestant's own. The plainness of the landscape is itself held up as evidence of the truth of Protestantism."[15] Protestant inspiration devolves from what is interpreted as an unimpeded relationship between the individual and Christ. Consequently, Protestants want to witness Christ and not his putative agents, and natural landscapes were seen as providing this unmediated access.[16] The prominence of the vista may also reflect the ambiguity of the Protestant relation toward holy sites. It is "the Jesus of the land rather than the sites" that is essential for Protestant pilgrims.[17] The concentration of focus on a specific natural object (a tree or stone) – or especially a man-made one (a relic or icon) – materializes sanctity and, hence, arouses Protestant theological opposition in ways that inspiration by a broad, more diffuse landscape does not.

Protestants also present Jesus as "a fellow-seeker after the unmediated Divine, as if He were not the object of the pilgrimage, the Divine person of the Trinity but as if He were himself merely the first and chief of pilgrims."[18] As one contemporary pilgrim commented on a tour I witnessed at the Sea of Galilee, "Jesus was a young man like me at the same age. We could walk on the same seashore together and He could have been my friend."[19] This narrative, as I will show, provides easier access for the Jewish-Israeli guide than Catholic or Orthodox pilgrimage, which situate the divinity of Jesus and ritual at center.[20]

Furthermore, from the Reformation on, Protestants have historically presented themselves as progressive and restorative – Protestantism saw itself as a movement seeking to restore the Church to the purity of the "original" true Church of Jesus's day, effacing a long intermediate past.[21] To construct themselves as progressive, truthful, and Western, they orientalized Catholicism, presenting it as traditional, obscurantist, and medieval. Hence, Protestant agendas played a prominent role in formative scientific research into the historical geography and archaeology of Israel-Palestine. The aim of nineteenth-century historical geography, according to Robinson, one of its leading practitioners, was "to lay open the treasures of Biblical geography . . . [that] had become so covered with the dust and rubbish of many centuries that their very existence was forgotten."[22] Biblical sites were to be verified and consecrated by historical references, archaeology, and geography – not by miracles, revelatory visions, and Catholic ecclesiastical authority.[23] Thus, most Protestants seek (and find) the "original stones" that Jesus might have walked on in order to walk with

Winnowing of grain in Nazareth Village Biblical theme park. The park corresponds to the Protestant imagination of the Holy Land. Some Evangelical groups prefer to visit and worship there rather than in the traditional church-covered sites in the Old City of Nazareth. *Photo © Amos Ron. Used by permission.*

Jesus. This Protestant paradigm fueled the research of the Palestine Exploration Fund (PEF), which although declared independent of any particular religious group, held their founding meeting in Westminster Cathedral.[24] The sites they chose to map and describe were shaped by a biblical agenda.[25]

The Protestant gaze will often seek out a large tree providing some shade, flowers, or thorns (depending on the season), a bird or a lizard, and a few comfortable rocks to sit on. These are usually perceived as an authentic and spiritually rewarding alternative to the formal, built-up, commercialized, and usually Catholic sacred sites. Elements such as olive presses, tombstones, and ruins of homes, were also perceived as visual aids that facilitated a simple and inspiring alternative to the congested traditional sites and added the allure of antiquity.[26] While at first, unmarked spots in nature provided the locus for the Protestant gaze and worship, with time, Catholic churches began to set aside nature spots for Protestant worship. Eventually, Protestants developed their own enclaval sites, such as the Garden Tomb, and finally, the Israeli government and private organizations have constructed themed sites, such as Biblical Resources and Nazareth Village, which correspond to the Protestant gaze.[27]

## ZIONIST PLACE-MAKING

If the Protestant pilgrim comes to the Bible Land with a partly unconscious set of expectations of what to see and how the land should look, the Jewish-Israeli guide is well-positioned to create a Bible Land that corresponds to Protestant preconceptions. Unlike Catholic groups, in which the authority of the accompanying priest is vested in sacraments and manifested (even if not exclusively) through performed liturgy, in Protestant groups, the authority of spiritual leaders is intimately linked to their performance of the biblical Word. As a "true Hebrew" the guide is granted speaking rights – and reading rights – to the Word. Furthermore, many Protestant presuppositions are engrained in the Zionist narrative that shapes the guide's training and habitus. The historically intertwined Protestant-Zionist relationship has engendered shared social-memory practices of viewing, classifying history, and orientalizing. These rely on shared ordering narratives and mythic discourses that maintain authorized meanings and promote ways of making and experiencing sanctified spaces.[28] Furthermore, as a Jew, the guide enjoys a certain traditional authority as witness to the Scriptures and as native. Insofar as he draws on Zionist practices and explicitly or tacitly encourages the view of himself as Hebrew, the overlapping Zionist and Protestant narratives cement the ties of both guide and group to the land and to each other while marginalizing Palestinian Arabs and Muslims.

The Protestant pilgrim guide of the nineteenth century served as one of the models for the *yedi'at ha'aretz* – "knowledge of the land" guide practices, although not the only one.[29] Other Protestant-inspired practices have been incorporated in Israeli archaeological practice,[30] cartography, and a view of the Orient as both backward and exotic.[31] The nineteenth-century Protestant attitudes toward the Orient (whether they were projected onto Arabs or onto Russian Orthodox pilgrims) and traditional shrines were taken up in Zionism's rejection of exile and tradition, as well as in the practice of in situ Bible reading as a way of laying claim to space and the past. The point is that the correspondence of the narrative and place-making practice of the Jewish guide and the Protestant pilgrim transcend political agreement or conscious manipulation (e.g., between Christian Zionist groups and right-wing Jewish-Israeli guides).[32]

Rather, Protestants of a wide variety of theological and political orientations share with Zionists a deep-structural historical legacy that generates similar doxa and bodily hexes, transmitted through Israeli education (both schools and tour guide training) and through Protestant preaching.[33] These historically sedimented ways of seeing and classifying include common practices of regarding landscape, the past, and the Orient that are seen to be natural, rather than the product of an ideological stance.[34]

## TRACING THE PILGRIM'S PATH: GUIDING PERFORMANCES OF SPATIAL ORIENTATION

I will now follow the Jewish guide/Protestant pilgrim joint project through guide orientations to four spaces. I chose these spaces because of the differing power distributions and discourses they seemingly authorize. I begin with the panorama, as a place shaped by shared religious and orientalist paradigms that lie beneath the surface of consciousness. I continue with a nonplace, the airport, a religiously neutral postmodern transitory space which may, however, serve as a blank canvas for narratives of belonging.[35] I then describe an enclavic Israeli space, "a single-purpose space . . . carefully planned and managed . . . [with] minim(al) underlying ambiguity and contradiction."[36] I then turn to a heterogeneous and potentially contested tourist/pilgrim space. Heterogeneous spaces are spaces of multiple crisscrossing currents of people and goods, with blurred boundaries that enclose a wide range of activities and people co-existing. In examining these spaces, I hope to show how various tactics are developed by Jewish guides and how such performances mesh with Protestant ways of seeing and behaving to make the Bible into a story that takes place not only at a specific time but in a specific space. Consequently, many little-known or hard-to-visualize spaces now become significant places, centers of the world, orientations for present and future experience.[37]

The central place I allot to guide orientation narratives reflects just how central orientation, naming, reading scripture, and viewing from heights are to Protestant pilgrimage practice. The dominance of the guide's voice within the following descriptions and the paucity of voices of resistance among the pilgrims reflects the usual dynamic at sites of orientation. In such places, even the most experienced pastors rely completely on guides' local knowledge, which includes awareness of road conditions, shortcuts, traffic jams, opening and closing times, and crowd sizes and lighting conditions at panoramic sites. The last two cases I discuss below reveal that, in spite of their authority, guides' interpretations are subject to a certain contestation.

### 1. Hosanna in the Highest – The Mount of Olives Panorama

It's six in the evening, fifth day of the tour. The tour bus climbs from the Dead Sea, lowest point on the face of the earth, up the road to Jerusalem. The travelers, most in shorts, many sunburned and dusty after their visit to Masada, doze in their seats. The pastor asks me to tell the driver to take the narrow back road to Jerusalem through the Arab village of A-Tur and stop for an outlook over Jerusalem before the group checks in to the hotel. Ten minutes before arriving at the overlook, the pastor hands the driver an audiocassette to place in the tape player. The baritone voice of a gospel singer belts out, "Jerusalem, Jerusalem! Lift up your voice and sing! Hosanna in the High-est! Hosanna to your king!" At the pastor's instructions, I stop the bus just before the view of Jerusalem, instruct the passengers to get off, and lead them on a short walk to the Mount of Olives panoramic view over the city. As the Golden Dome of the Rock first comes into view, outlined by the setting sun, some pilgrims emit gasps of surprise and joy.

After several minutes, I seat the group on the semicircular steps facing the Old City:

> You've just come in to Jerusalem as Jesus would have arrived as a pilgrim from Galilee. Do you all see the golden Dome of the Rock? [extending my arm full length and pointing at the building] . . . There's where the Temple was in Jesus's time. Twice the height and twice the width. And when pilgrims of Jesus's day caught their first glimpse of the Temple, as you are doing today, they would sing the Psalms of Ascent, *Shir Hama'alot*, the songs of the steps. Psalm 122: "I was glad when they said to me, let us go up to the house of the Lord."
>
> Do you see the black-domed church down there? [pointing and pausing while the pilgrims point out the site to each other] That's Dominus Flevit. The Lord Wept. Jesus wept there over the city that was to be destroyed. The Mount of Olives, where we're standing here was, already in the prophet Zachariah's time, the Jewish cemetery, like you see today. Right here. [pointing] That's why it became the site of the future resurrection of the dead.
>
> Do you see the wall? [pointing and pausing again] That's the Old City, East Jerusalem, the Arab part, and in back of it you see the skyscrapers of the New City, Jewish West Jerusalem. And there, do you see the tall white building? [pointing, pause] There, a bit below, just to the left, is our hotel.
>
> Take a couple of minutes for pictures if you like, and then we'll get back in the bus and drive there, and tomorrow we'll come out here again and begin our visit of the Holy City, Jerusalem.

This guiding performance builds on a shared historical process that shapes ways of seeing common to Protestants and Zionists, ways that enable landscape to be sanctified by both. At the same time, the guided pilgrimage provides a

The author/guide orients his group to the city of Jerusalem from the outlook point on the Mount of Olives. © *Salem Bible College and Thiessen Photography. Used by permission.*

frame separating the guide-group-landscape interaction from other stimuli as well as the quotidian world of the pilgrims in ways that create communitas and allow for suspension of disbelief and skepticism.

The panoramic view is an expression of power. As de Certeau writes of the observer viewing New York City from the top of the World Trade Center, "His elevation transfigures him into a voyeur. It puts him at a distance. It transforms the bewitching world by which one was 'possessed' into a text that lies before one's eyes. It allows one to read it, to be a solar Eye, looking down like a god."[38] Protestant viewing of the land, as I explained above, is historically, socially, and ideologically conditioned.[39] In Lock's words, "This implied space of viewing has much to do with the nexus of capitalism and Protestantism, with the distance that keeps us from the object, and that keeps us pure, uncontaminated by contact; and with the property that is owned and controlled from a distance."[40] This stance is part of the Protestant bodily hexis, a "political mythology realized, *embodied* and turned into a permanent disposition, a durable way of standing, speaking, walking and thereby of *feeling* and *thinking*."[41]

In tour-guide training, significant time is devoted to panoramic views and outlook points. Not infrequently, the outlook is the goal of the hike. In each case, the outlook depicts a similar desire toward domination through distancing and visual superiority.[42] Thus, when the guide orients pilgrims by pointing down at the city, Protestant and Zionist ways of looking, which developed in tandem, are strengthened and naturalized.

At the high point, the guiding explanation frames the city through the biblical text – "words lettered across the view." The pastor has already taken the initiative in this framing, requesting that the bus come up the old road to Jerusalem through the Arab village, and having them descend the bus before they can see the city to make its "revelation" as theatrical as possible. He also claims the microphone, playing gospel music to shift from touristic (Masada/Dead Sea bathing) to pilgrimic modes. The song provides the group's entry (on foot) into the city as well as the panoramic practice with the resonances of Jesus' triumphal entry into Jerusalem ("Hosanna in the highest!" Mark 11:10). This sets the tone for the guide, who then traces the group's future path through the city, having the pilgrims move from one geographical place to another, from one historical event to another, from one scriptural passage to another, by following his voice, his finger, and, finally, their own fingers across the landscape. As Georges van den Abbeele notes, "The illusion of authenticity depends on the tourist's feeling himself to be in an immediate relationship with the sight. This immediacy is assured by the sight's presence, to which the tourist can point."[43]

At the high point, the guiding explanation frames the city through the biblical text – "words lettered across the view." The pastor follows the story of Elijah in the Biblical text at the Mount Carmel outlook point. © *Salem Bible College and Thiessen Photography. Used by permission.*

This path tracing will be repeated in greater detail at the same spot early the next morning.

The guide's monologue names the elements of the scene through biblical references (Mount of Olives, cemetery, resurrection). He frames Jesus, in accordance with long-standing Protestant practice, as the first and chief among fellow pilgrims to Jerusalem.[44] Finally, he elevates the site by referring to future events that will take place there – the resurrection of the dead, partially supported by the Jewish graves, which can be marshaled as waiting witnesses.[45] Veteran guide Steve Langfur reported, "When they stand where Jesus was, the coin drops: these things really happened. They happened at a specific place, and we're here. It's an encounter between fantasy and reality. As long as the guide gives them enough time and doesn't ruin the experience. That's the power of the trip" (interview, June 2004).

The in situ reading of the Bible is a performative act of great force. As Jon Mitchell learned through his research among Maltese Christians, the habitual public performance of the biblical text "draws attention away from the content and emphasizes its form. The repeated words become almost forgotten; what becomes significant is the fact that they are written, and hence physically present in the Bible, which is an artifact of social memory."[46] The Bible becomes a conduit for direct contact with God and calls forth emotion. Through the repeated process of reading out loud, "the Bible is transformed from a representation of memory into its *actual physical recreation or embodiment*. More than just an isolated memory, it becomes memory itself" (id., emphasis added). As the pilgrims listen to scripture, view the site from above, point, and photograph, the scene itself becomes engraved in their minds and bodies, so that it – and the emotions that may accompany their first view of the city – can be easily triggered when they later hear the passages read in church or in Bible study back home. The primary act of consecration – the naming, framing, and pointing to elements of the site through the biblical text is one accessible to the Jewish guide, especially if he cites Old Testament texts. In his performance, the guide demonstrates his understand of his primary task not as the mere communication of information but as the building of a series of sites (chosen on the basis of a religious logic but sequenced by travel agents on the basis of geographical, logistic, or financial considerations) into a meaningful spiritual path.

The guiding narrative ignores the Muslim sites, overlaying the Dome of the Rock with the vision of the Temple. It makes no mention of current Palestinian Muslim habitation and history and refers to the Arab and Jewish parts of the city as "Old City" and "New City," respectively (although less than ten percent

Pastor Larry Tumbleson reading the Sermon on the Mount at the traditional site. The reading enables memories of the site to be easily triggered when pilgrims later hear the passages read in church or in Bible study back home. © *Salem Bible College and Thiessen Photography. Used by permission.*

of the city's population – Arab and Jewish – live in the Old City).[47] This is an allochronism, a denial of the coevalness of the Palestinian-Muslim-Arab that also reflects Zionist understandings of the Arab as belonging to the past and the Orient (Old City, East Jerusalem) and the Jewish Israeli as belonging to the modern West (New City, West Jerusalem).[48] Finally, the reference to the hotel emplaces the pilgrims in the landscape, cuing them to visualize the next days of their visit to the city as a reenactment of Jesus' pilgrimage to Jerusalem.

Indeed, the denial of coevalness – the relegation of the subject to a time frame different from that of the observer – is of two types, both mentioned by Johannes Fabian. Although the schema of modernity, which constitutes the West as opposed to the rest, is certainly in operation here, it works alongside a second schema, that of salvation history.[49] Not all pasts are of equal value. Those that are central for salvation history, such as Zachariah's prophecies or Jesus's triumphal entry, become contemporized, become near, become objects of identification, loci for reenactment. Others, such as Muslim presence, are effaced here through the guide's and pastor's silence. Thus, a second overlapping power relation is constituted – we, the people of the Bible, the significant subjects of salvation history, and they, the Muslim Others. This is reinforced through the guide narrative's movement from Zachariah to Jesus to the current Jewish cemetery to the future resurrection.

Finally, the frame of the pilgrimage encourages the suspension of disbelief and skepticism. The guide mentions the prophecies of Zachariah, the current Jewish cemetery, and the future resurrection in the same breath, thus implicitly attributing the same facticity to all three. The event of introducing Jerusalem to pilgrims causes both guide and group to be "caught up" in the flow of the prophecy narrative. Although they do not share the same beliefs, both guide and group share the desire that the landscape be seen through the eyes of scripture, that "the disappearance of the places established by a spoken word, the loss of the identities that people believed they received from a spoken word" be arrested. Furthermore, the religious language itself and its aural resonance may have transformative potentials, especially when the pilgrim has prepared him – or herself to be "there."[50] The Israeli tour guide too, has been trained to be not only a *moreh derekh* – a "teacher of the way" – but also an encourager of faith.[51] To encourage faith among the pilgrims the guide need not playact. Rather, he allows himself to be caught up in the performance, and his skepticism is suspended. In that sense, the ritualized performance not only reflects faith but also generates it.

### 2. Nonplaces: The Good Spies at Ben Gurion Airport

A Protestant group from California arrives at Ben Gurion Airport after nearly 24 hours in transit. After the group has boarded the tour bus and made a bathroom stop, the driver has loaded the luggage, and I have counted passengers, the pastor requests the microphone for a word of prayer: "We just want to thank you, Lord, for safely bringing us to this special place. . . . Continue to protect us and guide us, in Jesus's name, Amen." The pastor hands me the microphone, as the bus pulls out of the parking lot.

> Shalom, everyone and welcome to Israel. My name is Jackie, and I'll be your guide for the next ten days. Our driver's name is Muhammad, and he'll be driving us throughout the Land of the Bible.
> Now your pastor, Rev. Jones, tells me that you know your Bible. How many of you brought your Bibles with you on board?
> [Most of the hands go up. Some: "I left it in my luggage."]
> Good! Now I'm going to start off with a little quiz. Just to make sure you really know your Bible – okay? [waving the Bible at them] Now, I'm gonna

mention some names, and if any of you recognize any of them, just raise your hand, okay?

Michael, the son of Sethur. [no hands]

Yigal, the son of Joseph. Anyone here know Yigal? [no hands]

Hey, maybe I've got the wrong book. Let's see [looking at book spine]: Ho-ly Bi-ble. Right book. . . . Let's try again.

Geuel, the son of Maki. [no hands]

Hey Rev. Jones, I thought you told me they knew their Bible.

[Rev. Jones smiles conspiratorially. Another six names follow. No response to any of them. The participants begin to feel uncomfortable.]

Nah-bi, the son of Voph-si. [no hands]

Hey, you guys are 0 for 10. Bring on the designated hitter. We'll give this one last try.

Caleb, the son of Jephuneh. [half the hands go up] Joshua, the son of Nun. [all the hands go up]

Whew, I was getting worried! Well, the first ten names I read were those of the bad spies. Those are the ones that came back and said, "Israel! Dangerous place! You don't want to go there!" [pause, some laughter] Bet some of your friends told you that before you left, right? [murmur of assent] Well, forget about them – just like the ten spies – we forgot about them. But the other two, Caleb and Joshua – they said, "Don't worry, just put your faith in the Lord and He'll see us through." *They're* the ones we remember.

We're here in God's hands, and we're here in the hands of our excellent driver Muhammad, and I'm looking forward to a wonderful and fulfilling experience over the next ten days with you.

We're now traveling through the Sharon Plain, and in 45 minutes we'll be at our hotel in Netanya. I'll have maps for all of you tomorrow.

The well-rehearsed opening dialogue builds on assumed preconceptions of the land (dangerous and oriental – hence, threatening), Protestant practices and implicit theological understandings (Bible reading, the Jew as authoritative Old Testament witness), Protestant tropes of faith ("just put your faith in the Lord"), and popular US culture (baseball and quiz programs) as well as strategic shifts in pronouns (from *you* to *we*) and the use of enthusiastic feeling-tones to frame the tour, from its outset, as a pilgrimage.[52] By introducing himself, the tour, and the land through this dialogue, the guide seeks to imprint the group with his voice, to position his performing voice as the sound pattern that, along with that of the pastor, will serve as the gravitational center of the environmental bubble throughout the tour. As long as the pilgrims remain within earshot of that voice, the participants are part of the community, in step with the directed movement through space that is the pilgrimage. Without it, they may be "lost."

Furthermore, the exchange with the pastor attempts to fashion a model for interaction between the two authority figures. The guide, in charge of logistics, counts the passengers. He then turns over the microphone to the pastor, to lead the prayer. This duality positions them as both disciplined and disciples, two positions with which they are familiar. The travelers become engaged listeners in a biblical performance – also a familiar position. After the pastor invokes the "specialness" of the place, the guide then names the spaces and times of the voyage, giving voice to the story that transforms undifferentiated space into significant place.[53] Thus, the guide's voice also becomes the voice of the land – an auditory memory of something new that has entered into the visitors' personal and communal soundscape.

The dialogue places a unique stamp on the land not as another tourist destination but as the place of history, promise, and destiny. This is done by proclaiming the Bible as the authoritative text for the group, using the biblical story to "christen" or hallow the neutral airport nonspace. Both Protestantism and Zionism speak of recovering their roots in the land (and under its surface) and generally seek "the poetics of faith, rather than a hermeneutic of suspicion."[54] Pilgrims have made the long trip to the Holy Land to strengthen their faith rather than question it. The practice of naming places through the Bible is easily accessible to Israeli guides who have gone on many hikes, both during the guide course and as they grew up in Israel. For many, this practice of historical connection to the land is a significant part of the story they tell of themselves. By affirming the authority of the Bible, the guide attempts to increase the group's confidence in him while revealing the true land as the one inhabited by biblical "Israel."

The guide's questions test the waters of the group ("How many of you brought your Bibles?"), pay public homage to the pastor's authority, and initiate a pattern of mutuality for the tour ("Rev. Jones told me you know," the conspiratorial glance), unite the group in an interactive activity, affirm the spiritual and biblical goals of the voyage, and attempt to position the guide not only as local tourism expert and Jewish "witness" (affirmed through his pronunciation of the Hebrew names of the twelve spies) but also as cultural mediator and as interpreter of scripture.[55]

In grounding the nature of the voyage through Israel in the Old Testament narrative of the spies, the guide strives to bolster the authority of the guide-as-Israeli-local-expert with that of Jew-as-witness-to-biblical-truth. Assuming this position, the guide welcomes and praises the participants' decision to tour Israel not as a vacation option but as an expression of religious faith. By calling the travelers to become "the good spies," he affirms the legitimacy of their spiritual tie to the land. He also lauds their decision to overcome security concerns and fly to Israel as an act of trust in God.[56] By raising their hands to "volunteer" to identify (and identify with) Caleb and Joshua and laughing in appreciation of the point afterward, the pilgrims provide bodily assent to this role. At the same time, the guide implicitly assents to become a "true Hebrew," an Old Testament Israelite as depicted in the Protestant imagination. He also endows the tour bus with a supporting role, as a vehicle of God's goals. Although Ben Gurion Airport is a nonplace par excellence, through strategies of guiding performance, the bus can be hallowed as a home away from home; the profane parking lot of the airport becomes the starting point of a pilgrimage to spy out the land and bring back the Good News.[57]

At the same time, the joking tone and the reference to the tour bus and its Muslim driver as divine instruments—but not grounded in scriptural reference—mark a certain distance between the guide's mode of reading and applying the Book and the more reverentially intoned readings of the pastor; he implies that this pilgrimage will offer participants a good time, while negotiating a space between his role and that of the pastor's.[58] As a non-Christian member of the "witness people" or People of the Book, as guide-interpreter and as English- (in this case, American-) speaking Israeli, the guide is positioned in a liminal space that facilitates shifting between frames. This shifting is marked through a performance that straddles the categories of Israeli (Hebrew) and American (baseball references), game (quiz) and ritual (Bible reading). This shifting and separation between "serious" pilgrimage and "fun" touring will enable the visitors to enjoy both religious experience and hedonistic fun, without the two realms contaminating each other. I illustrate this further in my discussion of the Way of the Cross, below.

Unquestionably, performances such as these are facilitated by the guide's acquaintance and comfort with the Bible text and similar Israeli practices of naming and authenticating sites. They are also honed through mimicry of previous pastors and trial and error. Yet they do not become completely routinized. Had the group recited a Hail Mary and the Lord's Prayer on arrival, an experienced guide would not have referred to the Bible using popular TV program language. Had no one brought their Bibles with them, he might have suppressed the routine, suspecting that the group might not understand the punch line. Thus, although the sealed environmental bubble of the bus, with the guide commanding the microphone, minimizes possibilities for resistance from "outside," the response of the public is a dynamic factor fashioning the performance.[59]

### 3. Enclaval Space: Jesus, Rabbi of the Temple Steps

As part of their Old City tour, I brought a Protestant group to visit *ma'alot hulda*, the Hulda Steps, an excavation located within the Davidson Center heritage complex, adjacent to the Western (Wailing) Wall and below the Mosque of El Aqsa, on land expropriated from the Muslim Waqf. Gathering the group in a semicircle, I held up the archaeological drawing supplied by the site's management, which depicted the site as it looked during the Second Temple period:

> You see those steps? [pointing left]
> Those are the original steps leading into the Temple Mount. Jesus and his disciples must have walked those steps many times on their way into the Temple to sacrifice. The Mishna tells us that Rabbi Gamliel too taught his disciples here, in the shadow of the Temple.
> After the Romans attacked us and destroyed the Temple, those steps were covered over with dirt and debris for two thousand years until, after the Six-Day War, we began excavations, brought the steps to light, and restored them.

At the same time, a Reform bar mitzvah was taking place, with tallit-wearing worshippers reading the Torah on the steps nearby. After my commentary on the site, the group's pastor asked his congregation to climb the steps and be seated on the top ones. He then opened his Bible and read, "As (Jesus) was leaving the Temple, one of his disciples said to him, 'Rabbi! Look how beautiful these stones and buildings are!' And Jesus replied, 'Do you see these things? There will come a day where there will not be one stone left upon another that will not be thrown down'" (Mark 13:1–2).

The guide's presentation builds on the selective excavation and signposting of archaeological sites by the Israeli government authorities operating the site, in which materializations of knowledge that signify "later" eras, especially those of Muslim habitation are effaced.[60] The performance draws on a shared appreciation with the pilgrims of archaeology as "proof" of truths; these proofs may, in turn, engender ritual, national or religious.

The research of the mainly Protestant PEF spurred Zionist efforts to emphasize the Jewish nature of the land through Israelis' own exploration and archaeology projects.[61] Archaeology has been an important part of Israeli civil religion and makes up a substantial portion of the Israeli government tour-guide course.[62] Protestant and Israeli archaeology presents archaeological remains as embodiments of biblical textual traditions. These traditions enable belief, and their materiality serves as verification of those texts.[63] Protestants and Zionists also share commonly accepted ways of displaying "authentic" remains. The archaeological remains are exhibited at the site through partial reconstruction and a wavy line dividing the "untouched original" from the "reconstructed" portions of the excavation, accompanied by signposting (on the site and in the diagrams supplied at the entrance) referring to the appropriate biblical passages. This Zionist aesthetic corresponds to the Protestant pilgrim's view: science and the modern state recover the "natural" past of "Israel" buried under the dirt and clutter of oriental "tradition," whereas the wavy line is a graphic display of the celebration and the limits of human efforts to recover the past through science. Imagination and faith may do the rest.

This understanding of archaeology as proof of scriptural truth and national presence is also reflected by the common use of metaphors of "revelation" in Zionist Israeli and Protestant discourse on archaeology – in this case, "bringing the steps to light." This language obscures the extent to which archaeology constructs the past out of a limited number of material finds, in accordance with dominant, often politicized understandings of history.

The Jewish-Israeli guide's performance is facilitated by the aspects of historical consciousness shared by traditional Judaism and Protestant Christianity. Zionism's "return to history"[64] was interpreted as a return to national political sovereignty ascribed to the Israel of biblical and Second Temple times, whereas later periods of settlement were denigrated as "exilic."[65] In understanding its "return to history" and to Palestine as a return to the Bible, Zionism sought to return to the common Judeo-Christian source of Western tradition.[66] The biblical text, placed in opposition to the Catholic Church and papal (or Byzantine) "tradition" by Protestants, was placed in opposition to the Talmud and exilic Judaism by Zionism.[67] Thus, Zionism anchored its "return" in a place within the theological narrative that constituted the Protestant imagination – the *sola scriptura* of the Bible. Consequently, Zionist archaeological projects privileged the unearthing, restoration, and display of remains of the biblical and Second Temple periods. Similarly, Protestants seek the "original stones" of Jesus's day, ignoring (Byzantine Christian and other) remains of later periods as oriental clutter that can be removed to display the truth of Old and New Testament scripture. The orientalism inherent in this view was enforced when Zionist historiography extended the significant Jewish presence on the land until the Muslim conquest in the seventh century.[68] Thus, the onset of "exile" was merged with the Muslim/Arab conquest (as opposed to, say, Hadrianic Roman expulsion, Byzantine Christian exclusion of the Jews from Jerusalem, or gradual diminution of the Jewish population for economic reasons), and "exile" terminated with Zionist settlement, the end of Muslim/Arab rule, and Jewish sovereignty over the territory of Israel-Palestine.

Through his use of the pronoun we – "we fought the Romans, we excavated the site," the guide's implied continuity with ancient Israel and the excavators concords with the widespread Protestant view of both Jew and material objects in the land as witnesses (even if unwilling) to eternal truth and as representing Western science.[69] That "eternal truth," however, comprises aspects of the Christian view of Jewish history and faith that Israeli Jews reject. For the pilgrim group, the rabbi of "The Rabbi's Steps" is Jesus, the True Rabbi, the fulfillment of Jewish teaching and the telos of history. The guide and the Reform rabbi, as exemplary representatives of "Israel," are framed allochronically as Old Testament precursors of Jesus or as (unwilling) witnesses to Jesus as prophet of its destruction and (for some) judge of the future apocalypse.[70] If the guide develops a narrative designed to cast Jesus as a prototypical Jewish pilgrim and marshals the authority of the Gospels to support the continuity of Jewish-Israeli historical claims to the site and the teleological, restorative nature of Zionism, the pastor evokes Jewish authority (guide and rabbi) to attest to the eternal truth of the Gospels and the veracity of the Christian faith. He also reminds the group (and the guide) of Jesus's prophecy: as a result of the Jews' refusal to accept him as Messiah, there indeed would be "not one stone left upon another that will not be thrown down" (Mark 13:1–2) for 2,000 years!–that is, until the present-day Israeli excavators and builders uncovered the past and developed the site.[71]

As a Jew, the guide is a "reluctant witness," whose presence and scriptural knowledge testify to the truth of scriptural prophecy.[72] As Ora Limor has shown, for Byzantine pilgrims and writers, Jews were seen as possessors of the Book, as bearers of the longest memory, and as older natives of the land who possessed geographical and scriptural knowledge.[73] As they received and preserved the Law and the prophets throughout the generations and understood the Sacred Tongue, already in the Byzantine Period they became witnesses and authenticators of Christian sacred sites and truths, despite their rejection of Jesus as messiah.[74] The Protestant pilgrims' view of the Jew and the land, although based on theological assumptions the guide probably rejects, casts the guide as *hebraeus verus* – the true (biblical) Hebrew – thus reaffirming the Zionist historical claim to the land. Insofar as the guide employs shared social-memory practices of viewing, classifying history, and orientalizing in narrative performances, Zionist and Protestant narratives cement the ties of both guide and group to the land and to each other while marginalizing Palestinian Arabs and Muslims.

We see here how even a well-regulated enclaval space – a fenced-in, Israeli-government signposted archaeological excavation – may become a place of contestation over the issue of who is the true Rabbi and the subject of revelation. Yet such contestation notwithstanding, the site (on Islamic Waqf territory expropriated by Israel) is consecrated through narrative and ritual performance as Judeo-Christian holy ground.

Over the last few years, the Rabbi's Steps have become a "must" site for worship in many Protestant itineraries, encouraged, in part, by Israel Government

Tourist Office posters directed at the Evangelical market. The increased importance of the site has engendered Israeli government construction of a new museum, in the remains of the cellar of the eighth-century Umayyad palace. The museum's presentation includes an impressive audiovisual show that shuttles between the present-day ruins and the scene during Second Temple pilgrimage. Thus, the invisible Second Temple is made present and visible, whereas the Arab Umayyad palace is nearly effaced.[75] The performance of Protestant pilgrimage narratives thus displays clear political consequences in creating new "facts on the ground."[76]

### 4. Contested Space: Following Jesus through the Arab Market

On the second morning of their stay in Jerusalem, the Protestant group I am guiding is scheduled to walk the Via Dolorosa and visit the Church of the Holy Sepulchre in the Old City of Jerusalem before holding a communion service at the Protestant-administered Garden Tomb. I usher the pilgrims into the darkened Catholic chapel of the Second Station of the Cross. Although I assume that they might not care for the polychrome plaster statue of the condemned Christ, the cool benches offer welcome relief from the heat and noise on the street. The Palestinian vendor at the entrance hawks his booklets, "All the stations of the cross. One dollar."

Standing to the side of the altar, in front of the statue, I turn to the group:

> Look, many of you expect to find a peaceful, devotional path. But more than the sound of prayer, what you'll be hearing outside is the sound of business. Now, imagine what it was like in Jesus's day. People doing their last-minute shopping for Passover. A group of Roman soldiers comes up the street, dragging the bloodied Jesus on his cross. A sheep vendor along the way looks up at the cross and the sign above his head, [squinting] "Je-sus of Na-za-reth. Ah, another Galilean rebel." Then he turns back to his customer [putting on an Arab accent]: "so, how much you pay for the sheep?" Except for the bored kids, the rest are just going about their business. And Jesus dies alone on the cross: "Father, may this cup pass from me. But not my will, but thy will be done."
>
> Let's keep that in mind as we make our way out to the Via Dolorosa and up to the Church of the Holy Sepulchre. Now, please stay close together and mind your pockets. There are money changers out there whose ancestors were in the Temple, understand? [restrained laughter] I'll point out some of the stations and we'll have time for devotion and prayer at the Garden Tomb later on. Okay, Rev. Wilson?

Among tourist spaces, the marketplace is seen as one less controlled by the tourist industry and open to crisscrossing flows of people, noises, and smells. Such spaces, writes Tim Edensor, are "pregnant with possibility" and "frequently result in encounters characterized by improvisation."[77] They are conceptualized as the roaming ground of the pedestrian, spaces in which the walker–through his trajectories, shortcuts, and pacing–can perform tactics of resistance to hegemonic strategies. The marketplace is conceptualized as a space of process rather than structure, of subversion of the spatial order.[78] Group tourists, however, tend to prefer safety and structure over adventure, risk, and improvisation.[79] Their fears of Muslims and Arabs in the teeming marketplace have only been increased by the events of September 11, 2001, and media reports of the ongoing Middle East conflict.

The oriental otherness of the marketplace is assigned a secondary role in the pilgrimage text, which privileges the search for the center of one's own society over the seeking of the Other, the unknown, and the demonic that typifies the tourist adventurer.[80] Unlike the postmodern tourist (or "post-tourist") who may delight in rapid shifts from cynical distance to serious contemplation to hedonistic enjoyment, and enjoy the play of surfaces and the inauthenticity of tourist attractions as a mark of his own connoisseurship and "coolness," the pilgrim often comes in search of a "hotter" authenticity, a more profound sense of self. Yet, within the increasingly commodified frame of the group pilgrimage experience, often determined by peak- and low-season prices, availability of hotel rooms, opening and closing times, and competition with other pilgrims and tourists for space at the sites, the sought-after spiritual experience can get lost.[81] This complaint is frequently voiced by clergymen, especially Catholic custodians of sites and religious guides, who sometimes accuse (Israeli) tour guides of transforming the spiritual pilgrimage into a commercial tour.[82] What's more, these very pilgrims also engage in touristic activities like visiting Masada, swimming in the Dead Sea, and shopping. For the pilgrim to maintain the emotional tenor of spiritual experience and see him- or herself as performing pilgrimage (rather than "mere" tourism), the touristic elements must be bracketed off in separate spatiotemporal frames.[83] Through the guide's bracketing, the visitor can be both a true pilgrim and an eager shopper.

Perhaps the most important difference between tourist praxis and pilgrim praxis is in their understandings of walking.[84] Whereas most group tourists frame the exotic at the level of the episodic experience–the sight–Christian pilgrims seek the sense of walking a path, interpreting their bodily procession through space as a reenactment of the movement through time, as the Way toward a religious goal.[85] Through the pilgrims' simultaneous presence as a group, through their moving around in the landscape and leaving traces in it, they become "implicated in the landscape."[86] As they are loaded with sensations of kinesthetic movement and sensory stimuli, the gospel sites and stories take on new depth and meaning.

Through the guiding performance, the final path of Jesus, as the Protestant pilgrims imagine it to be, can be isolated from the sounds and smells of the oriental marketplace and the Other can be properly distanced and subsumed under a scriptural model. Invoking the authority of the written Word, the guide designates the walk as the path of the pilgrim rather than a stroll through the Old City Arab market. By framing shopping en route as a temptation, a deviation from Christ's footsteps, and the Palestinian vendor as akin to a contemporary money changer of Christ's day, the guide disciplines the group to move along quickly without stopping to shop. The walk through the Arab market becomes a procession, following Jesus all the way to the Garden Tomb.

By keeping their eyes on Jesus and their ears tuned to the guide, the pilgrims construct through their movement a Protestant Way of the Cross: a new Protestant devotional path traced by the guide – from the traditional First Station of the Cross, through the darkened Holy Sepulchre (the Others' – Oriental and Catholic – sacred site), to the Protestant archaeological-nature setting of the Garden Tomb (as the site of the resurrection).[87] As their shepherd through the dangers and temptations of the marketplace as well as through the apparent disorder and sensory overload of the Holy Sepulchre (a shrine Protestant visitors generally find distasteful, unaesthetic, and sometimes "idolatrous"), the guide increases his spiritual capital.

The guide's disciplining performance, including the exclusion of the Palestinians, is consistent with the Protestant view of the Orient. Like many other European national movements, Zionism identified itself with progress, as opposed to the unchanging "Oriental." Hence, unlike many other national movements of liberation, Zionism took on a Western self-image. In adopting a secularized Protestant schema of progress and nationhood, Zionism applied the category formerly applied by Christian thought to diaspora Jews in Europe ("Oriental" or *Ostjude*) to the Arab inhabitants of the land.[88] In the example above, the depiction of the vendor in the market as Temple money changer (a stereotype applied in Christian culture to Jews) is founded on the orientalism that is part of the shared legacy of Protestantism and Zionism. The postcard vendor's current speech ("Forty postcards, one dollar") is distanced from the coeval present and dubbed with the sales pitch of one of the "bad guys" of significant history (the sheep salesman's, indifferent to Jesus's suffering). Although I was not aware of it while I was guiding, by applying a traditional Christian anti-Jewish stereotype to the oriental Palestinian, I was aligning myself with the Christian West.

In the marketplace, however, the guide's performance may frequently be contested. Thus, in the case cited here, once the pilgrims left the church and got out into the marketplace, the Palestinian vendor (some of whom eavesdrop on guides' explanations), proclaimed, "Don't listen to your guide. He takes fifty percent commission. He does not want you to buy at my shop because he hates Arabs."[89] Although guides often foresee such challenges and, thus, build up their moral authority while pretending to ignore the sales pitches of the shopkeepers and vendors, this may not always be effective. In other cases, the group may have scheduled an evening meeting with a Palestinian spokesman, who may direct the group to pay attention to other elements on their walk through the Old City marketplace – such as Palestinian poverty or Israeli military presence.

## THE AUTHORITY OF GUIDING PERFORMANCES: TWO CAVEATS

1. The performances I have cited in this chapter show the guide at his strongest – in privileged arenas in which his words are carefully listened to and least open to contestation. They also demonstrate his superior authority in some heterogeneous spaces – such as the Via Dolorosa/Arab Market, where the "facts on the ground" do not always support him, and where the narrative is subject to potential challenge.[90] But tours also include in-between times – in lunch cafeterias or in tourist shops – when the guide's choices are open to disagreement and even dispute. Times during which he or she is silent – like at prayer services. And, of course, evening meetings, back-of-the-bus conversations, and group reunions, in which some participants – or pastors – may express the wish for a guide more Christian, less verbose, or perhaps less political.[91] This chapter reflects the confidence – sometimes verging on arrogance – of many guides in select theaters of performance.[92] From another perspective, however, the guide might be seen not as a player enunciating the strategies of Protestant pilgrimage but as a freelance worker "on the watch for opportunities that must be 'seized on the wing.'"[93] A *bricoleur* whose tactics carve a Jewish or Zionist text – and a means to livelihood – out of a Christian pilgrimage dominated by religious, financial, and security considerations over which he or she has limited influence.[94] The traditional Christian view of the Jew as "reluctant witness" to Christian truth may be skillfully employed by the guide to personal advantage, but, as I will show later, it often limits the guide's ability to present the country, history, the Jewish people, and himself as he would like.

2. The encounter between tourist and native, writes Bruner, takes place on the tourist "border zone" – "the distinct meeting place between the tour-

ists who come forth from their hotels and the local performers who leave their homes to engage the tourists in structured ways in predetermined localities for defined periods of time."[95] In the pilgrimage performances I describe in this chapter, this border zone is inhabited by a guide who is "in the middle" – empowered by scripture, but not Christian; Israeli but also American; a citizen but not quite a "native."

Undoubtedly, interactions will vary for native-born Israeli guides and Jewish immigrants from Western countries, for religious and secular guides, and for men and women. Likewise, such presentations will differ for US and German Protestants; for missionizing Zionist Christian fundamentalists (who sometimes attempt to convert the guide) and for liberal Anglicans. And, of course, they will differ significantly in the case of the "Living Stones" pilgrimages, conducted by Palestinian Christian (or Muslim) guides.[96]

My own subject position, as well as my personal inclination, leads me to venture into the "pastoral" role by listening to and adapting pastors' performances, choosing descriptions, phrases, and feeling tones that can "make the Word come alive" or, as the guide Galia put it, "open their eyes." As a guide, I understand my primary task not as the mere communication of information but as the building of a series of sites (chosen on the basis of a religious logic but sequenced by travel agents on the basis of geographical, logistic, or financial considerations) into a meaningful spiritual path. Other guides, as I will show, may choose other positions.[97]

Pilgrimage practices and stories are part of an ongoing struggle among actors who seek to appropriate space and remake the world in their own image;[98] such practices often draw on deeply engrained, if often unacknowledged, historical images and practices. Thus, if space is a "practiced place" and walking is a process of appropriation and an acting-out of the meaning attached to that space, pilgrims' walking follows well-worn paths traced by previous Protestant practices and Israeli guiding narratives.[99]

Yet it is precisely such shared social memory practices of viewing, classifying, and reading scripture that grant the Jewish-Israeli guide authority to shape understandings of Protestant Christian spaces and even create new ones. The Bible becomes an embodied text, and the guide's emplaced vocal and gestured narration of the Bible constitutes pilgrims as performing listeners and their movement through space as a pilgrimage. The pilgrim's gaze and reactions, in turn, may constitute the guide as a "true Hebrew." The guide's voice, along with that of the pastor, sanctify places in the Bible Land, direct pilgrims' movements and assign them religious and moral value, and draw together the pilgrims, pastor, and guide into a single group moving together through space and time. Through situated narratives, sacred geography is made, boundaries of community are affirmed or readjusted, and significance is granted to certain events, actors, and sites whereas others are read out.

The guide's emplacement and embodiment of an authoritative narrative to be consumed by a wide range of senses lends the link between biblical narrative and territory a facticity that places even disputed territory beyond political discussion. Through invoking scripture, and facilitating kinesthetic and sensory experiences, Jewish-Israeli guides and Protestant pastors shape the movements of travelers into the path of the pilgrim. Israel becomes not a site of political contestation but the eternal Land of the Bible.

# 4 CHRISTIANIZING THE CONFLICT: BETHLEHEM AND THE SEPARATION WALL

> Just as none of us is outside or beyond geography, none of us is completely free from the struggle over geography. That struggle is complex and interesting because it is not only about soldiers and cannons but also about ideas, about forms, about images and imaginings.[1]

THROUGHOUT THE CONTENTIOUS history of the Holy Land, the sacralization of places through scriptural attributions, reproduced images, and liturgical performance has been the common currency of political claims to space.[2] Insofar as pilgrimages often take place in contested public space, they serve not only as an affirmation of faith and belonging but also as a manifestation of presence to others, a staking of a claim to territory.

In this chapter, I will investigate how sites of violent conflict in Israel/Palestine become sacralized and imbued with transcendent meaning. What narrative and performative strategies make certain understandings of violence natural, and how do actors shape biblical landscapes and narratives in order to make their understandings of the conflict self-evident and justified to others – whose moral and political support they seek? I will focus on a recent but already canonical manifestation of the Israeli-Palestinian conflict, the "Separation Wall" and the passage between Jerusalem and Bethlehem, as experienced by Western Christian pilgrims.

If in the previous chapter I gave the place of pride to my own guiding narrations and performances, here I deal with tours whose political orientation is far more explicit than the ones I led. To illustrate models for these trips, I draw primarily on brochures and website itineraries used to promote the tours of the Holy Land/Bible Land. In an age in which media representations have become increasingly significant in shaping tourist and pilgrim imaginations and expectations, this perspective is essential.[3] Furthermore, many of these tours are organized, not by a local church or parish but by political or denominational movements whose members earn and sign up for the tour based on mediatized representations rather than word-of-mouth information. The data culled from media is supplemented by observation of touring practices and from interviews with Jewish and Palestinian guides and Western Christian pilgrims of varying theological and political orientations.

I chose to make the Separation Wall between Bethlehem and Jerusalem the focus of this chapter, since Bethlehem is the site in the Palestinian Authority outside of Jerusalem most visited by Christian Holy Land tours; sometimes it is the only one. Furthermore, over the past decade, the Separation Wall has become an icon of the Israeli-Palestinian conflict. The conjuncture of the religious significance of Bethlehem as the birthplace of Christ, with the political significance of the Separation Wall makes touring discourse and practice in Bethlehem a window into how theological and political players and prayers interact.

## THE SEPARATION WALL

The 790-km Separation Wall, whose construction was begun by Israel in 2002 in response to the mounting waves of suicide bombings, divides Israel from the Israeli-occupied and/or Palestinian-administered West Bank. Although it appears and is often referred to as a border (both by tourists and Israelis), it was unilaterally erected by Israel, often several miles within West Bank territory.

Physically, the Wall marks facts on the ground – it keeps some people out, others in; it separates the farmer from his fields, the worker from his place of employment, and the terrorist from his target. Much of its impact derives from other, less visible elements of power and policing: fixed checkpoints, bypass roads, flying roadblocks, ID cards of various colors, police patrols, the Israeli air force, "pinpoint assassinations," collaborators within the Palestinian Authority, and more.[4] But as the Wall serves as the most prominent material symbol of both security and power inequalities, it becomes a screen onto which people project a wide variety of imaginaries. As a former Palestinian tourism minister put it, "The matrix of control exists, but the Wall is what you can take a picture of."[5] Many pro-Israeli groups refer to it as the "security fence" and credit it with the drastic reduction in suicide bombings in Israel; pro-Palestinian ones often call it the "apartheid wall," emphasizing the disruption of the daily lives of West Bank Palestinians. As the Wall is the most visible, most material reminder of conquest or security, it has become a frequent object of media attention both local and international. And as the tourism industry (especially pilgrimage, heritage, cultural, and border tourism) relies so heavily on visual signs, the Wall has become a national and international tourist attraction.[6]

Previous anthropological studies of political tourism have tended to locate power in the destination country ("hosts"), with tourists sometimes serving as the discontents. For example, in Kobi Cohen-Hattab's study of tourism under the British Mandate, tourism becomes a battlefield in which Israelis and Palestinian travel agents, tour guides, press, and guidebooks often exploit tourism and manipulate images in order to advance distinctive political and ideological goals.[7] There, as well as in the articles of Richard Clarke and Eldad Brin on political tourism in Hebron and Jerusalem, the scene is often one of sophisticated, often wily, ideologically committed guides who become "soldiers in the national struggle," generating and manipulating images for a generally uncommitted, underinformed, malleable, and curious tourist.[8] Here, however, I hope to show how meaning is negotiated between foreign Christians and locals through a dialogue of religion and politics. New material objects and contemporary political struggles are granted Christian religious significance through their incorporation into existing Bible-directed Christian paradigms, thus Christianizing the landscape while granting religious legitimacy to political struggle. Moreover, I will portray the guide here as a mediator between State propaganda, commercial agents and the desires of tourists, as he attempts to communicate and realize his own interests within this space.[9]

Friedland and Hecht state, "Rites depend on Rights; the very construction and officiation of any sacred site, no matter how meager, has a component of authority."[10] As we have seen, there is a tight relation between consecration of holy sites, the performance of ritual, and imperial or colonialist power – whether we consider Constantine in the fourth century or the Palestine Exploration Fund in the nineteenth.[11] The diffusion of Holy Land images, relics, and reproductions also played a role in the consolidation of the sites. Subsequently, pilgrim stories and church rituals mapped movement from site to site in the Holy Land onto the linear course of the year-cycle and/or the space of the church as, for example, in Passion processions.[12] European miniature models too often served as inspiration for the consecration and construction of buildings in the Holy Land.[13] The material displays and narrations of the Separation Wall and the representations they engender illustrate how processes of sanctification and legitimation take place in an era of media images and by authorities not necessarily of the pilgrims' church or denomination.

I will begin by briefly surveying the intersection of theology and political orientations of various pilgrim groups and their reflection in tour brochures. I then focus on how Bethlehem and the Separation Wall are portrayed in brochures and itineraries of Christian pilgrim groups of various theological orientations. I then demonstrate how the Wall, supported by other Israeli security measures, creates geographical "facts on the ground" that amplify certain Israeli understandings of the conflict, while muting Palestinian ones, and how such understandings are contested through pro-Palestinian graffiti and Wall posters. Finally, I will demonstrate how sites of violence or suffering are narrated in Christian religious terms by Israeli and Palestinian guides in and around Bethlehem. Through these narrations, constructions, and performances, Christian beliefs may render particular political perceptions of the land natural, understanding violence as tragic, inhuman, or divinely justified.

## POLITICAL AND THEOLOGICAL POSITIONS OF PILGRIM GROUPS

Stephen Sizer has classified three orientations of Western Christian Holy Land pilgrimages:[14]

1. "Evangelicals [and most Western Catholic and Orthodox pilgrims – JF] go essentially to visit the sites of biblical significance . . . without addressing either the present Middle East conflict or necessarily engaging in theological praxis."
2. "Fundamentalist pilgrims visit the Holy Land for similar reasons but with the added eschatological dimension, believing themselves to be witnessing and indeed participating in the purposes of God, at work within Israel in these 'last days.' They believe they have a divine mandate to support the state of Israel . . . by participating in the purposes of God, at work within Israel in these 'last days' [Before the rapture and the Second Coming of Christ]. They believe they have a divine mandate to support the State of Israel."

The most widespread current Fundamentalist eschatological doctrine is based on the division of the world into time periods or dispensations. As Rosemary Reuther summarizes, according to dispensationalism, world history is divided into seven epochs, and the world is currently toward the end of the sixth.[15] Contemporary events, dispensationalists believe, show the hand of God protecting his chosen people, the Jews. The Jewish people's return to the land is part of an end-time scenario leading to the rebuilding of the Temple, the conversion of 144,000 to Christianity, Armageddon, and the destruction of unsaved Jews, Arabs, and Communists.[16]

Faydra Shapiro takes issue with Sizer's characterization of "fundamentalist" or Christian Zionist groups, writing that "the role of dispensationalism has been over-stated as a basis for contemporary Christian Zionist understandings of the Holy Land. Appeals to biblical literalism, prophetic fulfillment and covenant faithfulness, to name a few, are invoked far more often than complex theological/eschatological schemas. Doubtless a post-9/11 emphasis on a putatively shared Judeo-Christian heritage over and against Islam, together with the perceived threat of radical Islam, also play a role in strengthening recent Christian Zionist support for Israel."[17]

These groups support a security-oriented Israeli view and, like Israeli National Religious groups, see the return of territories to the Palestinians as contrary to God's will.[18] As one Biblical Israel website informed prospective pilgrims,

> If you are praying for peace in Israel, we do believe that to be Biblical, although we do not expect the situation there to improve until our Lord is on the throne here on Earth. Please, do not make a reservation with us based on the hopes of a calm future. If you are interested in the special blessings only available in Israel, we will take you there and most probably without a hint of trouble. Our expert driver and guide will keep you from areas that could present a problem and treat you to the riches of Israel as a special guest.

The site reassures prospective pilgrims that their visit to Israel is an act of faith in Jesus and that, consequently, they will be protected from harm: "All of our tours over the past 20 years have returned without a hitch and the souls that went were blessed beyond measure. Everyone has been stirred in their commitment to Christ and not once has anyone felt threatened or in danger."[19]

3. The third group identified by Sizer, a pastor and founder of a UK-based organization bearing the name "Living Stones" pilgrimages.[20] The theology supporting Living Stones tours is rooted in a New Testament passage (1 Peter 2:4–10) supportive of supercessionist theology, in which the Christian Church replaces the Jewish people as a nation of priests (Leviticus 19), heirs to God's promises to Abraham and agents of His will in the world.[21]

> He [i.e., Jesus Christ] is the Living Stone, rejected by human beings but chosen by God and precious to him; set yourselves close to him so that you too may be Living Stones making a spiritual house as a holy priesthood to offer the spiritual sacrifices made acceptable to God through Jesus Christ (v. 4–5).
> You [i.e., the (Gentile) Church] are a chosen people, a royal priesthood, a holy nation, a people belonging to God. . . . Once you were not the people, but now you are the people of God (v. 9).

"These pilgrimages," he writes, "seek to counter the ignorance of many Evangelicals and the harm caused by Fundamentalists, by engaging in acts of solidarity with the Palestinian church. These pilgrimages include opportunities to meet, worship with, listen to and learn from the spirituality and experience of the indigenous Christians."[22]

The choice of the term "Living Stones" tacitly acknowledges the penchant of Western Christians for visiting Holy Land shrine and archaeological sites while ignoring the local population. In Living Stones tours, Palestinian Christians are granted authority as "brothers and sisters of Jesus" and are represented as steadfast martyr witnesses to an unbroken Palestinian Christian presence in the Holy Land since the times of Christ. The focus on uninterrupted tradition makes such tours more attractive to Catholic and more traditionally liturgical churches (Anglicans, Presbyterians, many Lutherans), especially as their leadership often tends to be more liberal politically.[23] Also, these churches' iconographic and liturgical orientations are shared by some Palestinian Christians; thus, the shrines as well as shared worship with Palestinian Christians are a draw for such pilgrims.

Since the rise of the right-wing Likud Party to power in 1977, various Israeli governments have targeted American Evangelical and fundamentalist groups as a prime audience for garnering political support.[24] The government tourist ministry has sent speakers to Evangelical churches, publicized pastors' visits to Israel and speeches, invited them to be guests of honor at Israeli State events in their home countries, and brought many pastors to Israel on highly subsidized orientation tours. The visit to the Bible Land has heightened the authority of preachers, as it often serves as a locale for in situ devotional broadcasts, both live and taped. The leading of Holy Land tours also provides a source of additional income for pastors.[25] The marketing strategy has been successful, and Evangelicals have proven to be Israel's most loyal visitors in times of crisis, as during the second Intifada.[26]

Over the past two decades, Palestinian authorities and nongovernmental organizations (NGOs), such as the Jerusalem-based Sabeel, have worked with pro-Palestinian church groups and NGOs from the West to bring Anglican and other liberal church denominations on study tours that promote sympathy and political action for the Palestinian cause, such as through support of the BDS (boycott, divestment, and sanctions) movement against Israel.[27]

In the following section, I will characterize the two political poles of the Western pilgrimage spectrum – Biblical Israel or Christian Zionist tours (terms that are more accurate than "fundamentalist") and Living Stones tours – and illustrate their strategies of representing the Wall through itinerary choices and brochure narratives. While accurate estimates of theological (not to mention – political) orientations among pilgrims are notoriously hard to obtain, one scholar writes that American evangelical pilgrims not all following the Biblical Israel itineraries listed below – numbered 35% of American Christian visitors in 2011, more than their proportion in the American population. Americans are the largest group of foreign visitors to Israel.[28] The number of participants in Living Stones tours is even harder to estimate, but they probably do not account for more than several thousand a year. Most Christian visitors focus on the footsteps of Jesus or the holy sites and liturgies and ignore current events, although guides may introduce political messages into their narratives as well.

## HOLY LAND PILGRIMAGE AND THE TOUR BROCHURE

Most groups come through voyages organized by Christian travel agents who target specific publics through their webs of church contacts, as well as through the language of brochures, itineraries, and websites. The program itinerary is thus not merely an advertising teaser but is integrated into the spiritual mission statement of the sponsors as well as the contractual obligations of the travel agents. Dean MacCannell was one of the first to underline the importance of on-and-off-site markers in creating the meaning of the tourist attraction.[29] These markers, including brochures, websites, and guiding narratives, shape the visual and other expectations of the visitors, such that they often experience the site as real insofar as it corresponds to the image produced by those markers.[30] The field of off-site markers of the Holy Land is vast, including Bible readings and prints, sermons, altar paintings, returning visitors' stories and videos, computer screen savers, and even children's bedtime stories. The tour brochures provided to pilgrims, in print or online, illustrate as well as orient the expectations of visitors from sites as they prepare for departure – especially since many are integrated with contracts that specify mutual obligations of tourist and tour provider. Studies on tourist brochures show how they reflect orientalism, as well as colonialism and unequal power relations, often depicting the natives as exotic, unusual (yet typical), primitive, and often sexually desirable and available.[31] While some of those images (the exotic but not the sexual) are present in Christian pilgrim brochures, the brochures also draw on a series of iconic images propagated by churches.

The pilgrim tour brochure is a hybrid "glocal" product in which the trends and graphics of the global tourism industry interact with the sensitivities and wishes of local church groups and, sometimes, the Israeli government as well.[32] Usually, the foreign tour company selling the tour, the local (Israeli or Palestinian) tour company providing the services, and the group's Christian spiritual leader shape the final product together. While most local agents are more concerned with booking hotel and bus services and pricing the itinerary, leaving the language of the brochure to ministers and spiritual leaders, some are highly sensitive to the particularities and variants of Christian language. Thus, one described how in an initial telephone contact with a prospective Christian group leader, he listens and jots down the key words used. "The language is everything. If you get the language wrong, you won't sell the tour."[33] From my own experience writing brochures, the terminology for copywriting programs differed considerably for Catholics and Evangelicals, while there were certain key phrases that reappeared in brochures oriented toward the same market niches.

Among the prominent buzzwords of Biblical Israel (or Christian Zionist) tours that appear in brochures and websites are love of Israel, people of the Book, Jewish roots of Christianity, fulfillment of prophecy, return of Christ, eternal covenant, House of David, burden for Israel, and rapture. Among the prominent Living Stones buzzwords are contact with "real people," Palestinian brothers and sisters of Jesus, preservation of the authentic lifestyle of Jesus and his disciples, steadfastness of community, martyrdom and suffering, and love, compassion, justice, and mercy. Although these lists include theological terms as well as explicitly political ones, the concentration of several of them together in a single tour brochure suffices to mark it as belonging to one of the two orientations.

The photos that appear on brochure covers and website home pages for the tours also market the itineraries to groups with particular theological, liturgical, and political orientations. Witness, for example, two brochures produced by the same American tour agent for two different pilgrim groups in October 2007. The first, entitled "Israel: A Biblical Journey," sponsored by Full Faith Tours, shows a large picture of the menorah, the candelabrum opposite the Knesset; a picture of the Temple Mount foregrounding the Western Wall at prayer, a panoramic shot of the Sea of Galilee, and a picture of a Hebrew text of the Dead Sea Scrolls along with a young man with a digging trowel in a desert landscape (Qumran?). The upper left-hand corner bears an image of the "Messianic Seal" combining the candelabrum, a fish, and Star of David. This symbol has been attributed by Messianic Jewish and some Evangelical communities to the early Judeo-Christian church.[34] The second, with a Living Stones orientation, is entitled "Faces, Spaces and Places of the Holy Land." Its key picture shows the Lutheran Redeemer Church in Jerusalem at sunset with the Holy Sepulchre in the background, along with three insets depicting a pastor in casual ecclesiastical garb (the Palestinian pastor Mitri Raheb), an old Palestinian woman in traditional cross-stitch dress, and two children – male and female, with the younger boy holding a piece of bread.

The first brochure provides a "Jewish" point of view on the Temple Mount, Hebrew as the language of ancient Scripture, the candelabrum that serves as the symbol of the State of Israel, archaeology, and landscape. The logo on the cover announces, "If you read the Book, you'll love the land."[35] The brochure's short list of declared aims of the tour includes "to make known the Hebraic roots of our faith" and "to show our love for the God of Abraham, Isaac and Jacob, and for the Jewish people." The second brochure broadcasts the Lutheran character of the tour along with the themes of Palestinian Christian presence, indigenous tradition, and charity to needy children.[36] Inside, the brochure announces one of the primary goals of the trip as "to learn from and stand with the diminishing Christian community in the Holy Land, exemplified by Palestinian Lutherans."[37] In both cases, the title of the tour and the pictures that promote it index the itinerary that follows and transmit visual images that broadcast the political and theological messages of the group's organizers.

I now turn to the Bethlehem itinerary as depicted in the brochures of Biblical Israel and Living Stones tours.

### BETHLEHEM AND THE SEPARATION WALL IN BIBLICAL ISRAEL TOUR BROCHURES

One Biblical Israel tour outlines the Bethlehem day of their "Feast of Tabernacles Tour" itinerary as follows:

> *Day 8 – Hebron – Jerusalem*
> Today we will head south into Judea. The Kfar Etzion sound and light show will give you a picture of the price the Jews have paid to hold on to their land. Driving past Bethelem [*sic*], down the path taken by Abraham to the burial place of the patriarchs in Hebron and the Cave of Machpelah as well as the first capital of King David. We will meet some residents of the old city of Hebron and walk to the ancient neighborhoods and museum. Return to Jerusalem for dinner and the Feast Celebration.[38]

The tour bypasses Bethlehem completely, to make its first stop of the day at a sound-and-light show in a Jewish West Bank settlement. This corresponds with the Christian Zionist understanding, which sees the conquest of the West Bank ("Judea and Samaria") in the Six-Day War and its settlement by Jews as part of the end-time scenario. As religion scholar Faydra Shapiro explained: "it's not about where Jesus walked, it's about where he's going to walk" (Faydra Shapiro, personal communication, January 2011).

The remainder of the program includes encounters with the Jewish settlers in Hebron,[39] while the museum there frames the Muslim hostility toward the settlers (as expressed through the pogrom of 1929) as endemic, drawing parallels with the Holocaust. Clearly, it is only the Jewish "residents of the ancient neighborhoods" who are linked with the Patriarchs. This corresponds to the Christian Zionist ideology in which "Eretz Israel [the Land of Israel] is given under the Abrahamic covenant to Jews alone . . . and a strong Israel is seen as essential for the protection of Jews from 'another Holocaust.'"[40]

A second Biblical Israel brochure, after mentioning many of the biblical sites to be visited on the proposed tour ("descend the Mount of Olives on the Palm Sunday Road to the Garden of Gethsemane. . . . Visit Calvary, share in communion at the Garden Tomb") lists "View Bethlehem from the Shepherds' Fields."[41] The tour promises a view of Bethlehem but not a visit of the town or the Church of the Nativity. The Shepherds' Field mentioned is not one of the marked-with-a-church traditional sites in Beit Sahour under Palestinian Authority control but an unmarked site off the road, in Israeli-administered territory near Jerusalem. The choice of site corresponds to the larger Protestant love of panoramic vistas and, often, revulsion toward traditional shrines.[42] The choice of an outlook point on the Israeli-controlled side of the Wall (as opposed to another, more pastoral one in the vicinity of Beit Sahour) reflects Christian Zionist desire to avoid unnecessary contact with Palestinians.

Another itinerary with a Christian Zionist orientation reads:

> *Day 9: Bethlehem, Biblical Gardens, Messianic Lecture.*
> If we are permitted, we begin our day visiting Bethlehem and the Bethlehem Bible College.[43] If we are not able to go to Bethlehem, we will substitute the Southern Wall Excavations [at the foot of the Temple Mount).

Here, Bethlehem is included in the itinerary but is made contingent on "permission," namely, Israeli security considerations, as relayed by the (Jewish-Israeli) guide and the group's spiritual leader. In any case, the archaeological site of the Temple Steps in Jerusalem (i.e., "the Rabbi's Steps") is presented as a suitable alternative. Given the visual expectations of many Protestants, including participants of Biblical Israel tours, the Orthodox and Catholic Church of the Nativity, located in the midst of an oriental Palestinian (and largely Muslim) Bethlehem, is a disappointment for many Protestants.[44] Thus, some groups bypass it on their way to Hebron, where they visit the museum at Beit Hadassah (depicting the massacre of the Jewish community in 1929) and the homes of the settlers, while some make the visit optional. Others, eager not to skip the "must" site of the birthplace of Jesus, spend as little time in town as possible. As they see part of their mission in Israel as "blessing" the Jewish people and the State of Israel and "standing with Israel," many refuse to spend their money in Palestinian shops in Bethlehem or in the Old City of Jerusalem.[45]

Note that none of these tour brochures mentions the Separation Wall, although all will see it as they pass through the checkpoints, and some programs may even include an outlook on Palestinian areas from the Israeli side (see below).

## BETHLEHEM AND THE WALL IN LIVING STONES BROCHURES

Living Stones brochures and itineraries cast a harsh spotlight on sites that are either rendered invisible or interpreted favorably in Biblical Israel tours. One such organization, Alternative Travel Services, based in the West Bank town of Beit Sahour, advertises their tours as follows:

> Alternative travel in the Holy Land provides an added benefit to pilgrimage by connecting you with the Living Stones of Palestine who live under military occupation. Visit the holy Christian sites, worship in ancient Palestinian Christian churches, walk where Jesus walked and bear witness to the realities of occupation – military checkpoints, refugee camps, Israel's Apartheid Wall, bypass roads, illegal settlements and more.[46]

These emphases in their understandings of Christianity and the conflict are reflected in and projected onto the site descriptions in two groups' itineraries of visits to Bethlehem and the Wall:

1. *Mon 30 APR Bethlehem*
   Did not our hearts burn within us?
   This morning visit Shepherds' Field in Beit Sahour. Afternoon: Remembering that Jesus was a refugee we will visit Bethlehem's Dheisheh Refugee Camp, administered by the United Nations Relief and Works Agency for Palestinian Refugees.[47]

2. *SAT, 10 Nov, Bethlehem*
   Tour the recently constructed Separation Wall and understand its impact. This concrete wall is still being built around Palestinian villages, towns and farms by the Israeli government. In some cases, farmers cannot reach their fields because the Wall stands in between. Visit the Dheisheh Refugee Camp, where Palestinians have lived since 1948. Continue to Beit Sahour to see Shepherds' Field, where the angels announced the birth of Jesus (Luke 2:10). End the day with a relaxing Bedouin dinner. Abu Gubran Guesthouse (B, D).[48]

In the first itinerary, the opening quote refers to the disciples' late recognition of Jesus on the road to Emmaus through their common breaking of bread. Implied is that Jesus is revealed to present-day pilgrims not by viewing old stones but through their communion with the suffering Palestinian Living Stones. In this narrative, Jesus, the solitary traveler on the road, is depicted as a refugee. In such tours, the Separation Wall is often viewed where its path seems most oriented to cause arbitrary suffering to civilians, such as where it encloses one of the refugee camps in northern Bethlehem. Thus it is depicted as a sign of the Israeli government's oppression and (by making Jesus a Palestinian refugee) persecution of the Living Stones, who here become all Palestinians (not just Palestinian Christians).

## MAKING FACTS ON THE GROUND: THE VESTMENTS OF HEGEMONY AND RESISTANCE

At this point, I turn away from the brochures of the organized Living Stones and Biblical Israel tours, to show how through construction and graffiti, the Wall and the passage into Bethlehem are imbued with Christian meaning. If the Wall and the transition from Jerusalem to Bethlehem can be assigned widely differing symbolic values through itineraries, brochures, and touring practices that draw on varying Christian theologies, it can also be "dressed" in vestments of hegemony or resistance. This dressing of the Wall has the potential to affect a wider sector of visitors to Bethlehem, although their contact with it depends on the time (if any) allotted to viewing, touching, or praying by it.

The Israeli government dresses the Wall, concealing the matrices of control supporting the Wall and naturalizing it as part of a regulated international border landscape; Palestinians paint murals, scrawl graffiti, or draw cartoons of the Wall that emphasize its disruptive nature.[49] I will provide illustrations of each of these tactics insofar as they reference Christian understandings.

The main passage from Jerusalem to Bethlehem is in the vicinity of Rachel's Tomb, one of the most hotly contested and fortified points along the entire Wall.[50] Here, the thick Wall, cutting the main Jerusalem-Bethlehem-Hebron road in two, is 9.5 meters high and lined with numerous watchtowers. The imposing materiality of the Wall is muted through the construction of "Rachel's Crossing," an air-conditioned hall, with walls painted in pastel colors and a surrounding pavement of small brick-colored blocks. The façade is covered with large banners in several languages that bear the symbol of the Israel Ministry of Tourism – the two "good" spies carrying a cluster of grapes on their shoulders (from the biblical story in Numbers 13–14). The English sign reads "Peace be with you." The complex contains a parking lot, toilets, passport checks and metal detectors, and separation between tourists and Palestinian residents.

Banner "dressing" the wall on the Israeli side of the checkpoint named Rachel's Crossing. The peace greeting has since been taken down. *Photo © Amos Trust. Used by permission.*

According to Lieutenant General Dani Tirzah, one of the Israel Defense Forces liaisons on the Separation Wall, the crossing resembles the security measures currently practiced at airport terminals and international borders.[51] Thus, pilgrims are given the impression that they are crossing a normal, two-way international border rather than a unilaterally constructed military obstacle. The physical separation of international pilgrims from local Palestinians within the terminal renders the far longer waiting time and strict surveillance undergone by Palestinians crossing through invisible.[52] The name "Rachel's Crossing" frames the site as a gateway. In the Christmas holiday season, they are even handed certificates confirming their status as emissaries of peace. To quote an Israeli Ministry of Tourism newsletter,

> On Christmas Eve, thousands of Pilgrims and local Israeli Christians passed safely without delay between Bethlehem and Jerusalem. . . . Tourism Ministry staff manned Rachel's Crossing to greet the tourists and handed out Christmas greetings in Hebrew, Arabic and English, trinkets and candy in the holiday spirit. Pilgrims embraced the staff and sang songs of praise.[53]

www.goisrael.com

צליין יקר

מדינת ישראל שמחה שהחלטת לחגוג את חג המולד בארץ הקודש.

ראשי הכנסיות בירושלים קראו לעידוד הצליינות לארץ הקודש וחתמו על מנשר לצליין המבקר בה,

להתפלל למען השלום ובכך ליצור גשר בין כל העמים.

נא קבל שי קטן ומתוק זה לרגל החג.

חג שמח!!!


Dear Pilgrim

The State of Israel is glad that you have decided to celebrate the Christmas Season in
the Holy Land.

Christian religious leaders in Jerusalem have announced the promotion of pilgrimages

to the Holy Land and have signed an appeal to the pilgrims visiting

the Holy Land to pray for peace between all nations, thus creating a bridge for peace.

Please accept our token of sweets for the Holiday Season.

Merry Christmas!


عزيزي الحج

سرت دولة اسرائيل بقرارك الأحتفال بعيد الميلاد المجيد في الأراضي المقدسة.

رؤوساء الكنائس في القدس وجهوا دعوة لتشجيع الحج للأراضي المقدسة ووقعوا على كتاب يدعون

فيه الحجاج الوافدين اليها للصلاة من اجل خلق جسر السلام والتاخي بين الشعوب.

نقدم لكم هدية متواضعة بمناسبة العيد.

عيد سعيد!


Certificates produced by the Israeli Ministry of Tourism for pilgrims
crossing into Bethlehem on Christmas Eve. *Reproduced by permission
of Israeli Ministry of Tourism.*

Israeli Ministry of Tourism staff hand out sweets to pilgrims crossing into Bethlehem on Christmas Eve. *Photo by T. Sasson, Courtesy of Israeli Ministry of Tourism.*

The pilgrims are depicted as border crossers, harbingers of peace, and emissaries of the Prince of Peace consecrating free passage through their presence and movement.

If the Israeli side of the Wall is integrated into the landscape by being "cloaked" as a border, gateway, and an integral part of the landscape (in other places, the scenery hidden by the Wall is painted on its façade), the Palestinian side of the Wall has become inscribed with graffiti, murals, and posters depicting it as arbitrary, illegal, and disruptive of the quotidian and spiritual life of Palestinians. Palestinian graffiti emerged in Gaza and the West Bank during the first Intifada in the 1980s. Painting graffiti became an act of resistance to Israeli censorship, a means of symbolically reclaiming occupied territory, a statement in the struggle between Palestinian factions, a means of denouncing collaborators, and a rite of passage for youngsters joining Palestinian resistance movements.[54] Most of these functions have since been fulfilled by other practices, and in the 2000s, Palestinian graffiti became increasingly professionalized and commercialized.[55] In 2004, following the building of the Separation Wall, international graffiti artists, in cooperation with Palestinian authorities,

"Target Dove," a Banksy mural on the wall of a Bethlehem building near the Rachel's Crossing entrance to the city. *Photo © Amos Trust. Used by permission.*

came to paint on the Wall (sometimes even before its completion) in order to draw world attention to the suffering of Palestinians caused by the Wall's construction. Using Berlin Wall graffiti as their model, these artists attempted to depict the Wall as arbitrary, ridiculous, and an obstacle to freedom and democracy. The potential audience for these images was primarily Western and European, as made evident by the "windows" drawn on the exposed concrete, depicting Swiss mountain landscapes, tropical beaches, and European living rooms.[56] The best-publicized of these artists is the British street artist known as Banksy, who referred to Palestine as "the world's largest open-air prison and an unbeatable destination for graffiti-artists on holiday."[57]

Aside from a wide variety of more or less spontaneous graffiti, some of which compare the Wall to the Warsaw Ghetto, the Berlin Wall, or Sharpeville, several artistic examples employ Christian themes. According to Palestinian guides I interviewed, one of the most frequently viewed murals, on the main road between Rachel's Crossing and the Church of the Nativity, is that of the "targeted dove." Here, a dove carrying an olive branch wears a bulletproof vest, while the cross-hairs of a rifle scope target its breast. This picture has additional resonance for Christian visitors familiar with the biblical story of Noah and the dove sent out to find dry ground to make a fresh start after the great flood.

Another mural, often reproduced in catalogs, websites, and exhibitions elsewhere, depicts the three Magi following the star of Bethlehem, on their way to venerate the newborn infant Jesus. Just outside Bethlehem, their way is blocked by the Separation Wall, and one of the Magi dismounts his camel to dig a hole underneath it.[58] A second variant shows Joseph and the pregnant Mary (dressed as Palestinian villagers) being stopped to be frisked by Israeli soldiers. Joseph is spread-eagled against the Separation Wall while a soldier holds a mirror to check underneath Mary's donkey (and dress?).[59] These humorous cartoons draw parallels between contemporary Palestinians and Jesus, contemporary Israelis, and Roman soldiers. The Wall is thus portrayed as an obstacle in God's plan, as embodied by the Prince of Peace of Bethlehem, to bring peace and salvation to the world – an obstacle that through resistance (digging underneath it) will ultimately be overcome.

A similar theme is depicted in the "walled Nativity set," an olive wood Nativity set marketed in England by Amos Trust and available in some Bethlehem souvenir shops. I should note that Nativity sets are not just another souvenir; produced in Bethlehem since the Middle Ages for Western pilgrims, they are practically an icon of the city. I have never seen one bearing humorous motifs. Like the pilgrim brochures, the posters and olive wood Nativity sets are hybrid or glocal products, negotiated between Palestinians craftsmen and entrepreneurs, NGOs, and Western Christian churches and markets.

Further opposition to the Separation Wall may be seen in a permanent exhibit, mounted by the Bethlehem Municipality in Manger Square, adjoining the Church of the Nativity. There, huge ancient olive tree trunks cut down for the construction of the Wall are placed on display. Nearby, at the entrance to "House of Peace," a large old olive tree was planted, with a signpost indicating that the tree was rescued from the bulldozers constructing the Wall. One blogger reacted to the Manger Square olive tree monument as follows:

> When I visited Bethlehem, I was jerked into some deep dark place. As I came up the hill I saw them. . . . Once majestic and venerable . . . now with branches and roots trimmed back, the stripped trunks chained separately with padlocks securing them to the pillars of the building fronting the street. My heart leapt into my throat and hammered away . . . and I took out my camera to record their shameful end. It was like witnessing a crucifixion.[60]

In this Nativity set, the Separation Wall separates the three Magi from the infant Jesus. The set comes along with instructions on use of the crèche in Christmas services, to heighten solidarity with the "Living Stones," Palestinian Christians in the West Bank. *Photo © Amos Trust. Used by permission.*

The dressing of the Wall was further institutionalized through mechanical reproduction, when the Palestinian Authority posted a series of large banners around Manger Square and in Dheisheh Refugee Camp to welcome Pope Francis and his entourage on their visit to Bethlehem in May 2014.[61] These posters, designed by the Palestine Museum, provide huge renderings which juxtapose of classical European paintings of Biblical suffering with contemporary photographs of Palestinian life. They include a classical painting of Jesus healing the paralytic alongside an old man seated at the base of the Separation Wall. They were designed to "welcome the Pope in an altogether unique way by examining the Palestinian experience in relationship to one of the land's most famous martyrs, Jesus Christ."[62]

Another way of imbuing the Wall with Christian significance is through its incorporation into liturgy.[63] Pope Francis' stop to pray at the Separation Wall on his recent visit to the Holy Land in May 2014, increased the visibility

Pope Francis stops to pray at the Separation Wall during his May 2014 visit to the Holy Land. The televised stop increased the visibility of the Wall as a sign of unjust suffering. © *Ma'an News Service and Ramy Abu Diqqa. Used by permission.*

*Our Lady of the Wall*, painted onto a portion of the wall, serves some Orthodox Christians and Catholics as an occasional site of processions and worship.
© *Michael R. Jackaman. Used by permission.*

of the Wall as a sign of unjust suffering.[64] It remains to be seen if this visit will place the Wall on the Catholic pilgrim's liturgical map, as indeed happened following Pope John Paul II's 2000 prayer visit to the Western (Wailing) Wall in Jerusalem. Ian Knowles of the Bethlehem Icon Center also painted an icon, *Our Lady of the Wall*, onto a portion of the Wall, which serves some Orthodox and Catholics as an occasional site of processions and worship. Some Christian groups carry in procession a large olive wood cross made from trees uprooted for the building of the Wall.[65] The hewn trees serve as a metaphor for martyred bodies and are merged with the crucifixion of Christ.

Alternatively, Amos Trust provides detailed instructions for churches on various rituals to be performed using its "walled Nativity set" to incorporate solidarity with Palestinian Christians and protest against the Separation Wall into local churches' Christmas liturgies. Some of these have been performed in British Anglican churches over the past few years. A text provided by Amos

Trust in their "Bethlehem Pack 2010" to accompany their "Separation Wall Nativity Set" (see above) reads:

> "If Jesus was [*sic*] born today in Bethlehem, the Wise Men would spend several hours queuing to enter the town. As local residents of Bethlehem, the shepherds would have had much of their land confiscated for illegal Israeli settlements, and with a lack of freedom to travel and restrictions on trade, it would be very difficult for them to make a living from their sheep."[66]

One might contrast these pro-Palestinian rituals with another "tree ritual," performed by Zola Levitt's Holy Land Tours, which organizes groups with a pronounced Biblical Israel orientation:

> A special opportunity awaits those wanting to memorialize a loved one or leave behind a testament of your love for Israel by planting a young tree in the Zola Levitt Ministry Grove. The tree you plant could perhaps shade the King when He returns.[67]

Here, the planting of a tree in a Jewish National Fund forest fosters a rite of Israeli nation building and imbues it with a new dispensationalist meaning – seeing the greening of Israel as preparation for Christ's imminent return. In both cases, tree symbols identified with the nation and serving to lay claim to land – Palestinian olive trees and Israeli pine forests – are overlaid with Christian significance, which fortifies the national meanings.

### PERFORMANCE MATTERS – THE FRAMING OF THE SEPARATION WALL

In both Biblical Israel and Living Stones tours, the amount of time and extent of contact and economic exchange with the local Palestinian community is determined by theological and ideological factors. Many Living Stones tours explicitly encourage visitors to shop in Bethlehem and use Palestinian travel agents, hotels, and guides in order to contribute to the welfare of the Palestinian (or Palestinian Christian) community. Biblical Israel tours will often promote Jewish-Israeli (or sometimes, West Bank settlers') establishments for parallel reasons.[68]

For most Christian groups, however, Bethlehem is first and almost exclusively the place of Jesus's birth, and most groups will devote little time to the Palestinian-Israeli conflict, particularly if it is not an issue of religio-political consensus within the group. In such cases, controversy and conflict are often seen as inimical to the pilgrim experience.[69] Consequently, the amount of time they spend in Bethlehem and the information they hear from Palestinians (primarily the Bethlehem local guide) is determined by other touristic/pilgrimic factors, such as the desire to visit as many biblical sites as possible in a limited number of days. The Christian tour packages advertised through brochures and websites are arranged by local Palestinian (usually Christian) or Jewish-Israeli travel agents, in cooperation with travel bureaus abroad. It is the agents who usually choose the Israeli or Palestinian guide who will accompany the group throughout their trip. Guides may and do express their political opinions but will take care not to antagonize groups with views that do not coincide with their groups' positions, insofar as guides perceive them.

As a consequence of the negative image of the Wall surrounding Bethlehem and the threat of possible closures, as well as the image of Bethlehem as a dangerous place, most Christian groups prefer to overnight in Jerusalem and come to Bethlehem for a short half-day excursion. During a peak period in tourism, in May 2007, most tourist hotels in Jerusalem were overbooked, and during their tour days in Jerusalem, some tourist groups spent their nights at the Dead Sea (twenty-five miles away) or even in Tel Aviv (forty miles away), while space was still available in tourist hotels in Bethlehem (six miles away). In addition, some Israeli agents may refuse to support hotels in the Palestinian Authority on principle; nevertheless, if the client requests it, Bethlehem hotels will be booked. More recently (summer 2014), a Palestinian journalist informed me that Bethlehem hotels have been increasingly used by budget package tours from poorer countries in Eastern Europe and Africa (Alex Shams, e-mail communication, August 24, 2014).

Many Christian groups are guided by Jewish-Israeli guides, most of whom will not enter Bethlehem, dismounting the bus at the Wall-crossing point.[70] If the tour bus belongs to an Israeli company, the group will dismount, walk through the control point and, on the Bethlehem side, transfer to a local Bethlehem tour bus, often also provided by a souvenir store owner.[71] Alternatively, if the bus is of an (Arab) East Jerusalem company, the bus will drive straight through. In either case, a local Palestinian guide will board the bus on the Bethlehem side, taking the group to the Church of the Nativity, sometimes to Shepherds' Field in Beit Sahour (and occasionally, to Herodion), and shopping. The fact that the Israeli guide, who has become familiar with the group, sometimes through over a week of guiding, must leave the bus, is already a cause of insecurity for many pilgrims. This insecurity often results in the tourists' curtailing their visit to Bethlehem to the very minimum.[72]

Many of the local Bethlehem guides have limited command of the tourists' language (especially if it is not English) and have not undergone intensive guide training, as have the (Jewish or Arab) Israeli guides. Furthermore, the Israeli or East Jerusalem travel agent may ask the local merchants of large Bethlehem souvenir stores to provide local guides (often at a minimal salary of fifteen to twenty dollars for two to three hours, and with the expectation of tourist tips), some of whom who may double as salesmen in the shops.[73] The commissions from the groups' (often substantial) purchases in Bethlehem will be transferred to the Israeli (or East Jerusalem) driver, guide, and often the local tour agent as well. Thus, while the Israeli guide may accompany the group for a week and derive his authority from the extended time together, the local Bethlehem guide (and driver) may spend no more than two or three hours with them. The Bethlehem Palestinian narrator-guides are restricted by their inability to cross to the other side of the Wall. Only a handful of West Bank guides (50, as of 2013) have permits to guide in Israel (or in East Jerusalem). While the security regulations prohibiting Israelis from entering Bethlehem also afford some minimal opportunity for local Bethlehem guides, the guides fear that the crossing may be closed by Israeli security at any time, thus depriving them of their meager livelihoods. In light of the far lesser time spent with the group, and hence the lesser authority of the local Bethlehem guides as compared with their Israeli counterparts, the guide may worry about challenging the political opinions of the group and thus suppress political opinions critical of Israel. Some Palestinian guides also expressed fear that their guiding narratives might come to the attention of Israeli authorities or Jewish travel agents who, in turn, might ask the shopkeepers to furnish another, less political guide.

While I have no evidence of direct Israeli government intervention to silence Palestinian guides in Bethlehem, guides' fear of such intervention in the financially precarious environment of contemporary Bethlehem is very real. Short-term Palestinian guides in Bethlehem tend to avoid responding to tourists' questions on politics. One Palestinian tour agent explained to me that the groups' reliance on Palestinian Christian clergy (like Mitri Raheb of the Lutheran Church in Bethlehem) to provide explanations of the Palestinian "situation" in Bethlehem derives not only from the pastors' greater religious knowledge and eloquence but from their relative immunity to Israeli pressures.

Finally, Palestinian shop owners often instruct "their" guides to avoid any potentially controversial subjects and bring them to the shop as quickly as possible. Thus, the Separation Wall results in almost total dependence of most Bethlehem guides on the shopkeepers of major stores for their livelihood. Hence, while they speak of the need for peace and of Palestinian (or Palestinian Christian) suffering and often mourn the Wall as an obstacle, the Bethlehem guides tend to mute the intensity of the Israeli-Palestinian conflict to avoid arousing Israeli suspicion and to instill the minimal sense of safety and security that will make the pilgrims comfortable enough to do their shopping there, recommend the visit to friends, and return at a later date. Yet the initial feeling of insecurity that visitors may have is often difficult to overcome. Their Israeli guide must leave the bus at the entrance to Bethlehem for "security reasons"; the Third World poverty is manifested through the sometimes aggressive hawking by the child street vendors and is compounded, for some, by a fear of the Orient, especially after 9/11.[74] If, in addition, an undertrained (and underpaid) guide rushes them through the sites to get them to the shop on time, and if the church itself does not match their (Western or Protestant) imagination of the manger, on their return from Bethlehem pilgrims sometimes express a sigh of relief at their return safe and sound to "civilization."

The Jewish-Israeli guide may also shape the pilgrims' impressions of Bethlehem and the Separation Wall before their arrival there. Most Israeli guides will choose to explain the Wall from one of two sites – either from Gilo or from the UN headquarters at Armon Hanatziv. In Gilo, a Jewish neighborhood of Jerusalem built in West Bank territories captured in 1967, a deep valley separates Israelis from the Palestinians of Beit Jala. The outlook point is at a considerable distance from soldiers, roadblocks, and daily Palestinian life but across the street from the homes of Jewish-Israeli citizens. Often, guides explaining the separation fence will point to the half-destroyed houses that served Palestinian snipers during the second Intifada and explain how the Wall protects the residents of Gilo from terrorism. Thus, tourism practice reinforces the Israeli state and municipal laws annexing Gilo to Jerusalem and naturalizes the area as just another Jerusalem neighborhood, while the Palestinians are associated with the snipers "there" across the river bed.[75]

In the second case, near UN headquarters at Armon Hanatziv, the site is a panoramic outlook point where the Wall can be traced from afar. The outlook is an expression of power. It places the observer at a distance and transforms the enchanting world into a text that can be read by an omnipotent viewer from above and at a distance from immersion in the Orient.[76] In the case of the outlook on the Separation Wall, the panorama unites Jewish-Israeli guide and Christian pilgrim and constitutes them as Western and as opposed to the Palestinians on the other side of the Wall.

Yet panoramic views may also be appropriated subversively. Asked about the effect of Wall murals when guiding Christians in Bethlehem, Ra'ed, a Palestinian guide, responded

> The most impressive wall mural in Bethlehem is Har Homa, "Wall Hill," viewed from Shepherds' Field in Beit Sahour. . . . When they see the fortified village on the other side of the wall opposite, they ask me – "What's that?" I

An English-language exhibit posted on the Separation Wall in the vicinity of several popular tourist shops in Bethlehem, linking the wall with the message of Christmas and the Patriarchs. *Photo by Jackie Feldman.*

answer that this is the settlement built by Bibi [Israeli Prime Minister Benjamin Netanyahu] after the Oslo accords in violation of the agreements. So they ask me "can you live there?" And I answer, "of course not. No one there will rent me a house." (interview, January 24, 2010).

As Henri Lefebvre said of the practices of space in general, pilgrimage is a form of political power that partitions space in ways that make it possible for noncritical thought to accept the resultant reality at face value.[77] Performances may assert the right of the powerful to public or contested space, but they may also be a way of resisting the hegemonic order imposed on space.

While the Israeli and Palestinian guides and agents present conflicting narratives, they do not compete on a level playing field. The power inequalities manifest in the materiality of the Separation Wall filter into the marrow of narration. Israelis erect walls; Palestinians spray paint on them. Israelis build terminals and parking lots; Palestinians may try to slip through them. Israeli guides may justify the Wall; Palestinians may need to marshal the authority of priests and pastors to challenge it. Israelis guide for eight days, Bethlehem Palestinians for two hours. The meanings assigned to the Wall, what can be said about it, are not detached from the powers that build, patrol, or resist it.

The practices of display and narration of Bethlehem and the Separation Wall surveyed here promote particular political views of the Israeli-Palestinian conflict and lend them authority by saturating them with particular Christian meanings and associations: If a Palestinian refugee camp is inserted into a sacred genealogy that commemorates the events of Jesus's life and the martyrs who suffered and died for the truth, then a visit to the refugee camp is cast as an act of Christian witness. If the pilgrim worships in "ancient Palestinian churches," with the oppressed "brothers and sisters of Jesus," then communion with Palestinians is a revisiting of a founding moment in Christianity, with Israeli authorities sometimes cast in the role of the evil King Herod. Likewise, if visiting a West Bank settlement is following in the footsteps of the Patriarchs, then the pilgrim is performing sacred history through his feet and his show of solidarity. When he overlooks a "hostile" Palestinian village on the other side of the Wall from a Jerusalem Israeli neighborhood annexed after 1967, the panorama is cast as an act of standing with the Chosen People in the final days preceding Armageddon. Whether it is referred to as the security fence or the apartheid wall, linked with Palestinian (or Palestinian Christian) suffering or God's plan for the Jewish people, both Living Stones and Biblical Israel tours sacralize the Wall and its surrounding landscape by inserting the struggle into Christian sacred history.

As the tours described here are generally organized with a pro-Palestinian or pro-Israeli perspective, both expressed in religious terms, most of their pilgrims are exposed primarily to a single political view – the one their church adopts. As a rule, pilgrimage is far more about the confirmation of faith than about the hermeneutics of suspicion. It is rare that a pilgrimage will make efforts to present multiple points of view that risk "confusing people with the facts" – especially if on both sides, those facts, are given scriptural support.

This is not to say that all pilgrims come with belligerent positions. On the contrary, most proclaim their earnest desire for peace. But narrations of the past in historical and religious terms anchor the widely divergent claims in the sacred and minimize the room for compromise. Guides and pastors may choose to relay a more complex story of the conflict, but the itineraries examined here show that it is often difficult to accomplish.

The consumption of images and itineraries by contemporary Christian pilgrims should further emphasize the importance of tourism shaping opinion, and the need to include pilgrim and tourist productions as an important part of any understanding of political violence, power, and legitimation. It might seem at first that Christian pilgrimage and touring practices are an insignificant manifestation of the unequal and violent Israeli-Palestinian power. Yet pilgrim stories, travel narratives, and touring practices have long been an important means of laying claim to territory, expressing power relations, and shaping people's understandings of the world.[78] Government organs and tourism practitioners, in Israel/Palestine and elsewhere, frequently view incoming tourism as a venue for winning the hearts and minds of "world opinion" and invest accordingly in guide training and publicity.

Unlike in much mass tourism, in the case of pilgrimages, the narratives and performances of space on pilgrimages are not merely a leisure activity confined to the spatiotemporal frame of the tour. Rather, the experience of the voyage creates new memories as it continues to resonate in the practices of a community back home.[79] Church groups may pray for Israel/Palestine/Palestinian Christians, take up offerings for Holy Land charities, carry olive wood crosses in procession, lobby their congressmen, organize boycotts, hold solidarity evenings, and serve as the kernel promoting next year's church voyage to Israel or Palestine. No clear line can be drawn separating these activities into sacred and profane, religious and political. These everyday practices continue to incorporate the Separation Wall and the Israeli-Palestinian struggle into sacred Christian history. The prayers and rallies, charity and boycotts all feed into a hermeneutic loop that shapes future visitors' understandings and expectation of Bible Land and Holy Ground, of Israel and Palestine.

# 5 THE GOODS OF PILGRIMAGE: TIPS, SOUVENIRS, AND THE MORALITIES OF EXCHANGE

Second tithe may not be sold, nor given as pledge, nor exchanged, nor used for reckoning weights. . . . One may not say to his neighbor in Jerusalem, "Here is wine and give me oil (in exchange)," or "Here is oil, give me wine (in exchange)." But one may say, "Here is wine for you, for I have no oil," "Here is oil for you, for I have no wine". . . . But they give each other free gifts (*Mishna. Ma'aser Sheni* 1:1).[1]

DURING THE SECOND Temple Period, in four years of each seven-year cycle, second tithe, a tenth of the agricultural bounty, was set aside for expenditure by pilgrims on food, drink, and anointing oil during their pilgrimage to Jerusalem. Nearly 2,000 years ago, rabbis struggled with the contradictory tensions of the material and the sacred: how was one to enable pilgrims to make the exchanges that would give them variety and nourishment so that they could be joyous before the Lord, without turning consecrated foodstuffs into market commodities? The rabbis' regulations show that, in order to achieve a sense of fellowship among pilgrims and between pilgrims and spiritual goals, transparency is not necessary. Indeed, a certain amount of ambiguity and multivocality is almost essential. The teasing, hinting nature of the noncontractual exchange, the elusiveness of the boundary, the reciprocal quality of the declarative performance – "Here is wine, for I have no oil," "Here is oil, for I have no wine" – mark the trade as not totally determined, thus preserving something of the communitas of pilgrims, as "Consequently, they exchange and yet do not exchange, and do each other kindness" (*Tosefta. Ma'aser Sheni* 1:1–2).[2] Through such performances (to quote Victor Turner) "the other becomes a brother."[3]

Calvinist sermons notwithstanding, in Christianity, spirit and material are not antithetical. The incarnation makes God manifest through the material world; thus, through intention, good deeds, ritual, and revelation, the material world can be imbued with sanctity, can become an instrument of realization

*91*

of religious goals. Christians "create and maintain spiritual ideas through the exchange of goods."[4]

The tensions between law and grace, gift and contract, are also inherent in the "hospitality industry."[5] The tourist or the pilgrim is both honored guest and entitled customer; the pilgrimage itself is both a commodified package tour and a means for spiritual realization. In the case of organized pilgrimage, this tension is muted by lack of disclosure of all the financial arrangements and by setting up all-expenses-paid packages, so that the pilgrim is not forced to think about money all the time, once his reservation is secured. There are two areas, however, where such tensions may surface in the course of the voyage, and where I encountered them as tour guide – in the purchase of souvenirs and in the giving of tips.

The following chapter deals with the *goods* of pilgrimage – the souvenirs and services the pilgrim pays for – and the *good* attributed them by shopkeepers, pilgrims, tour guides, and bus drivers. I will show how objects acquired as souvenirs by pilgrims, as well as monies acquired by guides and drivers as commissions and tips, are assigned differing moral values by various agents; I then examine how those moral values can be transformed through ritual or discourse. The first part of the chapter involves transactions between shopkeepers and pilgrims, takes place in souvenir shops, and is based on my knowledge of tour arrangements, supplemented with stories from other guides and information on websites. The second part deals with exchanges in which guides and drivers play a highly visible role; its main venue is the tour bus and it is based mostly on my own experiences as guide. As I will show, the transactions of pilgrimage are not just about value for money, pleasure, and social status; they are profoundly colored by religious values, political conflict, and East/West power relations.

## THE PURCHASE OF CHRISTIAN SOUVENIRS: VEHICLES OF VALUES[6]

In Christian Holy Land pilgrimages, there are many opportunities for witnessing the bonds created among people in the group and between individual pilgrims and heavenly powers. Souvenirs are of special interest because they may extend such bonds beyond the communal and temporal boundaries of the traveling group, to Palestinian and Jewish-Israeli "natives" (craftsmen, store owners, salesmen, and bus drivers) on the one hand, and to pilgrims' friends and families back home on the other. Souvenirs answer to people's need to bring things home with them from the sacred, extraordinary time or space. As the nonordinary experience of pilgrimage is ephemeral, "when one puts his hands on a souvenir, he is not only remembering he was there but 'proving' it."[7] Souvenirs generate narratives which authenticate the possessor's experience.[8] The stories they tell of them may help pilgrims articulate religious experiences they could not do otherwise, transmit concern for the spiritual legacy that they pass on to their children and grandchildren, and create new bonds with casual acquaintances back home.[9] Through shared display on living room shelves, in showcases, and at family, church, or group reunions, the voyage may be linked with other significant life events.[10] The purchase and giving of souvenirs confirms the status of women shoppers as family ritual experts and the role of gifts in lubricating social relations. Christian souvenirs are material objects that "engage people in the social relations and forms of sacred imagination that structure relations to the divine."[11]

Christian souvenirs are of two kinds: manufactured items, usually purchased from souvenir shops or vendors, and found objects, such as stones and leaves picked up by pilgrims at significant Biblical sites. I will restrict my analysis to the former, sometimes classified as "souvenirs" as opposed to "mementos," showing how mass-produced souvenirs purchased in commercial souvenir shops or tour buses become vehicles of religious and moral values.[12] Through religious discourse and ritualized behavior, such objects may be imbued with the bonds of communitas, the marks of political-religious solidarity, the grace of charity, or the taint of insincerity.

The moment of purchase of a souvenir "marks the transference of origin to trace, moving from event to memory and desire. . . . Through narrative the souvenir substitutes a context of perpetual consumption for its context of origin. It represents not the lived experience of its maker but the 'secondhand' experience of its possessor/owner."[13] Thus, the purchase of the souvenir, particularly if that souvenir is visibly linked with religious practice, may be transformative – an attempt to saturate the ephemeral moment of the tour with the permanence of ongoing religious narratives, of linking individual experience with networks of kin and acquaintances. The religious souvenir may be a mnemonic of faith – it may bear witness, not only to one's socioeconomic capital but to Christ.[14]

## STANDING WITH ISRAEL: EVANGELICAL PURCHASES OF CHRISTIAN JUDAICA

While most Protestants officially reject the notion of holy ground, priestly blessings, relics, or brandea, their sanctification of material objects is far more similar to those of Catholics than they often care to admit.[15] Thus, pilgrims distinguish between purchases – as one explained to me, "I'd buy the T-shirt from anyone, but the communion set I want to buy from someone religious." This corresponds with Zaidman and Lowengart's observations that people visiting Jewish saints' tombs classify various religious objects as intrinsically religious (psalm books, candles), as things that receive sanctity through contact with a particular place (water, oil, earth), and as those that can be bought anywhere or from anyone (shirts, hats, toys), without consideration for the seller's honesty or religious beliefs.[16]

For Evangelicals, place counts too.[17] Many groups will wait to do their shopping at the Garden Tomb. Others will insist on purchasing a nativity set at Bethlehem, rather than say, in a hotel shop in Netanya.[18] The baptismal site, Yardenit, and the site of the "Jesus Boat" at Kibbutz Nof Ginnosar on the Sea of Galilee (where the wooden boats that take pilgrims for devotional sailings also dock) are two new places that have been particularly successful in creating an atmosphere that appeals to Protestant aesthetics of the sacred.[19] Both have thriving gift shops that cater primarily to Protestants, including a wide selection of Judaica for Christians. These include felt hangings with embroidered biblical verses, archaeological replicas such as "widow's mites" and oil lamps, and Jewish religious objects (often of a kind most Jews would not use for worship) such as small Torah scrolls, silver-plated mezuzah cases, gilded ram's horns, and prayer shawls with prophetic verses printed on their neckpieces. The Protestant aesthetics of the constructed "Biblical" site along with the selection of merchandise support each other to increase the authority and allure of such sites and make Protestants likely to shop there.[20]

Messianic Jews have served as major brokers of both Judaica for Christians as well as Jewish rituals adopted by Evangelicals (Passover *seders*, Shabbat services, etc.). They have even invented several items, such as pendants combining a cross with a Star of David as well as the "Messianic Seal" – a combination of the fish (an early Christian symbol), a Star of David, and a seven-branched candelabrum. This recent fabrication is supported by an urban legend that states that they were found by a Greek Orthodox priest in a cave on Mt. Zion and date back to the time of Judeo-Christian church of the first apostles. Furthermore, their website claims, the information was suppressed by the Israel Museum and, when the symbol was first put on display by its initial purchaser, the shop was stoned by Orthodox rabbis.[21] Thus, purchase of the item may be seen as an act of support for the ("persecuted") Messianic community, seen by some Evangelicals as the authentic descendants of the first Christians – by blood and faith.[22]

Another preferred shopping site for Evangelicals is the Galilee Experience, a multimedia edutainment center on the shores of the Sea of Galilee in Tiberias

The incomparable
IGM Regionaltour[SM]

ISRAEL

"Much MORE than crowded church shrines and souvenir shops."

IGM TOURS
WORLD WIDE

Wooden boats used for pilgrim services dock near the building containing the "Jesus Boat" and the adjoining shop selling Judaica for Christians. The boats, an icon of the Protestant Bible Land, appear on a tour brochure cover.
© International Group Ministries. Used by permission.

Authentic Gifts from the **Holy Land!**

www.JesusBoat.com

Bringing the Holy Land to You

The website linked to the shop near the "Jesus boat" at Ginosar offers a wide variety of Judaica geared primarily to the Evangelical market. © *The Jesus Boat. Used by permission.*

Selection of "Messianic Seals" and Judeo-Christian theme jewelry for the Evangelical market. Displayed at the shop at the Jesus Boat, Sea of Galilee. *Photo by Jackie Feldman.*

run by Messianic Jews. They promote "Jewish calendars for Christians" and ask them to support the local community, who in spite of attacks of the ultra-Orthodox, continue to reconcile Jews and Christians.

Still another Messianic website combines the themes of authenticity and support for the persecuted Messianic community in Israel with End Time apocalypticism:[23]

> Christian Gifts from here in Jerusalem
> During troublesome times as war continues to be declared on us in Israel:
> Thank you for visiting Jerusalem Christian Gifts Shop
> Israel is still at war against the forces that seek to "wipe her off the map." These are days to prepare and be prepared as war continues to be declared on many fronts. We thank you for your prayers and customer support as you shop for Christian gifts from the Holy Land.
> I WILL BLESS THOSE WHO BLESS YOU (Gen 12:3).

The advertisement hints at Evangelical readings of current events as signs of the incipient end-times ("be prepared"), and casts shopping as an act of participation in God's plan for His people in "troublesome times." Studies, however, suggest that Evangelical purchases of Judaica (and the adoption of Jewish-like rituals) among the rank and file have less to do with End Time scenarios than with cultural philosemitism, which "seem[s] to offer [Evangelicals] historical roots and a cultural richness that they feel is lacking in their churches."[24]

## SUPPORTING THE LIVING STONES: BUYING SOUVENIRS IN BETHLEHEM

One group I observed, a three-week American Bible College study program, chose to visit the Holy Land Cooperative in Beit Sahour for souvenir shopping, because one of the woman participants, involved in running a fair trade shop back home, insisted the group come there. For her, fair trade was a Christian principle and she saw this as manifested through their shopping in the cooperative.

In his presentation at the shop, the cooperative manager told the tour group that purchasers would support the continued existence of the dwindling Christian population. He then described the different qualities of olive wood and the long-standing tradition of carving, promoting the locally carved "traditional" olive wood crèches and sculptures, as well as the Jerusalem Cross, which he said, "you can only get here." Holding up one of the carvings, the manager told the story of a local olive wood carver, Rajah Baroun, saying that the group's purchases would benefit Christian laborers in hard times.

Thus, in his performance for pilgrims, Christian tradition, indigenous authenticity, support for Palestinian Christians, and fair trade are merged to make the purchase an act of charity and Christian solidarity with the Living Stones, the Palestinian Christian community.[25]

The manager's introductory sales pitch is expanded on the shop's website:

> The handicraft industry in the Bethlehem area is in danger of disappearing. This is a direct result of three things: constant political unrest, the resulting decline in tourism, and more generalized economic hardship resulting from the occupation. . . . The Cooperative strives to alleviate local poverty, decrease unemployment, increase the level of income, decrease emigration, and sustain the Palestinian handicraft industry for the benefit of the traditional handicraft artisans.[26]

The disappearance of traditional "Christian" crafts becomes a metaphor for the disappearance of the local Christian community. The performance focuses at-

Talit (prayer shawl) with verse of Biblical prophecy in Hebrew and English, destined for the Evangelical market. Displayed at the shop at the Jesus Boat, Sea of Galilee. *Photo by Jackie Feldman.*

tention away from price, as well as from the provenance of some of the (made in China) items being sold.

In another case, the proprietor of one of the largest souvenir supermarkets in Bethlehem, Bethlehem New Store, Ephram Nissan, commonly welcomes buses stopping by his shop by stepping on the bus, and welcoming the pilgrims and the group leader (by name). He thanks them for coming and tells them of the many Christian families supported by his shop. He then tells them that he sings in the choir of the Church of the Nativity in Aramaic, the Lord's language. He sings the Lord's Prayer in the microphone in Aramaic, and then welcomes "his brothers and sisters in Christ" by presenting each member of the group with a ceramic plate with the Lord's Prayer painted on it in Arabic.[27] (Many pilgrims assume it is in Aramaic.)

Following Hillary Kaell, we might see the purchase of Israeli Judaica by Evangelicals and the purchase of olive wood carvings from Living Stones Palestinian Christians as sharing in a common search for "roots" of faith and "a

Pastor Jeff Haney tries out a silver-plated shofar at the shop of the Jesus Boat, Sea of Galilee. *Photo by Jackie Feldman.*

personal connection to imagined genealogical or religious pasts."[28] The arboreal metaphors employed by both groups – "The living stones are the roots of our faith" or "We are grafted onto the Jewish people" – support this argument.[29]

## THE "MASS GIFT"

At the end of their shopping time, Nissan (like most Bethlehem shop owners) will present the group leader with a bag of olive wood communion cups. These cups are then used for communion at the Garden Tomb; subsequently each participant takes his cup home. These gifts may be considered as "mass gifts" – a hybrid form between gifts and commodities, which "establishes a relational space in which actors can negotiate the ambivalence of the cultural script of the 'gift.'"[30] The plate is presented to all as part of a quasi-religious welcoming ceremony, before they enter the store. It establishes the identity of the seller as a native host, a fellow Christian, and provider of jobs for other

Palestinian Christians. It thus calls on the group to purchase in his shop as an act of Christian solidarity. Unlike mass gifts presented along with purchases in supermarkets, its commodified nature is concealed by the bus ceremony of presentation, acknowledging the group's identity as Christian and welcoming the group's leader as an acquaintance and brother in Christ.[31]

The communion cups take on added aura of the gift, insofar as the group does not know that they have received them until well after they have made their purchases at the shop. The lack of opportunity to reciprocate in the short run enhances its status as a gift-like object of social exchange rather than an incentive to buy more. If souvenirs essentially tell the story of the purchaser rather than the maker of the object, the cup begins its career as souvenir as the object of a group narrative: it first acquires an individual owner, not through purchase but through the ritual of shared communion in a sacred place.[32] One pilgrim wrote in his blog: "Here we were, sitting perhaps 20 yards from the empty tomb, remembering our Lord's death and resurrection. We took home with us the communion cups carved from olive wood as a commemoration of that never-to-be-forgotten moment in the Garden Tomb."[33] Thus, the cup links individual pilgrim, the group experience, sacred place, and the broader Christian community. Its career also traces a significant cosmological trajectory, linking the birth of Christ (Bethlehem), his death and resurrection (Garden Tomb), and the pilgrim's home.

## RESISTANCE TO GIFTS AND PROTESTANT SINCERITY

Yet ritualized displays of Christian piety or solidarity display like those of Ephram Nissan may be rejected by pilgrims with alternative aesthetics or religious values. One Mormon group leader wrote of the shop in Bethlehem:

> People can tell when they are being "schmoozed" – spoken to with insincere icky-sweet talk – and assured of a "discount" and all the rest of it. This is especially weird at some of the fancy places where the salespeople are dressed like members of the mafia, smelling of heavy cologne, while surrounded by all sorts of poverty. This doesn't make the customers feel special. It makes them sick, sad, even disgusted.
>
> Where they come from, these people are used to prices and costs being quite straightforward. They can tell when a system is depressed and corrupt if just about everything they do has some extra hidden cost, or when they know very well that someone is getting a "kickback" from the deal. (They always seem to detect this and laugh about it later at the hotel, etc.) They go along with it, they accept it as part of the local culture. But, does it leave a good taste in the mouth? Of course not. Do they come away impressed? No. All

the strange and hidden dealings have the overall effect of compromising the respect they feel for the culture that is hosting them. . .

We would prefer to meet the real people of the culture under real conditions. We would like to pay straightforward prices. We would like to feel that our business is prospering the average person. We . . . would like to be free to love them without having to be on guard against sales pitches and schmoozing and being used. . . . Insincerity turns people off, it sets them at a distance" (v.a. email, 24.12.2005).

This response reflects the typically Protestant desire for sincerity as a supreme Christian virtue, a preference for simplicity and transparency, and an aesthetic that includes a measure of Orientalism (referring to the Palestinian salesmen as "members of the mafia, smelling of heavy cologne").[34] Such moral valuation would be contested by many of the actors for whom bargaining and praising of their wares and the donning of "respectable" dress in the contact zone with tourists is part of the game, and is seen as totally justified, especially given the inequalities of the encounter.[35]

The most popular shops for Mormon pilgrims to the Holy Land are run by Palestinians who send their children to Mormon universities, prominently display olive wood carvings of the Mormon Nauvoo sculptures and photographs of Mormon prophets and leaders, and imply that the seller is a believing Mormon (thought this is not the case). These shops allow Mormons to pay by personal check upon reception of their shipped purchases in their homes. This display of trust flatters the purchaser as one who can be trusted – because he is Mormon – and fosters word-of-mouth advertising, which is extremely important in a community with social webs as dense as those of the Mormons.

The Living Stones, as well as the Evangelical and Mormon cases, confirm the central role of the seller in religious marketing. As Zaidman and Lowengart wrote, "The meaning of sacred objects derives from the agents themselves. Retailers need to show they are authentic and can perform the process required by transferring meaning from the cultural mold to themselves."[36] As the emphasis varies within Christian cultures, so too does the nature of the display required of the seller. The pilgrims' choices in purchasing a souvenir and the ways in which sellers encourage them to do so illustrate "the relational space in which actors can negotiate the ambivalence of the cultural script of the 'gift.'"[37] It further attests how Christians, even those with negative theological views of materiality, "create and maintain spiritual ideas through the exchange of goods."[38]

We might note that just as objects take on different values as they are transformed through their "careers" of exchange, moving in and out of their commodity phase, so too do objects become souvenirs of pilgrimage through the contexts of their purchase.[39] The souvenir "moves history into private time."[40] The moment of purchase of a religious souvenir in the Holy Land brings a mass-produced item into private possession; it marks the transference "from origin to trace, from event to memory and desire."[41] By choosing to purchase a particular religious item only in certain (sacred, significant) places or only from certain (pious, Christian, sincere, Palestinian, or Messianic Jewish) sellers, or to earmark it for certain people and purposes, the pilgrim is initiating the object into the "pilgrimage souvenir" phase of its career. This career will continue with its transport and display at home or its gifting to significant others. The narratives subsequently told through the souvenir come to include the values that colored the initial purchase or the group experience of the pilgrimage.

### TIPS AND COMMISSIONS: SACRED OR PROFANE?

As the preceding discussion of souvenirs shows, in Holy Land pilgrimage human relationships and identities are affirmed and negotiated through acts imbued with spiritual or moral value. Such acts include not only prayer (for someone, with someone) and physical assistance on the voyage but also transfers of money and objects. I will now illustrate how complex relationships obtaining between Jewish guides, Palestinian drivers, and Christian pilgrims are mediated through tips and commissions.

Sacred and profane, as Jonathan Z. Smith reminds us, "are not substantive categories, but rather situational or relational categories, mobile boundaries which shift according to the map being employed. There is nothing that is sacred in itself, only sacred things in relation."[42] The words and/or ritual performance that accompany exchanges both express the moral value – what I call the "color" – of monies in pilgrimage, while also changing their "color" as they move from pilgrim to guide and driver.

### THE COLORS OF PILGRIM MONIES

Contrary to the famous quote which Suetonius attributes to Vespasian, money indeed does have an odor, or, in our case – a color. While Marx and Simmel understood money as a kind of universal "acid,"[43] alienating producers from the fruits of their labor and freeing transactions from moral distinctions, recent studies have illustrated how money functions in different ways in various societies and may take on different moral values in different cases within a particular society.[44]

Vivana Zelizer[45] demonstrated how monies of various origins are earmarked for various uses; money is thus inseparable from concrete sets of meaningful social relations and serves as a social mediator of values.[46] "Economic transactions," she writes, "are highly differentiated, personalized and local, meaningful to particular relations."[47] While some comparative studies have illustrated the ideology of exchange in traditional societies, other microstudies show how rituals transform the values of money within a particular society.[48] Janet Carsten documents how In a Malay village, the transfer of monies earned from fishing from men to women "cooks" the money and frees it of the negative moral value of individualistic competition that adheres to it.[49] Oren Kosansky demonstrates the spatial and ritual emplacement that underlies the classification of monies spent on *hilulot* – pilgrimages to Moroccan Jewish saints' tombs – as *dépenses* or *charité*.[50] Only the latter enhances the merit of the donor in the eyes of fellow worshippers and promises a divine recompense.[51]

In order to unpack the shifting social meanings of tips and commissions, I will first identify the "colors" of monies that change hands between pilgrims, guides, and drivers in the course of Holy Land pilgrimage. I then investigate how religious language, ritual, and authority may change the moral value of tips and commissions. Money may be "bleached" or "blackened," and the reciprocities of monies that change hands on pilgrimage may be diverted.

### PILGRIM MONIES: WHITE, GRAY, BLACK, AND GREEN

Israeli and Palestinian Holy Land pilgrimage guides, like all tour guides, are not altruistic mediators by vocation. As Heidi Dahles summarizes, tour guides

> sell images, knowledge, contacts, souvenirs, access, authenticity, ideology and sometimes even themselves. Their knowledge of the local culture is not limited to facts, figures and other *couleur locale*, it includes the art of building a network, of monopolizing contacts, a familiarity with the operations of the tipping and commissions system, a notion of trends in tourism and of the characteristics of tourists and their countries of origin – all this converging to make the encounter with tourists as profitable as possible for the guides themselves. Successful guides know how to turn their social relations and narratives into a profitable enterprise."[52]

Guides and drivers have three basic sources of income:

### 1. White Money: Salaries

Salaries are legally enforceable, taxable, and not subject to negotiation between the pilgrims and the guide/driver. They are paid at the end of the month, by check or bank transfer, with deductions made for social security, health insurance, pensions, and income tax. In accordance with local usage, I call this money "white." The vast majority of guides of pilgrim groups are freelance, and are paid a per diem fee, established by the Israel tour guides union ($200 gross income, as of 2014) regardless of their seniority or the size of the group. The tourist/pilgrim industry is both highly competitive and extremely sensitive – with any major security problem in Israel or in the region resulting in mass cancellations, for which there is no compensation. In order to compete, travel agents may cut prices by cutting wages (especially from nonunionized drivers or vulnerable novice guides) or generating additional means of income, including collecting commissions for routing tour groups to specific shopping places.

As guide salaries are fixed, guides are promoted by getting "better" groups, that is, those with greater potential to generate tips and commissions. Since the size of tips is linked with the size of the group and national character of custom, the result is a national hierarchy, with poor or nontipping national cultures at the bottom and wealthier countries with established traditions of generous tips (e.g., the United States) at the top.[53] Thus, I began my guiding career with multilingual day tours, then moved on to guide budget British groups, then Dutch Reformed, German Catholics and Protestants, and finally, American Evangelicals and (occasionally) mainline Protestants. Consequently, while in career advancement at large, tips often characterize low-paying jobs, and as one moves up the pay scale, the amount of legal, contractual money as part of the overall income increases, in guiding the reverse is true. We might say that the further a guide of pilgrim groups advances, in terms of his professional skills and network of contacts, the less of his money derives from "white" salaries, and the more dependent he becomes on tips and commissions.[54]

Drivers are usually salaried workers of bus companies. The companies pay drivers relatively little for almost unlimited work hours. This is particularly true among Palestinian companies where competition for jobs in a society with high unemployment is fierce. Over the years, some companies have required drivers to work for free or even pay a fee for the privilege of working for tourist tips and commissions.[55] The lack of an adequate salary, often combined with resentment of the occupying Israeli government collecting tax on it (and often offering only minimal services to the Arab sector in return) empties "white" monies of their moral value and makes them, especially for Palestinian drivers, simply more expensive monies. The inadequate salary often results in pressure on the part of drivers to frequent more commission-paying shops early in the tour.

## 2. Black Money – Commissions

Commissions are collected by guides and drivers from shops in which pilgrim groups stop to shop. The primary sources of commissions on Christian pilgrim groups are olive wood carving and souvenir supermarkets in Bethlehem and diamond factories in Netanya, Jerusalem, Tel Aviv, or Tiberias. These sites are referred to by Palestinian drivers as *hashshab* and *hajjar* – wood and stones, respectively. There are financially less important spots, such as glass factories in Hebron, Judaica factories and shops in Jerusalem and the Galilee, Dead Sea cosmetics factories and outlets, and more. Some standard tourist/pilgrim attractions have small- to medium-sized gift shops which may provide some additional income for the guide and driver, while several restaurants pay small commissions to drivers and guides, in addition to the free meals provided for them and for group leaders.

After the group visit, a percentage of the purchase price is given by store owners to drivers, guides, and, increasingly, to travel agents. In some cases, priests or group leaders will demand a cut of the commissions; this is a major source of conflict and of resentment among drivers and guides. Commissions are rarely fully declared, and, though legal, are kept out of the pilgrim's vision, even if many pilgrims assume that guides receive them.[56] Shops have devised a variety of tactics to veil the act of payment of commission monies: money is transferred in handshakes, cigarette boxes at parking stops, or paid at a later date; some shops have concealed booths or rooms for driver/guides, some equipped with closed-circuit screens. Many pilgrims refer to such payments as "kickbacks" (see the response of the Mormon group leader, above). Because of its concealed nature and negative moral connotations, guides and drivers refer to this money as "black." Nevertheless, the salaries and job insecurity of the tourist industry (especially in conflict prone Israel/Palestine) make commissions an essential component of income for guides and, especially, for underpaid drivers.

Shopping stops may strain relations between guides and priests/pastors. Some pastoral leaders feel that the act of shopping is, at best, a necessary evil – a profanation of the pilgrimage that replaces spirituality and communitas with materialism and conspicuous consumption, or a temptation that steals valuable time that could better be used for prayer or visiting additional biblical sites. Some are concerned about the economic competition that may arise between pilgrims of differing financial means. Occasionally, conflicts will emerge between pastors focused on prayer, teaching, and Biblical site visits, and participants, especially women, who want more time for shopping, in part in order to lubricate the social and familial networks they maintain through souvenir gifts. For many of them, the place of purchase is important – pilgrims are eager to bring back a nativity set purchased in Bethlehem, or from Palestinian Christians in Bethlehem (see above). Furthermore, for many, shopping is a social activity to be shared with other group members. The large spaces, wide selection, and ease of payment and shipping provide a comfort zone that makes them more attractive to many pilgrims than the cheaper shops of the Arab market of Old City Jerusalem. One suggestion frequently made by guides is making certain shopping stops optional after-dinner excursions, while restricting shopping time in the course of the day. Thus, the nonshoppers (mainly men, including the pastor) may remain in the hotel while their wives purchase olive wood carvings, diamonds, or souvenirs – without pressures of pastors or menfolk to limit shopping time. This solution may be made more attractive through religious language, delineating separate time-frames as sacred and profane – "Today we'll focus on the birth of Jesus in Bethlehem and tonight those who wish can come back with us after dinner and shop till you drop."

Religious language may also be employed by the guide to shape the itinerary in accordance with his (and the driver's) interests. In many cases, shopping times do not appear in the printed itinerary or are scheduled toward the end of the trip. Driver and guide often scan the program on their way to pick up the group at the airport to check this. Thus, in discussing the trip with the group leader on the first evening of the tour, the guide may note that the itinerary begins with four days in Galilee (where shopping opportunities are fewer), while Bethlehem is scheduled for the eighth and last day of the tour. The guide and driver worry that by then the group may have purchased their olive wood nativity sets in their free time in the Old City or in hotel gift shops, and attempt to move the Bethlehem visit up to an earlier tour day. Hence, in going over the itinerary with the pastor or priest the first evening, the guide may suggest: "Shouldn't we begin our Jerusalem visit with the Nativity in Bethlehem and end with the resurrection at Calvary?"

In addition to visits to shops, factories, and showrooms, several items are routinely sold to pilgrims by the guide and driver on the bus. These include primarily picture books, DVDs, and music discs produced for the Christian market. In addition, the guide may offer (or introduce salesmen who offer) personalized silver charms with Hebrew or Arabic names, ram's horns, or other items that he (or the driver) purchases or orders individually. A minor source of income comes in the form of water bottles or olive oil, usually sold by the driver. One guide I spoke to said of sales of bus items, "I hate the 'jams and jellies'! I let the driver take care of that. If they give me the money, I make a point of giving it to the driver in full view of the group. 'It's better this way,' I tell the driver. And in the end, [the drivers] admit that I'm right" (interview with G. J., 2003). Although commissions are normally divided equally among driver and guide, the guide may make it seem that the sale is a service done for the (lower-income) driver.

One early lesson I learned as a guide resulted from my selling videocassettes and books on the bus. As I walked through the bus, pushing the carton of books and videos down the aisle with my foot, distributing cassettes and making change for each passenger, I wound up with hands and pockets full of bills and coins. By the time I reached the back of the bus, I overheard more than one pilgrim comment on the money-changers in the Temple (driven out by Jesus – Matthew 21:12). Here the ambiguities of the contact between money and the sacred reinforced the stereotype of the Jew as businessman and money-lender. The guide's authority is compromised by his handling of money (and sales goods) in full sight of the group. By keeping his hands "clean" of cash, he can more easily maintain his role as spiritual leader or exemplary Biblical Jew, or expend his authority more strategically in promoting a future purchase.

### 3. Gray Money – Tips:

Tips are given by pilgrims directly to guides. The tip is an expression of thanks which is often difficult to quantify and goes beyond legal or contractual requirements – eagerness to serve, a smile, dedication, and in the case of pilgrim guides, a healthy measure of "emotional work."[57] As it is openly given as a sign of thanks but not legally enforceable and often only partially declared to tax authorities, I (as well as many guides) refer to this money as "gray."

Various theories have been advanced for the origin of tips in service industries. Tipping is supposed to be an incentive/reward for service. Marketing-oriented studies often cite tipping as an efficient way of monitoring service, and popular etymology derives the tip from the first letters of the words "to insure promptness."[58] George Foster, however, drawing on the link of the word for tips with drinks in most European languages (French – *pour boire*, German – *Trink-geld*), argues that the English word originates with the word "tipple." The tip, he claims, originated in the desire to deflect the harm of the envy of the waiter or person serving on the one eating or drinking by sharing food/drink or the means to acquire it: "The custom of tipping, at least as far as origins are concerned, is best explained as a symbolic device intended to buy off the envy of people less fortunate than the giver, since the recipient is, before or at the time of the tipping, in a position to work harm on the tipper."[59] "Tipping," he writes, "is not, as is often averred, a device in a class-conscious society for asserting superiority over servile people; it is payment, pure and simple, for protection, the need for which is sensed at a deep psychological level."[60]

In speaking of tips in the tourist industry, Boaz Shamir writes that "the gratuity . . . is not an expression of gratitude . . . but rather a defense against gratitude. This is perhaps the reason that the tip, in most cases, is given at the very end of the interaction . . . in a way which does not allow any reciprocal 'correction.'"[61] He adds: "The tip, like the gift is given under voluntary guise, but in fact under a constraining normative framework in situations where the mutual obligations are not exactly specified. The recipient . . . gets more than . . . he paid for. This creates in him a motivation to reciprocate and discharge his obligations, and thereby to balance his account." Shamir attributes the persistence of tips in service industries to the mystification of the quantifiable tourist product by the industry. Through tips, as through the rhetoric of "hosts and guests," the tourist industry maintains the illusion of hospitality, based on more generalized reciprocity, friendship, grace, and gratitude. As Boaz Shamir reminds us, "Many services, in contrast with the nature of most goods and commodities transferred in the economic market, contain elements which cannot be standardized and measured: no fixed price can be put upon them" (smiles, gestures of the service-giver).[62] "The tip," he writes, "is the mechanism which complements the regular fixed market mechanism in situations where the sold commodity contains nonstandardized and unmeasurable components" (ibid, 62).

Tips are usually given at the end of the voyage. Thus, pilgrims may seek to prolong the relation between themselves and the guide/driver by creating an indebtedness of gratitude and encouraging the guide/driver to reciprocate through letters, e-mail contacts, and even visits abroad. Alternatively, the tip may bring a close to the relationship of dependency that dominates the tour, in which the adult tourists are often infantilized and look at drivers and (especially) guides as "parents" in a foreign land. By giving a tip, the pilgrim may reassert the customer/service relationship at the close of the voyage, and demonstrate his own superior status by giving a gift which cannot be reciprocated in service. In either case, this is usually expressed through the individual pilgrim's personal presentation of the tip (often accompanied by his address or e-mail) to the guide or driver.

Tips are usually paid in cash in foreign currency and frequently are not entirely declared to tax authorities. Payment of tips cannot be enforced except by informal extralegal sanctions such as gossip, provision of poorer or surly service, or refusal to take another group of the same group leader in the future.[63] Thus, tips have the in-between status of gray money.[64] Expected but not obligatory. In many cases, especially in the case of groups from countries with a developed tip culture, tips have become institutionalized, with each participant giving the fixed amount per diem suggested by the foreign tour company, usually collected in advance by the group leaders.[65] In such cases, the tip is often presented in an envelope with the foreign tour company or church logo, with the sum printed upon it. Thus a 1990s Biblische Reisen tour envelope read "TOUR GUIDE: 9.5 touring days × DM 2.5 × 31 persons = DM726.25." The envelope contained DM730. The sums vary greatly by country and travel agency, ranging from one to five dollars per person per day.[66] Usually, guides and drivers are tipped separately, with guides generally getting 50–100 percent more than drivers.

Consequently, the tourist transaction is depersonalized, and the confusion on the part of the tourist (how much should I tip?) and the insecurity on the part of the guide and driver (will they tip?) are reduced. Through the standardization, tipping might become "a normative framework clearly understood by both sides in the transaction."[67] Yet, as we will see, even such arrangements may convey latent meanings, while the personal, discretionary element in tipping resurges nonetheless.[68]

## THE "GREENNESS" OF DARK MONEY

The uncertainty of the tips and commissions and its liquidity makes these monies "greener," more charged emotionally.[69] For many guides, the immediacy of the tip – the lack of time interval between the service provided and the tip given at the end of the tour – increases the tendency, especially among guides, to view the tip as an affirmation of his performance and his sense of self, especially in the case of nonstandardized individual tips. The form of the tip – in liquid, foreign currency, in envelopes thick with banknotes or heavy with coins – gives the tip a sensory element and solidity absent from bank transfers. Some guides earmark discretionary tips for treats or luxuries, rather than for paying bills.

Many drivers proclaim that the tips and commissions are *kulhu min Allah* – "all from Allah."[70] It is not, they proclaim, morally dubious "black" money but a source of blessing. Drivers dream of making the "big hit" and retell (often apocryphal) stories of extraordinarily large tips or commissions. The moral "grayness" of the tip or "blackness" of the commission is less marked in the Palestinian economy, where most transactions are made in cash, and informal loans and gifts among extended family members are an important part of the household economy.

The "greenness" of "dark" monies makes them more volatile. Because, unlike "white" salaries, their giving is not obligatory and cannot be enforced legally, they are more open to negotiation, more capable of carrying emotional, social, or religious charge. Thus, they are an important medium of establishing relations of trust between Palestinian drivers and Jewish-Israeli guides, who inhabit distinct social worlds. Like in the case of waitresses working for tips, acts of trust are required mainly where the rules of the organization do not spell out the obligations and rewards; where the recompense is neither negotiated nor specified by contract, it depends on trust and the anticipation of reciprocity.[71] Custom dictates that all commission monies generated in working together be divided equally by guide and driver. Some days, however, the group goes on day-long walking tours in the Old City of Jerusalem, and the driver is not present. He may even be sent by the bus company to work with another tour group. If the guide, upon returning to the bus, presents the driver with his share of the commission for items bought in the Old City, he earns the confidence and respect of the driver as someone who can be trusted.[72] This facilitates cooperation between the driver and guide for the rest of the tour. As the driver's social and professional network is extremely dense (unlike guides, who are mostly freelance workers, drivers are mostly salaried employees of a single bus/tour company), the guide's reputation as honest will spread and ease his adjustment to new drivers of the same (or other) bus companies on future tours.[73] Palestinian drivers may reciprocate on the group's visit to Bethlehem, where Jewish guides are unable to survey the group's purchases.[74]

Another common practice is for the guide or driver to collect and hold commissions from the first shops and refrain from dividing them for several days. This is both a display of mutual trust, as well as an act of wishful thinking that postpones what will be considered the "first" revenue of the trip until the time the money is counted out and divided. Thus, the initial purchase which "opens" the till (the ritual *siftach*) becomes larger, providing a better sign of blessing for future income.[75] The division of commissions often takes place in a semiritualized display of transparency that Israeli guides refer to as "Arab partition." The guide or driver tears open the commission envelopes and heaps the bills and coins on a hotel room table or the first seat of the darkened bus. The money is then divided into exactly equal piles: fifty/fifty, ten/ten, one/one, etc., with the last bill remaining undivided to serve as propitious "seed money" for future revenues.

## CHANGING THE COLORS OF PILGRIM MONEY

Money, as we see, does not necessarily reduce all human transactions to a universal and alienating standard. It may be of several "colors," each engendering a different set of reciprocities and charged with a different moral value. I will now show how religious ritual, language, and authority may serve to change the "colors" of pilgrim monies.

### 1. Bleaching Black Commissions – The DVD/CD/DISC as Devotional Tool and as Charity

As mentioned above, when selling merchandise (books, CDs) on the bus, money visibly passes from hand to hand, thus "dirtying" the hands of the guide and undermining his spiritual authority. This situation is altered if the pastor takes the merchandise from the guide and promotes it to the group as an excellent devotional tool for Bible education – and as a means for helping the driver and his family. Pastoral authority may elevate the object by making it into a devotional item, and also bestowing upon it the merit of charity (for the driver's poorer family). Insofar as the exchange is also a charitable act, the purchaser receives added value for his money; unlike trade, charity is recompensed by God.[76] The pastor's presentation also makes the guide invisible in the system of exchange: the guide's hands are kept clean, and the guide is now indebted for this to the group leader. He may "repay" the favor by obtaining free meals and refreshments for the pastor's family and accepting the pastor's request to guide his group in the future, even when it conflicts with another group.

### 2. Color Enhancement for Tips: The Love Offering

In many cases, tips have become institutionalized. They are fixed and collected in advance and paid to the guide in a sealed envelope at the end (or sometimes the beginning) of the tour. Thus, they become almost white, a supplementary salary. Nevertheless, individual tourists may develop close relationships with their guides and give them extra tips. Pastors, who may be eager to display their appreciation for the guide and garner their indebtedness, may choose to frame additional tips as offerings, or as love offerings in the case of Evangelical groups. In general, the group will pray or sing a hymn together on the bus or at the hotel at the end of the tour, and thank the guide and driver for their service and spiritual contribution. They often thank the guide not only for his knowledge and courtesy but for "bringing them safely through the land" and for "strengthening their faith in the Lord." In the case of Evangelicals, they often pray that their guide and driver see the light and accept Jesus as their Lord and Savior. The pastor or priest then passes around an envelope containing a greeting card, on which participants write their expressions of thanks, prayers, or missionary wishes or prophetic verses (Isaiah 53, John 2:14), and place a sum of money in the envelope. The envelope is then handed to the guide at a closing banquet or on the way to the airport for departure, sometimes as part of a short ceremony. Through the love offering, tip money becomes imbued with sanctity, since it engenders recompense from God, while casting the guide's service as a religious act worthy of such recompense.[77] It also may be envisaged as a way of spreading the Gospel and perhaps, leading to the conversion of the guide to the True Way. Thus, the gray monies become, so to speak, tinged with gold.

As the money is wrapped both in envelopes and in messages – biblical verses wishes and blessings – some guides keep the cards as tokens attesting to their ability to affect group participants and increase their attachment to the Bible or the land.[78] Others may regard the prayers for their conversion as offensive, and see the gift as an invitation to enter into a continuing relationship in which the donors desire that he convert. Some rip up the card and throw it away at the airport, pocketing the money. Others, less ceremoniously, toss the envelopes into a bottom desk drawer at home. This is an act of closure and purification – a ritual way of recasting the tip as recompense for performance already provided, and refusing the invitation to enter into a long-term relationship involving religious dialogue.

### 3. Black Is Black: "Outing" Commissions through Religious/Political Language

Just as intervention by religious authorities or use of religious language or ritual can lighten the "color" of money, so too, it can "darken" its moral value. One pastor, who came with his group in the middle of the first Intifada, consistently advised his group not to purchase items in Bethlehem, saying that the guide would profit from kickbacks from the shop. He encouraged group members to accompany him on the group's free day to a "trustworthy Christian shopkeeper" with whom the tour leader had established relations on previous voyages. These warnings led group participants to be suspicious of all items offered or promoted by the guide or driver. The driver reacted with fury: "Who does he think he is? He is coming to my country to make profit and to take the bread out of the mouths of our children?" Here, the driver defines the situation as one of colonialism and robbery, emphasizing the alleged kickbacks (in gifts) given to the group's spiritual leader. "It's all business (*mas'hara*). All that interests those priests is money," he added. The Palestinian driver includes the Jewish guide and his family ("our children") as those entitled to a legitimate living for their work. Given the size of drivers' salaries, the economic inequality between visitors and drivers, and the widespread nature of unofficial and undeclared income, what the pastor casts as cheating is seen by drivers as their legitimate, rightful income.[79] The pastor's display of transparency, asserts the driver, is merely a cover for imperialist self-interest. A bond is forged here between the Palestinian driver and the Israeli guide, even amidst the Intifada. This may be a further example of how utterances like "They are like me, because they also have kids to feed" demonstrate the ability "to recognize that 'Others' are likewise seeking a 'normal' life . . . (under) capitalist alienation and the dislocating effects of globalization."[80]

Other players can also get into the picture: shopkeepers on the Via Dolorosa in Jerusalem, frustrated by seeing many groups of pilgrims file by and none enter their shops, would yell at pilgrims: "Don't shop with your guide. He takes forty percent commission. He does not want you to buy from Arabs!"[81] Here we see that, whereas institutional forces (travel agents that require groups to frequent only stores where they receive commission) and some pastors tend to "bleach" the commissions, local merchants advance their own interests (in the hope that the pilgrims would then return to his shop) and frustrations by emphasizing the "black" nature of commissions as unethical, excessive, or politically motivated.

## GOODS OF PILGRIMAGE AS VEHICLES OF VALUES

The monies of Christian Holy Land pilgrimage – purchase payments, tips, and commissions – are not, contra Marx and Simmel, "a universal yardstick against which to measure and evaluate the universe of objects, relations, services and persons."[82] Nor are they an acid alienating people from the products they produce, transforming *Gemeinschaften* into *Gesellschaften*, liberating individuals from the claims of societies expressed through barter and gifts. Rather, those monies take on particular values depending on the human relations that they facilitate or impede. Different actors "color" monies differently and employ them to transmit messages across cultural divides – between pilgrims and Israeli/Palestinian natives, between Israeli guides and Palestinian drivers, and between Western pilgrim-customers and Palestinian Christian (or Messianic Jewish) salesmen. Just as in Malay society, the transfer of fishing monies from men to women "cooks" them, changing the moral values they convey, so too may the discourses and rituals of Christianity be employed to change the "colors" of gifts and commissions, altering the moral values attached to monies, products, and services.[83]

The exchanges of goods and money on pilgrimage reflect the blurred lines between commodities and gifts, sacred and profane, hospitality and professional service.[84] Through religious language and performance, the material object becomes more than a sales item, and the money given to the guide, more than a gratuity for good service. At the moment of purchase or change of hands, the material object or money may be imbued with profound religious values of communitas, solidarity, sincerity or piety – or alternatively, the taint of kickbacks and theft.

The circulation of goods and monies on pilgrimage thus provides a profound mirror into cultural classifications in situations of interreligious and intercultural encounter. The volatility of such goods and monies, their ability to absorb so many nuances of meaning and value, attests to the transformative potential of religious language and performance.

# 6 THE SEDUCTIONS OF GUIDING CHRISTIANS

SHORTLY AFTER I switched from guiding pilgrims to lecturing in anthropology, my wife remarked, "As a lecturer, your first responsibility is to instruct; as a guide it is to seduce." She was referring to the role of tour guides to convey the proper impression, to ferret out the desires and beliefs of the pilgrims, and "play the game" – *le jeu de la seduction* – in ways that would win their confidence, engage their emotions, satisfy their expectations, and yield compliments, requests for future services, and generous tips.[1]

The use of the term of "seduction" with respect to Christian pilgrimage may seem surprising.[2] For religion, "seduction was a strategy of the devil, whether in the guise of witchcraft or love."[3] Seduction was generally seen as evil, a sin, a diversion of mankind from its spiritual goal by the temptations of the flesh. Fornication, unfaithfulness, and idolatry are frequently linked in the Hebrew Bible (e.g., Hosea 2, Ezekiel 15). Numbers 15:39 commands the children of Israel to remember and perform the commandments of the Lord and "not seek after your own hearts and your own eyes, after which you prostitute (Hebrew: *zonim*) yourselves."

The realm of seduction, writes Jean Baudrillard, "is the sacred horizon of appearances."[4] On the surface, it would seem to be the polar opposite of the ideal pilgrim in search of transcendent meaning, his eyes fixed on the goal. As Zygmunt Bauman characterizes him, the pilgrim "can reflect on the road past and see it as a progress towards. . . . The world of pilgrims – of identity builders – must be orderly, determined, predictable . . . a world in which footprints are engraved for good."[5] The pilgrim, in Bauman's formulation, follows a life-long path to his chosen destination and avoids straying from the long and narrow trail in order to satisfy his momentary impulses or desires.

Yet the pilgrim approaches the Holy Land with a developed imaginary: "the constantly deepening, individually instantiated mix of remembered narratives and images that serve to inform an object or places' meaning."[6] The pil-

*116*

grim in search of Christ often not only projects his images and expectations onto the Holy Land; he also projects his expectations and (mis)conceptions of the Jewish people onto his guide. As we have seen, these images may effectively screen out other sites and meanings encountered on the ground, not least the realia of the Israeli-Palestinian conflict.

Here, I offer examples of my own seductive play in presenting pilgrims with the Holy Land, the Bible, and myself. In the initial encounter between Christian Holy Land pilgrim and Jewish-Israeli guide, appearances are of the essence. The guide must scan the pilgrim group for signs in order to place them on the Christian map, sometimes testing them through games or jokes,[7] and display a serious and empathetic demeanor in speaking of things sacred to the group. The performance does not follow a set script but involves risk-taking, double entendres, and a measure of playfulness. The guide must master "the sacred horizon of appearances" and charm the pilgrims and their spiritual leader in order to win their trust. He may seek to seduce them to accept his political positions, change their attitudes toward Judaism, or secure his own financial interests.[8] Alternatively, he may encourage them to transcend the boundaries of their previous faith commitments and join him in a common quest for a more authentic life, as guided by the prophets and Jesus.

In this chapter, I will look at three aspects of the seductions of guiding pilgrims, all related to the boundary between Judaism and Christianity: (1) the attempts of Jewish guides to seduce their groups through Christian (and Judeo-Christian) scriptural language and ritual performance; (2) the ways that Jewish guides of Christian pilgrimages become caught up in the game of seduction, "by which discourse becomes absorbed within itself and emptied of its truth in order to better fascinate others";[9] alternatively, they may get "caught up in play" of their own ritual and seductive performance, in spite of their initial, conscious reservations;[10] and (3) guides may be seduced by the beauty, truth, or warmth of community of Christianity as displayed by the pilgrim groups they lead.

In the latter two cases, the practices and discourses may leak out of the frame of the tour and affect guides' long-term Jewish identity. I will support my claim by showing how guides internalize their pilgrims' faith or incorporate Christian categories into their own Jewish self-definition. Alternatively, I will demonstrate how they resist seduction through discursive and performative acts that mark a separation between themselves and Christian practice, and I will describe several acts of "purification" done by guides to limit or neutralize the effects of Christian seduction. I conclude with a reflection on the ambiguous attraction/repulsion of Christianity for Jewish Israeli guides.

Most of the information presented here resulted from twenty-five interviews with Jewish-Israeli guides and tourism workers, conducted between 2001 and 2004 by myself, my colleague Yael Guter, and my research assistants Smadar Farkas and Matan Shapiro. We chose interview subjects with at least fifteen years' experience guiding, primarily with bus tours of Christian pilgrims of various countries, languages, and denominations. The interviews were supplemented by my own experiences as tour guide. The guides interviewed were traditional or secular,[11] some Israeli born, and others immigrants from Europe or North America (as are many tour guides). Except for the case of Steve Langfur, all interviewees' names have been changed.

Because the ethnography privileges the guide's perspective, what it seeks to show is not the guide's success in seducing his public but rather the tactics he devises for such seduction, his loss of control over the performance, and his thoughts – or second thoughts – on the role and dynamics of seduction. In doing so, the chapter should complement chapter 1, by placing my personal experiences with pilgrims within the wider cultural frame of other guides' practices.

### APPEARANCES: THE OPACITY OF THE PILGRIMAGE FRAME

The importance of appearances is built into the way guided pilgrimages are managed by the pilgrim/tourist industry. Witness this e-mail exchange between myself (as Jewish tour guide and consultant for Holy Land itineraries), the American agent specializing in Evangelical groups, and the local Palestinian (Christian) agent:

> (American agent): I think something like this would be very helpful [in our advertisements for the] Evangelical market:
> 1. [Our company's] guides believe in and stress Biblical inerrancy.
> 2. Your group will feel right at home with our Christian guides or Messianic Jewish guides because their beliefs and worship experiences are similar to your church.

I replied:

> Dear (American agent),
> Do you really think that all (company) guides "believe in Biblical inerrancy" or that all group leaders think that they do?
> I would say something like:
> "Our guides listen closely to the pastors and leaders of the groups and support them. They will keep your spiritual message at the center of the group's experience."

The Palestinian agent responded:

Dear (American agent),

I agree with the point raised by Jackie. It is not a question of guides believing in the inerrancy of the Bible. It is whether the guides are sensitive enough to the belief systems of their Evangelical audiences so as not to create doubts about the authenticity of the Bible within their guiding expositions. That also goes for the Jewish guides who do guide Evangelical groups. (e-mail correspondence with the author, January 2012).

The local tour operator acknowledges the guide as someone who does not necessarily share the beliefs of the pilgrims but who is sensitive and proficient enough to provide explanations and enable practices that correspond to pilgrims' expectations. A full matching of guides' identities with group leaders' (or here – the American agent's) requests would be impossible. In the case of this agent's public, there aren't enough skilled licensed Messianic or Evangelical guides living in Israel/Palestine. Nor would local agents want to rely exclusively on this group if there were.

While some pastors and priests clearly and publicly demarcate the roles of pastor and guide, Christian and Jew, many don't. Group pastors may know of the non-Christian religious identity of the guide and cooperate in keeping that identity ambiguous.[12] Several guides who worked with Italian or Latin American Catholic pilgrims told me that they were instructed by the priests who led the groups that they not tell the group that they were Jewish. Hillary Kaell quotes one of the Texas Baptist pilgrims she interviewed as saying "the guide's job is not to show his religion to you. If we had a Jewish guide, I would expect he would keep it to himself."[13]

In one case, at the end of a twelve-day tour, a group leader and dean of an Evangelical American college suggested I come to the States to teach a winter semester course. When I asked him whether it mattered that I was Jewish, not Christian, he replied: "It's just three weeks! The students will never figure it out." This admittedly extreme formulation illustrates the tensions of the frame in which Jewish-Israeli pilgrim guides operate: the pilgrims' (or agents') desire for religious sincerity[14] conflicts with their desire for a consummate performance on the part of the guide, one that could strengthen pilgrims' Christian faith. At the same time, a kind of conspiratorial "winking" often takes place between guide and group leader, over the heads of the pilgrims.

While different groups may tolerate – or desire – varying public expressions of Judaism on the part of their guide, impression management is clearly essential in the guide/group encounter. Performances of sincerity and repression of cynicism are as essential for guides as performances of feminine care were for the stewardesses studied by Hochschild in the 1980s.[15] Furthermore, as with the air hostesses, the boundary between performing oneself and performing for the client is shifting and fluid. As with the hostesses' behavior, the interactions of pilgrimage often leak out of the frame into the daily life of guides.

## POWER RELATIONS ON THE PILGRIMAGE STAGE

In the study of tourism, the issue of impression management and accommodation is related to the unequal global distribution of power. As the tourists often come from richer and more powerful countries (and classes) than the service workers and guides at the tourist destination, guides often feel obliged to accommodate tourist expectations by providing services and producing tourism narratives that will accord with what tourists expect to receive and hear. While toured cultures have some agency in adopting the power and money engendered by tourism to strengthen their own culture, in most cases, tourists' narratives and gazes refashion politically and financially weaker areas in the image of the more powerful touring culture.[16] Thus, Crang finds that tourism workers not only produce a product but produce themselves as part of their jobs: "Identity politics are at the heart of tourism labor processes . . . identities are not just brought to work by employees; they are forged through it."[17] Some of the pressures and rewards that determine the way guides perform their role are common to many service industries.[18] As guides spend an average of 8–10 hours a day interacting with their groups, speaking of things that often matter to the guides themselves, they often become dependent on the admiration and applause of pilgrims/tourists to reaffirm their own sense of worth. As I once faxed a travel agent, after a tense experience with a group leader, "Guides like me can feel rejected when someone in the group won't swear on a stack of Bibles that you've given them the time of their life."

Some of this interaction takes on particular shapes in the Jewish guide–Christian pilgrim–Holy Land encounter. In addition to the power differentials of hosts and guests, the historical and theological relations of Christians and Jews inflect the guiding performances and lead guides to craft strategies and devise tactics to fit the circumstances. From the point of view of the Jewish-Israeli guides, certain tensions between performing oneself and performing for others come into relief: What parts of the everyday world of guides are brought onto the tour guiding stage, given the nature of the actors and the roles assigned them by the pilgrimage industry? How do the conflicting demands of (many of the) pilgrims for both sincerity and consummate performance manifest themselves in the guide/group encounter, and what price do such demands entail? How do guides shield themselves from the missionary influence of many of the groups? To what extent are new realities created as the performance emerges?

In order to understand how onstage and offstage roles interact, I first summarize the path that leads many Jewish-Israeli guides to choose their profession and remain in it.

## THE GUIDE'S BAGGAGE: THE MAKING OF THE PILGRIM TOUR GUIDE

I have described the guide course from the point of view of the tourism/pilgrimage industry. But what brings Jewish Israelis to take the course and become guides? Many do so to broaden their general education and have no intent on making a career of tour guiding. Others, on graduation, opt to guide Israelis in Hebrew. Among the many tour guides born outside the country, their decision to guide is often integrally woven into their decision to leave their places of birth and come to live in Israel, though they may realize this only in retrospect. For some immigrants, it is a realization of the Zionist or Jewish religious motivation that brought them to Israel, and many enjoy the status of "Jewish/Israeli ambassador" that the tourists/pilgrims accord them. For others, it may be a way to live in Israel while avoiding some of the frictions and disadvantages suffered by newcomers. For native-born Israelis, the choice of a career interacting with foreign visitors may offer an escape from some of the entrapments of stability; many proclaim they could never work at a nine-to-five desk job.[19] For many, guiding offers the opportunity of being tourists in their own lives. Yet it exposes them, time and again to an outsider's view of Israel and Judaism and raises what might otherwise be taken for granted to the surface of consciousness.

The guide spends 8–12 hours a day performing in places he does not usually inhabit, speaking another language. Guides avoid commitments to the rhythms and obligations of daily life (parent-teacher meetings, holidays, birthdays, scheduled classes, etc.). Often, the holiday season in Israel, when families gather to celebrate, is the time of guides' most intensive work away from home.[20] Even the guide's sense of time is changed: he loses track of the day of the week, the month, the season of the year and the city he is sleeping in as he wakes in yet another anonymous hotel. In the most intensive tourist season, guides may pick up one group when they bring another to the airport – with their family members arriving to switch suitcases and bring clean clothes. For guides, there are no days of the week, except perhaps as expressed through sites' opening and closing times. Rather, there are seasons and off-seasons, work days and occasional "free days" – and sick days in bed to recover immediately following an intensive group (or several groups back to back). The difficulty in readjustment from work to home life is expressed by most guides and creates considerable strains in many guides' family lives,[21] as any tour guide's spouse will attest to.

Yet this other sense of time may be attractive. Many guides speak of the "aroma of abroad" (*nih'oah hutz-la'aretz*), the sense of being elsewhere while continuing to live in Israel. As Dalia expressed it,

> In every group, I feel a little bit like a tourist. I'm in the bubble too, and participate in their enthusiasm. It's an escape from my reality. That's what's addictive about this job. You're always on vacation. It's not just the hotel or the bus. People are in elevated spirits and you're with them. It's an imagined vacation from daily life. Even though you know that outside the bus life goes on, and it's their vacation, not yours (interview with Dalia, 2002).

Although most Jewish guides come into the guide training course with minimal knowledge of Christianity, they learn the basics in the course and increase their knowledge through their cumulative experience with Christian groups. Guides attempt to develop long-term relations with group leaders and agents abroad who may specialize in selected Christian markets (Southern Baptists, Church of England, Bavarian Catholic dioceses, California seeker churches, etc.). The quality of guiding, so say most agents, is a crucial element for the success of the pilgrimage tour.[22] Consequently, once a group leader finds a guide he is pleased with, he is likely to request him for his future groups.

In addition to the four guide functions specified in Erik Cohen's typology[23] – path-finding, mediating, facilitating social interaction, and communicating, the guide of pilgrim groups performs an additional spiritual function, forming the diverse sites of the tour into a spiritual path.[24] In doing so, he will employ appropriate feeling tones,[25] create empathy with key figures of the past,[26] and provide imaginative and personalizing descriptions of historical events. As Katz summarized, the Israeli tour guide (like the group's pastor/priest), has been trained to be not only a *moreh derekh* – a "teacher of the way" – but also an encourager of faith.[27]

Christian theologies may also play a role in the group's expectations and classifications of the guide. While Jews' "external" verification may bolster the authority of the sites,[28] the guide's possession of knowledge of Jesus without faith in Jesus may be a challenge to many pilgrims, a challenge that must often be carefully negotiated by guide, pastor/priest, and pilgrims.

Evangelicals are more active in missionizing their guides than Catholics and are more likely to take their guide's sympathetic explanation of Christianity to be a profession of faith in Christianity. Several factors may account for this: (1) The importance of inspired speech as a sign of conversion or at least of "coming under conviction";[29] thus, if the guide talks the talk, he must be walking the walk. On the other hand, the more communal nature of Catholic affiliation, as well as the importance of sacraments like baptism, makes the Jewish-Catholic divide in the guided tour clearer: if you haven't been baptized a Catholic, if you don't take communion in the Catholic church, you're not Catholic. (2) The prominence of seeker churches within Evangelicalism. Hawaiian megachurch members told me, "We have Mexicans, Buddhists, Catholics, and Jews in our church. What they share is a personal relationship with Jesus." Because of the rapid mobility of worshippers from one denomination to another,[30] the relative lack of importance of doctrinal orthodoxy or ritual initiation, and the (admittedly confusing) overlap of Jewish religion and ethnicity, Jewishness is not seen as excluding one from the church. (3) The role assigned by many Evangelicals to the Jews as "God's people" in the present (i.e., as ongoing partners in the Abrahamic covenant) and as active role-players in the approaching eschaton, makes Jews (and especially, educated Israeli guides!) particularly valuable prizes for the church.

## SEDUCTION, RESISTANCE, AND THE PERFORMANCE OF JUDAISM FOR CHRISTIANS

I now provide a series of examples that illustrate how guides negotiate the contact zone between foreign Christians and Jewish-Israelis through the seductive force of performance – and to what ends. I then show how the guide's attempt to seduce the group may result in a slippage, a loss of control, and a measure of "leakage" into their offstage lives; such leakage may divert the life trajectories of Jewish-Israeli guides:

*1. Confirming the Primacy of Judaism through Ritual and Discourse:*

Some pilgrim guides come from immigrant backgrounds in which their contact with Christians has been significant. Their decision to be Jewish and move to Israel is also a decision favoring Judaism – or at least, life in a Jewish environment – over Christianity. Roberto, an immigrant from Italy describes the path that led him to guide Italian Christians follows:

> From the outset, I felt that my home was more in Jerusalem than in Italy. It's such a unique place . . . an enchanting place. The people interested me and Judaism interests me intellectually. . .
>
> For me, Judaism is morality and the direct connection to God. I don't need anyone to be my mediator, I don't need the shepherd with his staff.

> My father was a Christian and my mother was Jewish, so I lived in the Christian world my entire life. . . . Whoever grew up as I did, in an Italian village with few Jews, and went to mass to pray. . . . Whoever grew up that way has a special understanding of things. He knows what the Christian has in his head.
>
> Until thirty years ago, the Vatican prohibited the study of Judaism and the Hebrew Bible. The Italian Christians date back 2,000 years and don't know who Jesus was. What a Jew is. The common people don't link up to the intellectual theories. So, when they arrive here (in Israel), we construct their knowledge in their language and in their mentality, and that's a great accomplishment. . . .
>
> I prepare them a picnic on the Mount of Beatitudes, where you see the entire lake. People get high from that. I prepare them sandwiches and fruit. . . . I read to them from the Hebrew Bible after I've led them to understand the story from the territory, and then, when I read to them from the Hebrew Bible, they react with "Wow!" (interview with Roberto, 2004).

He sums up his guiding work:

> There's an element of mission in guiding in Israel. It's not a vacation but an experience. I also believe that contributing to knowledge is contributing towards peace. . . .
>
> I chose Judaism and it's the best thing I've done in my life and I have no regrets and not the shadow of a doubt. I chose and I'm at peace so I can live with others and have no reason to fear. Many Italian guides don't go into churches, and in their position they transmit that they don't want "to get dirty." I go inside, and provide the complementary Jewish part to the priest's words – all if the priest agrees, of course. . . . Every Christian is also a Jew, he just doesn't know it. But when he gets here, he discovers that.

Roberto has chosen Judaism over Christianity. He sees the education of Christians about their Jewish roots as a mission that leads him to guide pilgrims. The location of the Judeo-Christian encounter in the State of Israel/Bible Land empowers Roberto to instruct Italian Catholics in ways he could not in his Italian hometown. As he remarks, "No Jewish community in Europe can be an educational force towards the Gentiles. . . . They don't want to disturb their lives, they just want to be obedient to the authorities; they're still searching for themselves." As tour guide, Israeli citizen, host (note the making and serving of sandwiches) and native, he can enter a church, not as the child of an insignificant minority but as "elder brother" to instruct Italian Christians about the Jewish Jesus and the Hebrew Bible. By offering them food at the site of the Beatitudes (overlooking the traditional site of Jesus's feeding of the multitudes with loaves and fish!), he positions himself as host, hence as proprietor of the symbolic landscape of the Sea of Galilee. One might say that as a member of the family of Jesus the Jew, he invites the Gentile Christians into his home. The contact with Christians as proximate other enables Roberto to enact his life choices through guiding, and reaffirm the correctness of his choice to be Jewish and to immigrate to Israel.

A second example of seductive Jewish ritual is the welcoming ceremony to Jerusalem. We have seen in chapter 3 that groups seek to intensify the experience of entry into Jerusalem through the ritual of playing a Christian hymn of Jerusalem on the bus audio system and descending from the bus to travel their last stretch to the panorama of the Old City on foot – "as Jesus did." An alternative entrance ceremony, which I often practiced and which has become extremely popular among both Christian and Jewish groups, is the Melchizedek bread and wine ceremony.[31] Here, on the group's arrival in Jerusalem, usually just before sunset, the guide will take them up to the panoramic platform on Mount Scopus. The guide sets up two small loaves of bread covered with a napkin, a packet of salt, and a cup of wine or grape juice (which he has purchased en route or taken from the previous hotel) atop the low retaining wall of the panorama platform. He reads the passage Genesis 14:18–20, describing Melchizedek, King of (Jeru)Salem's reception of Abraham with bread and wine, following Abraham's victory over the Kings of the North. Following his reading of the Genesis passage, the guide continues with a passage from the pilgrim psalms, most frequently Psalm 122 (121): "I was glad when they said to me, let us go up to the house of the Lord. My feet were standing within your gates, Jerusalem." Some groups then sing the final verses of the psalm, using a Jewish melody taught them previously by their guide. The guide then recites the Hebrew blessings over the bread and wine and the *Shehechayanu*: "Blessed art thou, God, our Lord, king of the universe, who has kept us alive, and sustained us and brought us to this day." Usually, these blessings are also translated into the pilgrim's language. Sometimes, the blessings are followed with a passage read by the pastor, describing Jesus's entry into Jerusalem. Subsequently, the bread is broken, pieces dipped in salt, and distributed to the members of the group. The wine/grape juice is poured from the guide's cup into small individual ones for the pilgrims to drink. The guide concludes: "Welcome to the Holy City of Jerusalem, capital of Israel."

This ceremony situates the guide as native host and ritual expert (like Melchizedek, the priest of God most high) and the pilgrims as honored guests to the city – like Abraham. The recital of the Biblical passage acknowledges common spiritual descent from Abraham (and Melchizedek, linked with Jesus in the New Testament – Hebrews 6–7) and a shared sacred book. The prominence of the Hebrew language and Jewish customs (covering the bread, blessing wine first and bread second, using two loaves as in the Sabbath ceremony) marks it as authentically Jewish. Although it was invented by guides only several decades ago for Jewish groups from abroad, it dovetails with traditional Jewish customs of ceremonially marking pilgrims' first glimpse of Jerusalem.[32] This ritual is often requested by returning Christian groups and sometimes specifically mentioned in tour itineraries.

The ritual seduces the pilgrims with its inclusiveness and familiarity (it's like Communion), but it is tinged with perceived Jewish exoticism. It reaffirms Judaism (including latter-day Jewish customs) as the ground of Christianity[33] and the native religion of the city, seemingly dating back to Abraham. As the guide Roberto said, "Every Christian is also a Jew, he just doesn't know it. But when he gets here, he discovers that." If the ceremony is followed by the identification of the major sites of the city (as in the Mount of Olives panorama), the sequence of ritual mediator/expert communicator further reaffirms the Jewish guide's status as bearer of the keys to the city.

### 2. Contact with Christianity as Return to Judaism:

Many guides born in Israel grow up with minimal knowledge of Christianity and a negative view of the little they do know. For Israelis with minimal religious instruction, Christianity is often perceived as idolatrous and as heir to a long tradition of anti-Semitism. One Israeli-born guide, Zaki, expressed it as follows:

> I remember at a certain point, when I specialized in guiding Christians, my father [a Polish-born survivor of Auschwitz] expressed his disapproval: "After all they did to us. . . ." I answered that I work with them to make up for it, so that it won't happen again. There is an abyss of ignorance between both sides. In some ways, I even see a link between the fact that I am the second generation of Holocaust survivors and my occupation guiding Christians.

Thus, guiding Christians becomes a rectification of historical Christian anti-Semitism (through teaching and personal example), as well as an affirmation of his legacy as child of Holocaust survivors.

In his first year or two of guiding, Zaki led a group visiting during the Jewish High Holy Days. On Yom Kippur Eve, at the end of the touring day, the British pastor took the microphone and said: "Now, Zaki won't be with us tomorrow, because tomorrow is Yom Kippur, the Day of Atonement, and Zaki will fast and be in the synagogue and hear the passages in Leviticus being read, of how the scapegoat atones for the people's sins." As a secular Jew, Zaki had never fasted nor attended synagogue on Yom Kippur, and was embarrassed. He relates:

As a result, I became more religious than before. I began reading the Hebrew Bible and came closer to my own religion. I look at other religious people and I have more understanding. I also became more spiritual than I was before working with pilgrims. . . . I offer thanks for every small goodness that I have in life. Not to accept things as self-understood. To give thanks to some supreme power, whoever He may be, for the small good everyday things (interview with Zaki, December 2001).

The positive spiritual atmosphere manifested by the pilgrims combined with the British pastor's intimate knowledge of Jewish sources led Zaki to see the pilgrimage encounter not only as means of combating Christian anti-Semitism but as a place where he could witness an expression of attractive moral and spiritual values. The Christians' indebtedness to Jewish sources, and their pointing him to his "home pasture" – the Yom Kippur synagogue, led Zaki to turn to Jewish sources as part of his search for spirituality.

### 3. Reexperiencing Ambiguous or Traumatic Events:

A very different intersection of a Jewish life trajectory with the seductions of guiding pilgrims is that of Bernice, a Francophone Orthodox Jew in her 60s:

I am Jewish, born and raised. But I had an interruption – when I was hidden [during World War 2], I learned Christianity. We were in hiding with my parents, living in a small village as a Christian family. I went to school and learned religion; it was very interesting. My grandmother made sure I would learn well, but every Sunday before Mass would whisper in my ear in Yiddish: "*farges nisht az du bist a yidineh*" – "don't forget that you're a Jewess."

In her mid-40s, Bernice chose to become a licensed tour guide and often chose to work with Christians: "I want to show them the Jewish sources of their faith. To show them the history of their religion in its natural setting. To show how Christianity separated from Judaism and why." She also tries to educate her French-speaking publics about the history of Christian anti-Judaism:

In the beginning, Christianity was in competition with Judaism. The borders between Christianity and Judaism were unclear. So there was a need to separate, to show that the Jews don't have the truth. It's written black on white that the Jews must be preserved, but only in a state of humiliation, that attests to Christian truth, that Judaism is passé. Like the Germans who prohibited Jews from going to the bathhouse and then said that the Jews are dirty and smelly.

I tried to make them understand that instead of humiliating the Jews and saying they were punished, they can observe their religion in peace. . . . But I also tried to transmit that Christianity is one of the three monotheistic religions, although it is not so monotheistic. I tell them that the worship of Isis persisted very late in the Roman Empire and the only way to deal with it was to dress Isis up in a blue robe and call her Mary, mother of Jesus. . . .

They sincerely believe that they worship one God. When the Creator created man, he placed in him a spark of divinity. That's how we come to a recognition of the Creator. If we're lucky and are born to the Jewish people, we're closer to the source. . . .

I want to transmit the Jewish message, that people will understand what Judaism really is (interviews with Bernice, 2002).

Bernice finds herself leading Catholic pilgrimages, sometimes spending entire days in churches: "After a day of churches, it's a pleasure to take a shower. I have the feeling that some kind of impurity weighs upon me.[34] In addition, there's the thing that almost all the churches I know of are built on sites of idolatry. And in fact, they continue to worship idols."

Like Roberto, Bernice sees her work with Christians as a way of justifying and announcing her choice of Judaism as a religion closer to the source, as a purer expression of monotheism. In addition, she continues to relive the paradoxes and tensions that have marked her attitude toward Christianity since childhood: "It's idolatry, but because of their idolatrous belief, my family and I are alive today." While she is repulsed by the "idolatry," she is grateful for the moral courage that was instilled in the French villagers by the church, courage which led them to risk their lives to save her family from the German occupiers. Like during the war, Bernice continues to frequent the church, though now as a career choice, all the while remembering and reminding her public that she is "*a yidine* – a Jewess."

### 4. Flirting with Christian Religious Experience:

Some guides get caught up in the pilgrim performance to the extent that they undergo Christian religious experiences which they describe as being beyond their control. Gila, a native-born Israeli in her 40s, related:

With the Mormons . . . I participated in their confessions and sometimes shared personal experiences with them but did not participate in communion, except a few times abroad, when I went with them to their neighborhood church. During their prayers in church, I prayed to my God in my heart and asked forgiveness if I was committing a sin towards Him. I divided myself – between outside and inside. . . .

When I was working with Mormons, I had visions of Jesus. . . . Once a woman appeared to me in a dream. She said she was coming especially to me to give her testimony that Jesus was God. In the dream about Jesus – which was very scary – I dreamt of a scene like that of the Creation: there was darkness, and suddenly light began to appear . . . I felt that God was going to appear to me. I saw angels who came down from the sky, and I knew that in a minute He was going to appear to me, and I was paralyzed with fear. Suddenly I saw a boat, and in it a figure half–lying down, half-seated. I understood that God was Jesus and that the boat was on the Sea of Galilee. Then it was over. This dream really upset me.

It happened in Israel, when I wasn't working but at a time when I had worked a lot with Christians. Apparently it was the influence of the New Testament stories. It made me think that maybe it's a hint that I should convert or recognize Jesus as part of my religion. I told this to my husband and also to a group of Mormons, in the course of their emotional confessions. They were very moved and hugged me.

She described another guiding situation:

The group was playing a CD of music, about Jesus and the Sea of Galilee. It was when we were on the Mount of Beatitudes; they had communion. Then they played the music. I was standing at the side, and on the passage about the Sea of Galilee, I started to cry emotional tears. Tears that fell incessantly. The music described the Sea of Galilee. Even though He wasn't there before, now He was there without being there. The group told me that the Holy Spirit has filled me. That's how you feel when the Holy Spirit enters you. That's the response. In my entire life I never cried like that (interview with Gila, 2002).

One way of understanding these experiences is that the power of in situ reading of Scripture (and music) is not limited to believing Christians alone. Shared storied sites, like the Sea of Galilee, as well as the pilgrims themselves, are charged with valences that "give the . . . audience the feeling of witnessing scenes and heroes of the past, as if they were taking place here and now."[35] Such storied sites may draw the guide out of her "Jewish" orbit and cause her to "jump the synapses." Undoubtedly, the guide's familiarity with Mormon iconography and religious experience and her previous willingness to participate, if not wholeheartedly, in Mormon rituals, provided the necessary conditions. The guide recognizes Jesus based on popular Christian (Mormon?) iconography and through descriptions of Jesus in the prayers and sermons of the pastors and does not deny that her inner state was a real manifestation of Jesus and the Holy Spirit.[36] At one point, she tells us, she and her husband seriously considered conversion to Mormonism, though in the end, they drew back. The fact, however, that she was willing to share her thoughts of conversion to Mormonism with the pilgrims indicates the seriousness of the proposition. Thus, we see, the guide may be sufficiently seduced by the spiritual experiences of pilgrimage, the pilgrims' expressions of warmth and mutual support – and the truths of Christianity – to consider conversion.

## 5. Confirming One's Commitment to Messianic Judaism[37]

Kobi, an Israeli-born guide and Messianic Jew in his early 50s at the time of the interview (in 2002), got his guide's license in 1981. On one of his tours, he met a Christian woman, whom he later married, and came to accept Jesus as Messiah, crafting a "Biblical Judaism" (as opposed to "Talmudic Judaism") heavily influenced by Evangelical tropes.

Although he speaks Swedish as well, Kobi prefers guiding American Evangelicals, among whom he is known as a Messianic guide. He shares many of their right-wing political and religious views on Israel and attempts to convince them to become more politically active in supporting those views. He provides an account of a remarkable guiding practice that he has developed around the Biblical site of Ein Harod, where, heeding God's word, Gideon tested his men before setting out for battle against the Midianites (Judges 6–8). Gathering the group around the spring, Kobi, Bible in hand, tells them the following story:

> I was a bad soldier until the Six-Day War broke out. In the war, I was an infantryman. The good soldier is thirstier, hungrier, more tired . . . he takes care of the other soldiers. He is always prepared. That's how, one night, I caught four Egyptians who would have killed us. The next day I saw how the Russian tanks [of the Egyptian army] fled from our tanks for no reason. It was really a miracle. I think that the entire Six-Day War was a miracle. . . . But the generals did not give God any credit.

Kobi relates to us how he reads a passage about Gideon from the Bible, saying

> The bad soldiers were the first to come to drink. The good ones walked slowly, checked that there was no trap, drinking with one hand, while the other held their sword.
> Then I get down on one knee and drink from the waters of the well. This demonstration is one they won't forget for the rest of their lives.

Following his explanation, many members of the group kneel down to lap up the water from the spring. Occasionally, the group leader will conclude with a prayer.

Kobi repeatedly performs a narration of his life in accordance with both the Biblical account of the Book of Judges (which sketches a cycle marked by fall into sin, oppressive punishment, crying out to the Lord, God's intervention, salvation, recognition of God's deeds, followed by forgetting, and a second fall into sin . . .) and Evangelical understandings of contemporary history. Kobi is Gideon's good soldier and a grateful agent of God's plan for His people in the present. Through his proclamation of a shared faith in God and in Jesus as the fulfillment of Biblical prophecy, Kobi seduces the pilgrims by implying that they too can be good soldiers – "those who give the credit to God." Initially, they do this by imitating Kobi in lapping up the spring water and by reciting a prayer. All that remains to be done is to become active players in realizing God's word on the world stage. They can do so, Kobi encourages them, by supporting God's people of Israel in these times of conflict: "They return to the church, write their senators and conduct pro-Israeli propaganda."[38]

The factors that brought about his acceptance of Jesus as Messiah are not available to us,[39] and Kobi's acceptance of Jesus as Messiah apparently preceded at least some of these performances. Yet the appreciation they engender (not to mention invitations and honoraria for speaking at Evangelical churches in the United States as a Messianic Jewish Israeli), confirms for Kobi each time anew the value and correctness of his decision.

## RESISTING SEDUCTION – PROPHYLAXIS, PLAY, ATONEMENT, AND PURIFICATION

Until now, we have seen how the intensiveness, acclaim, and communal spirit of Christian pilgrim groups (and the religious language of guides' own performances) may seduce the Jewish guides and become integrated into the stories guides tell of themselves. Many guides, however, are aware of this seductive force and perform a series of boundary-marking procedures designed to protect themselves from the seductive influence of Christianity and the missionizing tendency of Christian (especially Evangelical) pilgrims. I call these "prophylactic rites." Others perform rites of separation or purification to counter or neutralize Christian impact. The invention of these minirituals attests to the seductive power that Christianity, as embodied practice of the pilgrim, exerts on the Jewish guide.

Some group (spiritual) leaders specifically instruct their guides not to read Biblical verses.[40] Some even prefer silent guides who will provide government-licensed accompaniment but let them do all the talking. In most cases, however, the group is eager to have the guide provide a narrative that can help strengthen the faith or commitment of pilgrims and provide a supportive "native's point of view."[41]

Gloria told us: "Immediately when I get on the bus, I tell them that I am a native-born Israeli Jew *(tzabarit)*. So they know who's standing before them." Thus, she marshals the authority of the native in an attempt to draw a red line, an essential boundary, between herself and the group and repel proselytizing attempts.[42] Of her guiding narratives, she says: "I will never call him by his Hebrew name, Yeshua. Because he doesn't belong to me. Only "Jesus," never another name" (interview with Gloria, 2002). While such linguistic strate-gies often goes unnoticed by the group, sometimes frictions develop, as Tuvia reports:

> One day I received a group of Protestants. After several hours, I noticed that the pastor was dissatisfied. I asked him, "What happened?" He answered, "Nothing . . . maybe you have the number of the office?" I understood that he wanted to request another guide. I answered him, "But today is Saturday and the office is closed. What's the problem?" "How come you never say Jesus Christ?" I said there was no problem. I'll say it. Really, I have no problem with it. I don't express through that that I believe that Jesus is the Messiah, I don't baptize myself into Christianity. They were satisfied. A guide who isn't prepared to say "Jesus Christ" shouldn't work with pilgrims (interview with Tuvia, 2001).

Often, because of the guide's sympathetic readings and explanations of New and Old Testament sites and events, the group will assume that the guide is a Christian and may ask him when he discovered Christ. Alternatively, they may ask why he does not believe in Christ. Or, more frequently, "How can you know the Bible/the New Testament so well and *not* believe in Christ?" When con-fronted outright with the question if they believe in Jesus, some guides provide ambiguous answers that they know will be taken by the group as affirmations of faith. Thus, Hillary Kaell quotes a guide of one tour she observed as respond-ing to a female pilgrim, "You can't be a guide without developing a relationship with Jesus." Pressed by Kaell, he explained in private, "I've developed a relation-ship with Jesus like I've developed a relationship with [Roman-era historian] Flavius Josephus or any other historical character. So it's not a lie, how she takes it is how she takes it."[43]

Some guides never read from the New Testament. They will always hand the book over to the pastor[44] or find a volunteer in the group to read, so as not to voice the Hebrew Bible and that of the New Testament with the same author-ity.[45] Still others carry two separate volumes – a New Testament and a Hebrew Bible (rather than a Christian Bible containing both) and shift between them, in order to make the difference between the Hebrew Bible and the New Testa-ment visible. In a similar vein, Bernice says that she consistently uses the term Gospels (*Évangiles*) rather than New Testament: "The pilgrims noticed the fact only a few days later. . . . I can't accept the fact that the New Testament came to replace the Torah." In a similar vein, the guide Steve chooses to refer to the Gospels as the "Second Testament."

Still other guides mark separation through spatial practices. Thus, Gloria and Bernice take care never to speak from the ambo, the place of preaching of priests, even in inactive churches that have long become archaeological ruins. Others make sure not to attend communal meals until after they have begun so as not to have to hold hands with members of the group as they bless the food in Jesus' name.

Some groups may try to convert the guide or have him participate in Christian rituals. Guide reactions vary. Gloria said

> Once I felt this pressure – "we pray for you." So I gathered them all and told them that I was raised in a nonreligious household, and when I came to Israel I studied the history of the Jewish people and the guide course, and the New Testament, and I found out that I knew more about the New Testament than about the Hebrew scriptures. I have to thank the Christians for bringing me back to my Judaism. That was the end of it (interview with Gloria, 2002).

In my own guiding, I wound up performing an Orthodox Jewish ritual (donning phylacteries at the Western Wall), as a way of marking myself as Jew as opposed to the Christian group (see chap. 1, p. 6-7). Eventually, however, I was disturbed by the implications of my performance of an Orthodox Jewish ceremony in order to represent myself as a "true Jew" in the eyes of others.

Steve, in line with his exceptional aim of challenging the group's faith (and reflecting the mandate given him by group leaders to do so) tells us:

> If there is an attempt on the part of the group to make me into a Christian, I tell them, "I'm with Christians a lot. If I felt that their relationships were those of openness, that they had a better quality of life than others, I would join. But I don't see it. I don't see a community of perfect people. I see people with the same worries, problems and complexes as others. . . .
>
> [I tell them that] in Judaism, the Messiah is someone who brings salvation, redemption. Jesus was here and the world hasn't improved much. Sometimes I would feel their adrenalin mounting, and I said, "Good! That's the way it was 2,000 years ago, when Jesus was here in the synagogue, and some left the synagogue. And now it's a good time to eat St. Peter's fish." Who in their surroundings talks with them in that way? (interview, July 2004).

Note that here, Steve's provocation marshals his power as tour leader and organizer of logistics to cut short what could be a confrontational discussion – "time for lunch."

Another way of neutralizing or limiting potential seduction or conflict is by framing it as a joke. Witness Tuvia's story:

> On the way to the Jordan River site Yardenit, I told the group about the site and said that whoever wished could be baptized. One lady at the back of the bus said that she wanted to be baptized but that we had no pastor. So I said,

in jest, that I could baptize her. She replied, "But you're Jewish." I answered, "And John the Baptist wasn't Jewish?" They all laughed. I treated it as a joke. When we got to Yardenit, after the explanation, I gave them a quarter of an hour to wander around the site. And then, that woman comes up to me and asks me to go down to the river with her. I said that I wanted to drink coffee on the break. She said, "But you promised that you would baptize me." In the end I agreed, and that's what happened. And then another 6–7 women stood in line behind her, and I had to baptize them all. I hoped that other tour guides wouldn't arrive at the site and see the embarrassing moment. As soon as I finished, three Moroccan-Jewish matrons approached me and asked me that I bless them. Raising an eyebrow, I answered that I wasn't qualified. They answered that they saw how I blessed the women of the group, placing my hand on their foreheads during the baptism. As I had no choice, I had to "bless" them too[48] (Interview with Tuvia, 2001).[46]

Tuvia frames the entire event as a game: he "places his foot over the border-line," joking that if the Jewish John the Baptist could baptize, so can he. But the pilgrims, who don't want to miss the opportunity to be baptized in the Jordan, take him seriously—and take up his gambit/offer. In the dynamic of mutual seduction, Tuvia becomes caught up in his own game, and is unable (or perhaps not entirely unwilling) to pull back.[47]

As Koepping observes, "the dialectic between awareness and unconsciousness, between playing as active form of enactment and the process of being taken over by the text (the word, the movement) also entails the risk of loosing [sic] the self in the game."[48] Play, like ritual, Richard Schechner reminds us, creates its own [permeable] boundaries and realms that are slippery, porous, and full of creative lying and deceit—or at the least, capable of mere pretense and impersonation. "The fun of playing, when there is fun, is in playing with fire, going in over one's head, inverting accepted procedures and hierarchies."[49]

To what extent was the baptism ceremony a game for Tuvia all the way along? Might it represent a deep desire of Tuvia to be pastor to the Gentiles (but not rabbi to the Jews?), if only for a moment? Perhaps it was framed as a game only in retrospect. We'll probably never know. But in seduction, going too far is always one of the risks of the game.

Witness a similar situation, in which another guide succeeds in deflecting the seduction:

Gershon became very friendly with the pastor of a bus group. The group leader then says that something great will happen today, because Gershon is about to convert and that he (the pastor) will baptize him. The whole bus screamed in joy and excitement. . . . Gershon described the real ecstasy in the

Jewish guides may get caught up in the performance of Christian ritual, in spite of themselves. A pastor baptizes a pilgrim at the Yardenit – Jordan River baptismal site. © *Salem Bible College and Thiessen Photography. Used by permission.*

> bus, and also understood that he had to get out of the situation. The pastor too understood that the joke had gotten out of hand. . . . So Gershon took the microphone and said "I'll let the pastor baptize me, if he lets me cut (circumcise) him" (fieldnotes of interview with G., October 2003).

Here too, we see how playfulness and ritualizing "both deal with the negotiation of boundaries, holding in tension not only their creation but also the very promise of their transgression."[50] Although framed as a joke, the threat of violence ("I'll cut you") reinstates the boundary between Jew and Christian (drawing on circumcision as the mark of difference between Jew and Gentile in Paul's writings). If baptism/immersion was presented by the pastor as an act of loving incorporation dissolving boundaries, Gershon's joke recasts it as an act of violent erasure of boundaries that calls for a counter-act of violence reestablishing the boundary ("I'll cut/circumcise you"). Framing it as play "shifts the issue at hand [orthodoxy, power negotiations] from the forefront to a more discreet position, and in doing so seems to create room for maneuvering and accommodation."[51]

Sometimes, guides feel that they have traversed the border with Christianity in the course of their guiding performance. In such cases, they may perform acts atonement or purification. Frank relates:

> Once, a Catholic group I was guiding was making a film. They had me sit with them when they took communion. I tried to think of it as just a ceremony, without relating to its religious meaning. During their prayers in church, I prayed to my God in my heart. I asked for forgiveness if I committed a sin. I split myself: one thing outside, another inside (interview, 2002).[52]

"Seduction" proves to be a fitting term for such behavior, since it implies a previously marked morally/religiously correct life path, highly emotional interactive contact with another, embodiment, pleasure, spontaneous deviation, and movement. Seduction is often followed by remorse, purification, and return.

The Orthodox guide Bernice spoke of taking long showers to rid herself of the impurity she feels adheres to her body after a long day in "idolatrous" churches. Roberto comments that some Jewish guides of Italian groups don't go into churches, transmitting "that they don't want to get dirty" (interview, 2004). One is reminded of Mary Douglas' exposition of uncleanness as "matter out of place" and the disgust we feel toward bodily fluids outside the body or that stick to the skin.[53] Christianity "sticks" to Judaism, especially in the case of the Orthodox guide Bernice, who owed her survival to the idolatrous beliefs of the French Catholic peasants who hid her family during the Holocaust. Before reentering her strictly kosher kitchen, a shower was necessary.

Another practice of purification performed by guides, deals with the greeting cards that accompany the "love offerings" presented by groups immediately preceding their departure; these cards, tucked into envelopes stuffed with money, are inscribed with New Testament verses, prayers, and wishes that the guide see the light of Christ. Several guides told me that they enter the airport bathroom, remove the money, rip up the card and flush it down the toilet. This is done to violently remove the effect of the missionary verses, and cast the love offering as recompense for services already provided, rather than as an invitation to continue a theological dialogue with missionizing Christians.

## PERFORMATIVITY, GUIDED TOURS, AND THE SEDUCTIONS OF CHRISTIANITY

This discussion of the seductions of guiding pilgrims poses two major questions: Insofar as seduction is linked with a fixed (moral, religious) life path and the straying away from that path – what is it about the interactive tour frame that enables such seduction to take place? The second question arises from the vehemence of the expressions of fear and disgust on the part of guides, emotions that go beyond the discomfort that tour guides sometimes feel when working with groups they disagree with. What makes Christianity so repulsive – and seductive – to (mostly secular) Jewish Israelis?

## 1. The Seductions of the Guided Tour Frame

Judith Adler recognized the potential of travel, as a performed art, to effect change: "Travel lends itself to dramatic play with the boundaries of selfhood, and the character ideals of the performers and their audiences are as various as the performances. . . . Enduring identities are often narratively constructed on the basis of brief adventures."[54] The detachment of guiding work from both daily life and the rhythms of Israeli family and society facilitates more intense interactions inside the environmental bubble of the tour.[55] The limited time frame and definition of roles and goals for guides and pilgrims foster a sense of security that enable each to open up to each other. The frame also lends the tour environment a detached intimacy reminiscent of one-night stands. The worst and the best of groups leave within ten days. If he so wishes, the Jewish guide may even become "priest for a day" with minimal commitment (as we saw in the case of the guide's baptizing pilgrims).

The guide who acts more pious, more honest, or more respectful of his pilgrims' beliefs than he feels in private, offstage life is not necessarily duping his audience. As Schieffelin noted, "performances, whether ritual or dramatic, create and make present realities vivid enough to beguile, amuse or terrify. And through these presences, they alter moods, social relations, bodily dispositions and states of mind."[56] Just as stewardesses and hotel workers perform emotional labor as part of their jobs, so too, pilgrim guides may perform "spiritual labor" as part of theirs.[57] Both get under the skin. The pilgrims may encourage such "spiritual labor" through their readiness to suspend disbelief when they are presented with "authentic sites." Most seek facts that will confirm their faith rather than the systematic application of critical inquiry. They have come to be seduced, not challenged.

We should not be surprised that, in spite of its enclaval nature, what happens inside the tourist frame affects the guide's larger life. We get "caught up" in the play.[58] "We are, in effect," as Schieffelin wrote, "more performative than we intend, and we are in good measure 'submitted to' our performativity as part of our active being-in-the-world."[59] Even the most adroit performers experience 'leakage' between the public persona of the guide within the tour frame and the stories they tell themselves – and others – in private life.[60] What happens inside the frame not only reflects who we are but shapes it. As Arlie Hochschild wrote:

> When our feeling are vague and inchoate, the reactions of others to our ges-
> tures may help define what we really come to feel. . . . In such cases our ges-
> tures do not necessarily "express" our prior feelings. They make them avail-
> able to others as a sign. But what it is a sign of may be influenced by their
> reactions to it. We, in turn, may internalize their imputation and thus define
> our inchoate feeling. The social interaction of gestures may thus not only ex-
> press our feelings but define them as well.[61]

Most guides experience difficulty readjusting from work to home and family
life.[62] The taxing emotional labor or "spiritual performance" required of the
successful guide may also result in self-alienation at the end of the day or the
tour.[63] It may be difficult not only to relax facial muscles and "peel off" the
forced smile of attentive service but also to peel off the reverential expression
toward Christian practice when leaving the bus.

For the Israeli guide, as well as for the pilgrim, the liminal spaces of Israel/
Holy Land are charged with storied sites that connect to the world of childhood, of communal roots and of belief. The tour enables a vicarious experience
of spirituality or community missing from many guides' daily lives, as well as a
place in which the (common as well as specialized) knowledge and status of the
guide as Jew or as Israeli are appreciated. In the broad sense of MacCannell,[64]
tourism serves as a rite of affirmation of belonging, a balm against alienation.
While the guide can safely frame his actions and interactions as "just a job" or
"pleasing the customer," such discourse ignores the extent to which the decision to become and remain a tour guide for Christians, cannot be bracketed
off. It is often a result of identity processes that brought many current guides
to Israel in the first place or that keeps them in Israel in spite of the tensions of
living in a state of war. For the guide too, pilgrimage performances may be an
affirmation of faith.

In this sense, the research on guides is an inquiry into formation of identity in the contact zone between native and visitor, self and other. There are
things about this contact and about ourselves that are only revealed to us in the
performance. Some guides are acutely aware of how guiding Christians is part
of their Jewish-Israeli life path, while others only come to reflect on it in the
interview situation. However, the possibility of being seduced by the pilgrims'
faith, rituals, and commitments is always there.

## 2. The Seductions of Christianity

Beyond the dynamics of touristic performance, what is it that makes Christianity more repulsive – and seductive – to Israeli guides than other religions or
belief systems? After all, all guides suppress negative emotions in working with

guests; yet few feel the need to ritually purify themselves afterward. While I can hardly provide a full explanation, nor do I believe there is a single one, I will offer some suggestions:[65]

Theologically, as David Satran formulated it,[66] "at the heart of Christian faith and practice is the embodiment and humiliation of God, something which 'normative' Judaism has always found bizarre, if not repulsive. Paul may have said it best (1 Corinthians 1:23): "We preach Christ crucified, a stumbling block (*skandalon*) to Jews and foolishness to Gentiles." The Trinity, the adoration of Mary, and the notion of redemptive suffering were all mentioned in interviews as sources of repulsion, even among guides who identified themselves as "secular."

Christianity made the claim to be the "true Israel" or the "new Israel," in some periods actively humiliating the Jewish people so their abjectness would prove the superior truth of the New Covenant. Historically, the legacy of Christian anti-Judaism provided fertile grounds for active anti-Semitism. Thus, conversion to Christianity is seen by many Jews as an act of treason. The proximity of Christianity to Judaism, accentuated in the shared attachment to Biblical places and stories, reinforces Christianity's status as the significant other, the one from which Judaism must be distinguished. Whether the origins of Christian anti-Semitism are conceptualized as sibling rivalry, or as a defense against the potential violence of the heretic,[67] either may account for Jewish fear of Christianity. Thus, disgust is an expression of border maintenance, a reaction to that which is at the limit of the communal Jewish body and threatens its integrity,[68] even as the possibilities for openness of that body offer temptation: "There is neither Jew nor Gentile, neither slave or free, nor is there male and female, for you are all one in Christ Jesus" (Galatians 3:38).

The attractiveness of and revulsion toward Christianity lies not only in its rituals and aesthetics but in its status as the religion of the West. As Adoram Schneidleder wrote me,

> Within Western Judaism and within Israel proper, there is such a powerful quest for love shown to us by the European/Western Other, that any relations between Jews and Christians are infected by this collective pathological force. . . . If millions of Arabs hate us . . . it doesn't really affect us in our intimate world order. But whenever we are reminded of how much Westerners may dislike us, we are like Freudian patients squirming on the couch in self-tormenting agony (e-mail correspondence, August 2012).

The attachment of Christians to the land of Israel may create a shared desire but also resentment and envy. As Schneidleder suggested, the "pathological force [of Jews' need to be loved by Christians/ the West] greatly hampers the way

Jewish guides would relate to Christian groups traveling through Israel unrolling their "invented Holy Land geography carpet across its soil." The reversal of traditional majority/minority power relations between Christianity and Judaism in the State of Israel may provide opportunities for reconciliation but also for symbolic revenge, as is evident in Bernice's explanation of the idolatrous origin of veneration of the Virgin Mary. Such reversed power relations may even manifest themselves as Orientalism, as among secular Israelis, who attend Christmas Eve services to witness Catholic worship as folklore (which Diaspora Jews would not do). As in Orientalism, for many guides, the disgust and the seductiveness are inseparable.

### 3. Beyond Seduction – toward a Spiritual Synthesis

Notwithstanding the conceptualization of Christianity as attractive or dangerous seductress, guides may find common ground with Christian pilgrims in furthering spiritual goals or creating deeper mutual understanding. As Zaki attests,

> I became more spiritual than I was before working with pilgrims. [I have come] to give thanks for the little things of everyday life. Maybe that's part of growing up. To understand that there are things directed by a superior force. To be spiritually kinder to yourself. Not all the responsibility rests on your shoulders (interview, 2001).

For guides, the Jewish-Christian encounter in the Bible Land is charged with the pleasures and dangers of seduction. But it also contains the possibility of a shared striving for existential authenticity.

Steve Langfur, an American-born PhD in religion and a veteran tour guide, sees guiding as an opportunity for seeking together an I-thou relationship present in Jewish and Christian sources, but it is one that transcends much accepted religious belief:

> There's a level here deeper than the question of God. It's the question or the feeling that some people have, including myself and some of the members of the group, that you're not living your life fully, as a whole person, and you search for a way to lead this life. In that sense, I am a religious person – *religio* in the sense of a binding, according to Jung. We are together in the same stage and go searching. Prior to the question of God. From the beginning of the trip, I pose questions about the suffering of the righteous. People know I'm not making fun of them, I'm serious. I know the Second Testament. I too am seeking. So there's no problem....
> I seek perfection, presence, purity of heart (as in Matthew 5). To be there without being divided or split. This amounts to a relation to the other which I

define as Buber's "I-thou." . . . If the Christian's relationship with Jesus enables him to enter more fully into a relationship with others, if it raises the importance of others in my sight, then Jesus is not an idol. . . .

I seek brothers everywhere, and I found them (in the Second Testament) too. That's how I am able to take Jesus' teaching seriously. For me, Jesus is not God; he's a person whom I take seriously as a teacher.

Without significantly altering the travel agency's itinerary, Steve develops the tour as a pilgrimage to three mountains: Mount Carmel, the Mount of Beatitudes, and the Mount of Olives. At each of these, he expounds the scripture at length and poses questions designed to challenge his listeners' accepted faith:

There's sometimes a heated argument on the Mount of Beatitudes, because I present them with a Jesus they do not know. A Jesus who demands, who is more demanding than the God of the First Testament, the Hebrew Bible. [Who demands] that you be perfect, and if you're not, then you won't enter the kingdom of heaven.

I say that what he teaches on the Mount of Beatitudes is important. It is important to be a complete human being in my impulses and my actions. It is important to be present. So what good is his forgiveness? What does it help if I find myself in paradise, if I am still divided and incomplete? That's what the argument is about.

If it succeeds, we end the trip with the sense of having achieved a link with our most important questions. They say something like "You may not understand why, but you deepened our faith." All the themes of the trip join up to a single experience together. It includes understanding but not just an intellectual understanding. It's an understanding of our entire being.

This understanding – guiding as a cooperative spiritual search – is a challenge. Few guides take it on as seriously and as skillfully as Steve, but some do. Some pastors request Steve's guiding services so that he, as a Jewish outsider, in the liminal space of the pilgrimage, can challenge people in a way that the pastor in church cannot or dares not. Steve comments:

"I make it a point to ask them how they feel about me, as a Jew who does not believe in Jesus, reading to them from their holy book, but the fact is, it is a book that I take very seriously in my searching, and in that spirit I read from it to you. . . . If I were a Christian I couldn't tell them all the things I do. Because then I would be part of the club."

Not all participants appreciate it; some would rather be soothed and confirmed in the faith they brought in to the trip. Some would rather have less explanation and questioning and more time to meditate in silence.[69]

Some groups, Steve adds, react defensively:

They write me [after the tour] that they pray for me that I find Jesus. This disgusts me.... I think that it's something like "we are the winners, we've got the answer." When they were with me, they didn't have answers to the questions. But it doesn't matter, let them find Jesus and everything will be all right. "We are forgiven," they say.

The success of Steve's aims depends, of course, on the active support of the group leader (who sometimes reins Steve in if he's gone too far) but also on the group dynamic:[70]

There are three of four who support you and give you the charge, and then you're ablaze and you ignite others, and that, but the fact is, it is a book that I take very seriously in my searching, and in that spirit I read from it to you. I need three or four [people] at the beginning, and it will accumulate. It's a mutual charge (interview with Steve Langfur, 2002).

For Steve, pilgrimage is a charged space indeed, in which the active participation of participants is essential to success. But his aim, as a guide, is not to navigate or confront the two orbits of Judaism and Christianity but to employ the spiritual charge generated by the Jewish-Christian encounter in the Bible Land to achieve existential authenticity, an I-thou relationship.

# 7 CONCLUSION: PILGRIMAGE, PERFORMANCE, AND THE SUSPENSION OF DISBELIEF

JERUSALEM. MIDNIGHT, AUGUST 2014. Another round of fighting between Israel and Gaza. I sit typing on my terrace, opposite the Jerusalem Palestinian neighborhood of Sur Baher. The rocket warning sirens blare; someone in Sur Baher fires off a string of firecrackers, I assume as a sign of solidarity. I wish the rocket would fall on his head. Two weeks ago, my neighbors marched to the edge of the Palestinian village, waving huge Israeli flags and shouting "Death to the Arabs." On the hillside opposite, Palestinian youths have burned tires each evening in protest against Israeli actions in Gaza. Bumper stickers on cars in my street proclaimed God's blessing on the Israeli army in defeating their enemies. Hamas rockets continued to fall on Sderot and Ashkelon. Israeli fear and loathing of Arabs bubbled up to new levels, as some voices encouraged the Israeli army to smash their heads and level Gaza to the ground. The Friday muezzin sermons, blasting from the loudspeakers across the wadi sounded angrier than ever.

A police car has been parked at the entrance to Sur Baher each night for the last few weeks to keep the Palestinian village youths from entering the Jewish neighborhood, where I live. When tensions seem to quiet down somewhat, I drive across the wadi to Halil's grocery store to buy labaneh – sour cheese. Halil was, sometimes still is, a tour bus driver for the company I worked for. Somehow he managed to save up enough money in tips and commissions to set up a store for his family. "*Weinak, ya zalameh*?" he greets me, "Where you been, man?" I explain that I was afraid to enter the village, what with the fireworks and the police cars. Halil cursed the kids who were "making a mess" and keeping Israeli customers out of the village and out of his shop. "Are there still tourists coming?" I asked. "Very few. And those who do come are crap tourists. Not like the groups we worked together."

Meanwhile, circles of anthropologists in the States were planning a resolution to boycott Israeli academia. In calmer places in the West – in France and

*143*

Switzerland, enraged mobs of north African immigrants turned their frustration into violence vented against local synagogues and Jewish communities. In the midst of such turmoil, the Spanish Catholic group I had planned to observe and the Evangelical group I had hoped to guide both canceled their visits to the Holy Land.

On my last visit to the Old City, I saw pilgrims raise their heads to snap pictures of the sculpture of Simon helping Jesus to carry the cross at the fifth station of the Via Dolorosa. They didn't even see the Palestinian youth, head inclined, who stood waiting on the corner outside the chapel, as border patrol soldiers checked his papers. They were just keeping their eyes on Jesus.

In such a polarized situation, could pilgrimage possibly become a meeting ground, a place for reconciliation? Or perhaps, in spite of lip-service to transformation, is it just an enclave within real life, where pilgrims – and their guides – find only what they are programmed to look for before they leave home?[1]

## DR. JACKIE/MR. GUIDE – DOING ETHNOGRAPHY/ GUIDING PILGRIMS

The first time I presented my autoethnographic account "How Guiding Christians made Me Israeli," I employed various accents and feeling tones as I shifted from the enthusiasm of the pilgrim-guide to the critical voice of the scholar. Professor Yoram Bilu wittily commented, "What we have here is Dr. Jackie and Mr. Guide." As with the "leakage" of the guide persona into one's off-stage Jewish identity, in the end, here too, the lecture hall and the tour bus refused to be isolated from each other.

The experiences of pilgrims that I encountered while working as a guide have undoubtedly affected my research as an anthropologist. Certainly, my understandings of youth voyages to Holocaust Poland have been shaped by the quests and concerns of pilgrims.[2] Sometimes, reflecting on my experience with Christian pilgrims makes me more compassionate of the Israeli youth pilgrims' naïveté – and more tolerant of their limitations. The frameworks of pilgrimage have enabled me to see in the Poland voyages connections that would otherwise have remained submerged or invisible.[3] What Robert Orsi reminds us about historians applies equally well to anthropologists: "Abundant events . . . which are characterized by the face-to-face experience of presence may well draw the historian himself or herself, too, into an unexpectedly immediate and intimate encounter with the past. . . . The effort to write abundantly about events that are not safely cordoned off in the past, but whose routes extend into the present, [filters] into the writing of history itself."[4]

In my work as tour guide too, at sites where I found myself granted sufficient authority (as exemplary Jew and Israeli), I attempted to introduce an irritating sand grain of doubt into the shell of the tour, a subtle reference drawn from my academic studies of collective memory or critical history, not only to entertain myself but also to open up the closed circles of prooftexts and to provide a narrative other than the one the pilgrims came to confirm – if, of course, I felt I could get away with it. So Halbwachs and Foucault percolate into the story of Masada,[5] and the questions of power and representation, of archaeology and nationalism, become part of the guided tour of the Temple Mount and the Western Wall.

Although I learned to shut up when hearing things I didn't like or felt I couldn't change, I also found that the intensity of the pilgrimage encounter and its relative isolation from daily life can provide guides, as well as pilgrims, with the confidence and security that facilitate self-exploration and intimacy. There were times when I found that my story, as Jew, American and Israeli, and those of the Christian pilgrims I guided resonated together in ways that surprised me.

Like the time at Masada when I spoke with an Asian-American Christian group about how Jewish understanding of the Zealots changed throughout recent Jewish and Zionist history. I spoke of how remembering the past enriched us, but that that past needed to change in order to serve as a model for the present. At the end of the tour, I stopped under the sun-shelter to recite the passage in which Josephus provides us with the final speech to the defenders of Masada made by their commander, Elazar ben Yair before their mass suicide. I recited it with all the scriptural passion and pathos I could muster:

> My loyal followers, long ago we decided we shall not serve anyone but God, who is the true and righteous Lord of men. . . . For we were the first to revolt, and shall be the last to continue the struggle. . . . And I think it is God who has given us this privilege, that we may die nobly, unlike others who were unexpectedly defeated. . . . Let our wives die unabused, our children without knowledge of slavery. . . . Because we chose, as we resolved in the beginning, death rather than slavery!

I took a breath and turned to the group:

> A beautiful speech. But if your former enemies are ready, under certain conditions, to negotiate, and the only historical model you have before your eyes is Masada – it doesn't leave many choices. The desert behind you, the Dead Sea a thousand feet below, the sun blazing down and the Roman armies coming up the ramp.

The fifty-odd participants stood in respectful silence. Later that afternoon, one of the pilgrims called me aside. He told me of how his great-grandfather was brought over to Hawai'i as an indentured servant to work the pineapple planta-tions; of how his cousins were interned in detention camps in Arizona during World War II, and how his father, a Hawaiian Japanese, volunteered for the US Army's Nisei unit, whose soldiers had to prove their loyalty by fighting harder and suffering more casualties than all others. "America is my homeland," he said. "But the history of America is a painful one for me and my family. Yet Jesus told us to forgive."

I had come to deconstruct, to present a picture of contemporary Israel more nuanced than the myth "Masada shall not fall again" while indirectly questioning the pilgrims' confidence in their exclusive possession of divine truth. To insert, as Pierre Nora put it,[6] a knife between the bark of history and the living stem of memory. Yet I found myself embraced by community. Per-haps, then, the critique of commemorative narratives is not just an acid corrod-ing placid certainties but a solvent that catalyzes new interactions and enables new relationships and solidarities to take shape. An emotional and spiritual charge jumped the synapses of conflicting faiths and histories and made me stop and think hard. The tourist's final question posed a new challenge: in liv-ing with our past here in Israel, are we prepared to forgive without forgetting? Is forgiving our enemies anywhere in our cultural repertoire? And is it possible?

## FAKING IT: THE UNIMPORTANCE OF BEING EARNEST

Among the skills required of guides in their communicative role, Erik Cohen notes the centrality of "fabrication."[7] Guides invent stories or pass on stories whose truth value is uncertain. Sometimes, they repeat stories they have in-vented so often that they come to be convinced that it is the truth. While this capacity for fabrication is considered a major asset in most guiding situations,[8] there is something disturbing in constructing an experience, one that for many pilgrims is a search for ultimate truth, on the base of stories that for the guides are often mere legends.

This gap between guides' and pilgrims' perceptions of stories and facts can be of several kinds – Christian religious truths may arouse skepticism or even opposition among Jewish guides. On another level, guides must select or sup-press truths found in historical materials and guidebooks (such as those under-mining the "authenticity" or antiquity of religious sites) to match the sensibili-ties of groups. The often repeated mantra "according to tradition," with which guides often preface the mention of a Gospel event linked later with a particular site, is perceived by many groups as an expression of skepticism on the part of the guide. For those not seeking a critical archaeological-historical analysis, the tone often dampens their enthusiasm, and pastoral group leaders often invoke rhetorical devices or charged feeling tones to overcome the distance[9] – or else request "Christian believers" or less critical/rigorous guides for their groups. One Baptist minister criticized his Jewish tour guide: "I didn't come all the way here to see where Jesus wasn't; I came here to see where Jesus was."

On the other hand, if the guide fails to use prophylactic distance markers like "according to tradition," he will be seen either as providing scientific verification for sites he is highly doubtful of, be perceived as a believing Christian himself, or both.[10] Among the many tropes used in Christian devotional literature and sermonizing, some are difficult for Jewish guides to learn or preach. A Christian volunteer-guide working for the Garden Tomb, after briefly summarizing evidence for the Garden Tomb versus the Holy Sepulchre as the place of the resurrection, concludes, "Well, folks, it doesn't matter so much if it was here or it was there, the main thing is *the tomb is empty*! Praise the Lord!" Few Jewish guides would do this. Even fewer would do so in good conscience. Any guide can read the New Testament. Only a Christian will end the reading with the solemn declaration "palabra de Dios" – "the Word of God."

The multiplicity of often-conflicting religious beliefs and truths, contradictions and conflicts, commercialization and naïveté, ignorance and prejudices encountered in the course of guiding Christian groups make some guides feel that the whole thing is a fake. Some Jewish-Israeli tour guides I know extend this to religion as a whole. Their work leads them to distance themselves not only from Christianity but from Judaism as well. True, there are some guides whose ardent faith in Judaism or Zionism fuels their narratives and who refuse to remain silent when presented with contrary views of pilgrims. Others stop guiding Christian groups and build themselves niches as guides for Zionist fundraising missions, family Bar Mitzvah tours, foreign diplomats, or just plain tourists. Most, however, just try to make a living. For some, including myself, guiding involves a willingness to overlook some personal principles or self-evident truths in order to create a positive experience for the majority of pilgrims who come to confirm their faith rather than confront it. In time, I have grown to appreciate that for guides and pilgrims, a certain suspension of disbelief, along with a willful overlooking of differences may be a necessary step on the road to mutual understanding.[11] In my personal practice as guide, I learned where to shut up and smile, where I could inject the subtle double entendre that only the pastor and the learned would fathom, and where (like at Masada), I had license to present a subversive narrative and get away with it.

Certain aspects of guiding still leave me uneasy. In order to attain an experience that reaffirms pilgrims' profoundest religious truths, the guide must conceal certain facts and sometimes lie. Never mind the Trinity or the Resurrection. There, the guide can and will remain silent and defer to the group's spiritual leader. But when a Pentecostal pilgrim, euphoric after being granted the gift of tongues at the Upper Room, or an Evangelical, uplifted after the group's final communion at the Garden Tomb, asks me if this indeed was the authentic site, what should I say? That the Upper Room is a thirteenth-century Crusader structure based on a Latin mistranslation of the Gospel text, and that the Garden Tomb has no tomb of Jesus's day? Should I describe the mystical vision by which General Gordon located the Tomb in the nineteenth century based on the shape of contour lines on the Palestine Exploration Fund's map? Should I provide the archaeological facts if it will mar the authenticity of their experience? If I do, it may undermine the intimacy established with the pilgrims, an intimacy that increases the emotional warmth of the tour well as the remuneration given to the guide at its close.

Another source of discomfort relates to the authenticity of pilgrims' faith experience. In their capacity as guides, how do Jews react to faith experiences whose objective nature they deny?[12] I once guided a Malayalam-speaking Indian group from Cochin, to which the travel agent had attached an elderly Hindi-speaking woman from the north of India. She had saved for years to make the voyage to the Holy Land, because her Pentecostal pastor told her that God had granted her the gift of the Hebrew tongue. She asked me to listen to her charismatic speech and translate her message. After listening to two minutes of what sounded to me like pure gibberish, I said to her, "You know, Hebrew is a very old language – since the time of Abraham. And it has changed tremendously over the years. Perhaps you're speaking a dialect I don't know." I think I made the right decision.

If I were to sum up my advice for beginning guides it would be: "Don't lie, but God help you if you tell the whole truth."

## FAITH THROUGH PERFORMANCE

### 1. Hawai'i 2010

In the summer of 2010, I was recruited by a Christian travel agent to travel to Hawaii and write up Holy Land tour programs for Evangelicals and Catholics. As part of my work, I was asked to address church groups of prospective pilgrims. I had prepared a talk on "How Guiding Christians made Me Israeli" (an early version of chap. 1 in this book), a behind-the-scenes look at contemporary pilgrimage to the Holy Land. But in the Hawaiian Bible school hall, the Evangelical minister, who had served as a pastoral group leader on two of my tours, introduced me as "a pilgrimage expert from Jerusalem, who has a heart for the Bible and a heart for the Lord." I spoke of religious boundaries, of how my work with Christians bolstered my standing as Jew and Israeli, of how I chose not to recite the New Testament stories I liked to my daughter before bedtime. Following my talk, the first question from the audience was, "So when did you discover Jesus?"

I replied, "I didn't."

As an uneasy silence began to take hold, I added, "Look, you're traveling to the Bible Land to strengthen your faith. You haven't come on my pilgrimage. I've come to help you do yours."

The group was a seeker church. As one explained later, "We have all kinds of people in our church on a Sunday – Asians, Mexicans, Whites, Buddhists, Jews . . . the main thing is they all have a personal relationship with Jesus." For them, even if I wasn't born again yet, by talking the talk, I had demonstrated that I had "come under conviction."[13]

Several days later, I gave a very similar talk to a Catholic group several miles away. One retired participant turned to me with a heavy New York accent asking, "So where ya from in New York? "Washington Heights," I answered. "Yeah? What synagogue you belong to?" No question here. Catholics belong to their church, Jews to their synagogue.

A lesson to take back with me to the university: following *Writing Culture*, many anthropologists placed great faith in reflexivity. As if the open declaration of one's positioning in the field could counter the often exploitative power relations that had typified the ethnographer at least since Malinowski. Yet, as Geertz wrote,[14] each reflexive anthropologist "constructs a different sort of quasi-journal, places a different sort of being-there persona at its center, and arrives at a different sort of sincerity crux at its end." I-witnessing, whether in the anthropological text or the guiding performance, is not a once-and-for-all revelation of the true backstage.[15] "The 'I's' these writers [and guides] invent . . . correspond to the text-form employed."[16] The frame of the guided tour or the travel promotion talk in church defines part of the tacit contract that gives particular meanings to words – no less than the best intentions of their authors. There is no certainty at all that the "I" of the guide, even a smart-ass guide like myself, will not be interpreted by pilgrims and tourists in ways that I cannot imagine or control.

Later that week, my host, Mr. Chan, a Chinese-American tour agent and businessman, set up a promotional lunch meeting with Reverend Simon, an assistant to the Catholic bishop of Honolulu. After a ten-minute wait outside the restaurant, a middle-aged man with a pale complexion and thick-rimmed glasses approached and extended his hand. "Ah! Mr. Chan, Dr. Feldman!" I smiled and answered, "So, how did you know who was who?" Not missing a beat, he retorted, "Well, my father was Jewish and my mother was Japanese, and my father converted to Catholicism and they got married, so they had to come to Hawaii to live. And that's probably why I became a priest."

The waitress called us into the restaurant and led us to our seats. I thought I had best not order pork sausage on my pizza – why raise questions?[17] We introduced ourselves; Mr. Chan spoke of his company and the Evangelical church he attended, and I showed him and Reverend Simon the texts and itineraries I had written for Catholic pilgrim groups. Reverend Simon peered over his glasses: "Tell me," he asked, "are you a practicing Jew?"

"I don't practice all that much," I answered, "but I live for the performance."

### 2. Jerusalem – A Cantor for the Gentiles

Yom Kippur Eve, 2014. The light fades on the Mountains of Moab across the Dead Sea; traffic in the streets below slow to a standstill. I hasten to finish the bowl of chicken soup before the fast begins. I still don't know if I'll trek up the hill to a synagogue this year. The words of Yom Kippur prayers I learned at school, abjectly entreating our Father for forgiveness repel me from the synagogue door: "Our Father, our King, we have sinned before thee." "Forgive us for Thy sake, if not for our own." "Redeem the spilled blood of Thy servants." As a teenager, my freshman high school rabbi provided us with a supplementary list of sins to confess as we beat our breasts, including "spilling seed in vain." Yet the High Holiday music of my childhood lures me in. It conjures up warm memories of my huddling under my father's prayer shawl during the priestly blessing, listening to the words swell in the cantor's mouth until they ripened and dropped on our tallit-tent like ripe apples.

For several years, my solution to this tug of war between the content of the words and the music of the music was to find a synagogue where I could lead the High Holiday congregational prayers myself. On *Yorzeit*, the anniversaries of my father's and grandparents' death, I find synagogues that will let me lead the weekday prayer. This is my flight into performance. By becoming the *sh'liach tzibur*, the emissary of the congregation, I can hitch a ride on their devotion, on the trust they place in me as prayer leader, on the contagion of their sincerity and the homey nonreflexiveness of their routine.

This same flight into performance takes place at one of the sites I enjoy guiding most, St. Anne's Church in Jerusalem. The white Crusader pilgrim church, stripped of its frescoes by iconoclasm, age, and misuse,[18] provides an oasis from the tumult of vendors, wide automobiles on narrow streets, pickpockets, and jostling tourist groups. The sign inside requests visitors to sing religious songs only. I usher my group in and seat them on a bench halfway back in the nave, facing the altar. I go back to the corner chapel nearest the door, focus on the opposite diagonal corner, and fill the church with a mournful rendition of *"Yu Riboin Oilam,"* a Sabbath hymn praising the Creator of all universes, in plaintive Hungarian Hasidic pronunciation and melody. The sound reverberates off the stone pillars and echoes back to me. I sing three stanzas, stopping abruptly after the final sounds *"meilekh malkha-a-yu,"* King of Kings. The final minor chord resounds for a full seven seconds. The group members, once they discover where the sound came from, come up to me – "That was beautiful – what was it?" "A Sabbath hymn praising the King of the Universe," I respond.

My father was deaf and couldn't sing. His brothers were tone-deaf and couldn't sing either. When they did voice this hymn, it was a cross between a drone and a croak. Only after spending a Sabbath meal at the table of a friend of the family with a good voice did I finally learn – "so that's what they were singing!" Among the family members of my generation, I am the only one to sing this melody. So I give voice to a traditional past that my father and uncles could not voice well enough to transmit. My audience, though, is not my children at the Sabbath table, or fellow Jews in the synagogue, but Christian pilgrims in church.

Is this a sacrilege? My uncle Mendel would undoubtedly have thought so. When, as a teenager, I once wished him *"a git kretzmach"* – merry Christmas – on Christmas Eve, smoke nearly poured out the phone receiver: "That's not funny. You don't know how much we suffered because of *oisoi ho'ish* – that man." My standing at the threshold, unseen by "my" pilgrims in the back of the church, yet filling the space with my presence, is another expression of my playing with the boundary between Judaism and Christianity. Something in the church recital is empowering. The voice – silenced in my deaf father and among his tone-deaf brothers, and extinguished within the larger Hungarian Jewish community by the Holocaust, is now amplified in this Crusader building, by an Israeli guide who, in Jerusalem, bears the authority of the native and of God's people.

The sound pulls me into the performance as well. For me, in this church, it is a prayer. As, indeed, it is for the pilgrims. The swelling echo of the music and the reception of my song as prayer, enable me to overcome the distance – even if only for a moment – between my performing self and the words "you are the King, King of Kings." And, for as long as the melody reverberates, between Jewish guide and Christian pilgrim. As Victor Turner wrote, the sensory sur-

The author calling his pilgrim group to enter St. Anne's church for hymn singing.
© *Salem Bible College and Thiessen Photography. Used by permission.*

round of performance and the action situation of ritual may jump cognitive gaps, transcend logical refusals, and suspend alienation.[19]

The encounter in St. Anne's Church contains something playful too. In their book on religious toys and games, Bado-Fralick and Norris[20] conclude that "ritual play enables us to let go of rigid definitions, to acknowledge the sacred as permeating all aspects of life . . . and to understand that to be playful is perhaps the most serious of all." Ritual play, they write, shifts power issues "to a more discreet position, and . . . create[s] room for maneuvering and movement and accommodation."[21] As the pilgrims bow their heads, I remain standing, hidden near the threshold, in the church yet not of the Church, projecting my voice towards the altar, chanting my father's family *nigun*.

In this Spartan but resonant Crusade church, the often painful history of Jews under Christian rule cannot be erased. Neither can the conflicted history of the Holy Land; nor my own conflicts with the Judaism of my childhood. St. Anne's Church is not, and cannot, be home for me. But the reason that spaces of pilgrimage work on people, their power in providing healing and integration for the fragmentation in people's lives, may be because they are both part of their ongoing practice, yet separate from the lived experiences of home. Unlike spaces of home, pilgrims' sense of place is impermanent; specialness is marked by not dwelling.[22] The pilgrim may claim to seek a spiritual "home," but the decision to go on pilgrimage involves the desire to go out of place – to uproot oneself from the quotidian home to get to a "center out there."[23] As Bonnie Wheeler writes, pilgrimage demonstrates that "life is the struggle of restlessness against rest; this piercing into life exiles us from our quiet roots."[24]

At the "center out there" where pilgrimage takes place – for me as guide, as well as for the pilgrims – the sense of separateness and disbelief, and the conflicted histories and territories of Judaism and Christianity can be suspended for a moment. Out there, we may be able to open ourselves to other experiences, other persons, maybe even the wholly Other.

## AFTERWORD

Nearly thirty-five years after I first took the microphone on a tour bus, the Jewish-Israeli/Christian encounter through pilgrimage continues to fascinate me. In pilgrimage, scripts, sacred texts, images, and categories that the pilgrims bring with them interact with what they are shown and told on the contested ground of the Holy Land. The shared yet differing attachments of differing groups of Jews and Christians to the Land of Israel and to the Bible made me aware of the role of imagination in understanding the Holy Land and of "the symbolic labor that goes into making space sacred."[25] The pilgrims' stories and questions rendered familiar sites and texts strange and contingent.

The practice of pilgrimage encourages faith, or at least a temporary suspension of radical doubt and a willingness to entertain the "as if" of religious truths. True, guiding pilgrims may lead to cynicism and to a strengthening of religious or national borders against encroachment and contestation. But the guiding of Christians by Jews, especially for a Palestinian company, may also provide a more inclusive view of humanity and belonging in a land so often marked by religious and political strife. The foreign and Euro-American Christian gaze may also lead Jewish guides to reflect on and perhaps reconstruct their own traditions and values through the confrontation with partially overlapping otherness. As Lanfant asserts, "The evaluation of the affirmation of [one's] own identity can only be accomplished by reference to the Other."[26]

Guiding pilgrims is not just work; it is a form of ritual play. As formulated by Bado-Fralick and Norris,

> The transformation of breaking down traditional ways of being or seeking requires acts of intentional vulnerability and self-conscious exposure. It demands courage and skill – a willingness to explore, to engage, to reveal that mixture of play and seriousness that intertwines in our perspectives on the multiple worlds within which we live. . . . In short, it demands playfulness, a willingness both to create and transgress boundaries, to engage in multiple and partial identities, and to simultaneously challenge and transcend limitations.[27]

The practices and narratives of guides may result in changes not only in the beliefs and orientations in listeners but in themselves as well. As I continue to pose questions to fellow guides and to my own experiences, I become increasingly convinced that, as guides engage pilgrims in making places, they engage in remaking themselves.

# NOTES

### 1. How Guiding Christians Made me Israeli

1. cf. Urry, *Consuming Places*, 140; Ritzer and Liska, "'McDisneyization' and 'Posttourism,'" 107–109.

2. Brown, "Genuine Fakes"; Selwyn, *The Tourist Image*.

3. Turner, "The Center out There," 191–230.

4. Safrai, *Pilgrimage in the Second Temple Period*.

5. Turner, "The Center out There"; Turner and Turner, *Image and Pilgrimage in Christian Culture*.

6. Cohen, "The Tourist Guide," 20.

7. Cohen, "Towards a Sociology of International Tourism."; Schmidt, "The Guided Tour"; Holloway, "The Guided Tour"; Cohen, "The Tourist Guide"; and Quiroga, "Characteristics of Package Tours in Europe."

8. Limor, "Christian Sacred Space and the Jew," "Christian Sanctity – Jewish Authority."

9. Crang, "Performing the Tourist Product"; Black, "Negotiating the Tourist Gaze." Anabel Black wrote: "I was struck by the number of ways in which one becomes involved in colluding with a remarkably strict set of expectations and ideas about one's own culture. These may bear little resemblance to the parameters which structure one's own world outside the context of acting as a host, and yet they somehow make sense, or at least contain an internal logic, irremovable from the spaces marked out and sometimes constructed through tourism" (112).

10. Malley, *How the Bible Works*; Bielo, *The Social Life of Scriptures*.

11. Harding, *The Book of Jerry Falwell*, 59–60.

12. When eating at a nonkosher restaurant while on tour, some pilgrims would inspect my plate to see if I was eating pork.

13. Urry, *The Tourist Gaze*; Black, "Negotiating the Tourist Gaze."

14. See Chapter 5.

15. Hochschild, *The Managed Heart*.

16. Zipperstein, "Ahad Ha'am and the Politics of Assimilation."

17. The Yiddish words *sheigitz/shiksa* referring to non-Jewish men and women, from the Hebrew root *sheketz*, an object of disgust. Both have connotations of animality and sexuality.

18. See Almog, *The Sabra*, 160–184.

19. See Gurevitch, "The Double Site of Israel."

20. Festinger et al., *When Prophecy Fails*.

21. MacCannell, *The Tourist*, 44–45.

22. On the City of David and the practices of El-Ad, the settler organization that runs it, see Greenberg, "Towards an Inclusive Archaeology in Jerusalem," and Paz, "Guiding Underground Jerusalem."

23. Harding, *The Book of Jerry Falwell*, 88.

## 2. Guided Holy Land Pilgrimage

1. Cohen, "Towards a Sociology of International Tourism"; Quiroga, "Characteristics of Package Tours in Europe."

2. Turner, "Pilgrimage," 7145–7146.

3. Eade and Sallnow, *Contesting the Sacred*; Turner, "The Center out There"; Turner and Turner, *Image and Pilgrimage in Christian Culture*.

4. Coleman, "Do You Believe in Pilgrimage?"

5. Rodman, "Empowering Place," 212; Wheeler, "Models of Pilgrimage."

6. Coleman, "Do You Believe in Pilgrimage?," 362.

7. Turner, *The Ritual Process*, 30.

8. Graburn, "Tourism"; Candea and da Col, "The Return to Hospitality," S1.

9. Bruner, *Culture on Tour*.

10. Schieffelin, "Problematizing Performance"; Stromberg, *Caught in Play*.

11. Kaell, *Walking Where Jesus Walked*.

12. Handelman, *Models and Mirrors*, xv.

13. Ibid.; Handelman, "Introduction."

14. Crang, "Performing the Tourist Product"; Edensor, *Tourists at the Taj*; Ness, *Where Asia Smiles*, xvii; Bruner, *Culture on Tour*, 1–29.

15. Turner, "Pilgrimage," 7145–7146.

16. This corresponds to one or more of the definitions of "tourism imaginaries" in Leite, "Locating Imaginaries in the Anthropology of Tourism." See also Salazar and Graburn, "Introduction."

17. Orsi, "When 2+2=5."

18. See also Orsi, "Abundant History," 215–226; Taysom, "Abundant Events or Narrative Abundance," 1–26. Taysom's adaptation neutralizes the gist of Orsi's insight by reducing emergent sensory experience to something always already mediated by narrative, subordinating performance to text.

19. Knott, "Religion, Space, and Place," 37.

20. Preston, "Spiritual Magnetism."

21. Halbwachs, *La topographie légendaire des Évangiles en Terre sainte*, 151–152.

22. Halbwachs, "The Sacred Topography of the Gospels," 199.

23. Ibid., 196.

24. Urry, *The Tourist Gaze: Leisure and Travel in Contemporary Societies*, 1–2; Kelner, *Tours that Bind*, 96–97, 203–204.

25. Thomas, "'The Politics of Vision' in Landscape," 28; Fernandez, "Emergence and Convergence in some African Sacred Places," 187.

26. Box, *Philonis Alexandrini in Flaccu*, 45–46.

27. Amir, "Pilgrimage According to Philo," notes that *metropolis* in Philo is synonymous with *hieropolis* – the holy city, a term particular to Philo (111).

28. Jeremias, *Heiligen Gräber im Jesu Umwelt*; but see Satran, *Biblical Prophets in Byzantine Palestine*; Hunt, *Holy Land Pilgrimage in the Later Roman Empire*; Markus, "How on Earth Could Places Become Holy?"

29. Ibid.

30. Smith, *To Take Place*, 74–95.

31. Lefebvre, *The Production of Space*, 280.

32. I am indebted to Yvonne Friedman for much of the historical background in this section.

33. Friedman, "Francescinus of Pontremoli."

34. Richardson, "Being-in-the-Market versus Being-in-the-Plaza," 75.

35. Thomas, "'The Politics of Vision' in Landscape." In speaking of the importance of the shift in painting in the fifteenth century in forming Western perceptions, Julian Thomas writes: "Perspective art represents a form of visual control, which freezes time and presents things as they empirically appear to be, At the same time, perspective establishes . . . a fixed relationship between object and subject, locating the viewer outside the picture, and outside of the relationship being depicted. Landscape painting is thus a representation of space which alienates land, such that it can be appropriated by a gaze which looks in form the outside" (ibid., 21–22). He then links this way of looking and the development of modern strategies of monitoring and surveillance, as put forth by Foucault. also, Mitchell, "The World as Exhibition"; Ibid.; Wharton, *Selling Jerusalem: Relics, Replicas. Theme Parks*; Long, *Imagining the Holy Land*.

36. Said, *Orientalism*; Obenzinger, *American Palestine*; Vessey et al., *The Calling of the Nations*.

37. Ben-Arieh, *The Rediscovery of the Holy Land in the Nineteenth Century*; Said, *Orientalism*; Abu el-Haj, *Facts on the Ground* and "Producing (Arti) Facts."

38. Halevi, "An Italian Nationalist and a Religious Artist."

39. Ron and Feldman, "From Spots to Themed Sites"; Feldman and Ron, "American Holy Land."

40. Gurevitch, "The Double Site of Israel," 208.

41. Ibid., 208, 213.

42. Amichai, *Open, Closed, Open*.

43. Goldin, *The Fathers According to Rabbi Nathan*, ver. A, chapter 35.

44. See Ezekiel (45:1–8; 49:9–22) and Zimmerli, *A Commentary on the Book of the Prophet Ezekiel, Chapters 25–48*, 469–470, 542–543. Zimmerli comments on Ezekiel's characterization of the Temple as a *terumah*, a gift to God, in Ezekiel (45:1–8): "Yahweh is the owner of the sacred *terumah* and . . . neither priest nor Levites have any property in it" (Zimmerli, 469–470). "No human hand is to reach out for it as if it belonged to him. Rather this 'selected area' which lies around the historical center of the land is to be an area which is freed from the possession of the twelve tribes – the permanent reminder that the land is a gift" (ibid., 542–543).

45. Bax, "Female Suffering, Local Power Relations, and Religious Tourism."

46. The struggle between the Israeli tour guides' union and Catholic pastoral guides over the right to guide in Israel/Holy Land will be examined by Prof. Yvonne Friedman and myself, as part of an ongoing research project on priest-guides; There are a restricted number of Palestinian guides from the Occupied Territories who have government permission to guide in Israel (and a corresponding number of Israeli guides who may

guide in the Territories) as well as a small but growing number of Palestinian citizens of Israel who have completed the Israeli Government guide course.

47. Katriel, "Touring the Land," 12; Almog, *The Sabra*, 160–184.

48. Katriel, "Touring the Land," 8; see also Katriel, *Performing the Past*, 28–29.

49. Katz, "The Israeli Teacher-Guide," 63, 62.

50. Israel, Ministry of Tourism website – http://www.tourism.gov.il/GOVheb/Ministry%20of%20Tourism/MoreyDerech/Pages/default.aspx, accessed August 28, 2015.

51. Hercbergs, "Narrating Instability." Policing of the political content of guides' narratives by government representatives and site managers is common in many places throughout the world. Tour leaders report such policing in Jordan and Palestinians in the West Bank speak mostly of policing by pastoral group leaders (see chapter 4). For Indonesia, see Dahles, "The Politics of Tour Guiding."

52. After their certification, guides must attend a one-day refresher course each year and pay a fee to renew their national licenses.

53. Geva and Goldman, "Satisfaction Measurement in Guided Tours."

54. Cohen, "The Tourist Guide."

55. In some groups, the social functions may be performed by the pastor's wife or an assistant pastor.

56. Guter and Feldman, "Holy Land Pilgrimage as a Site of Inter-Religious Encounter."

57. Fine and Speer, "Tour Guide Performances as Sight Sacralization"; Modlin, Alderman, and Gentry, "Tour Guides as Creators of Empathy"; Katz, "The Israeli Teacher-Guide."

58. Belhassen and Ebel, "Tourism, Faith and Politics in the Holy Land"; Kaell, *Walking Where Jesus Walked*.

59. Adler, "Travel as Performed Art," 373.

60. This is less true for some Catholic pilgrim tours, which are structured around liturgy and masses. They have a more restricted range of sites and many return to the same site (such as the Holy Sepulchre) several times in the course of their tour for prayer.

61. Cohen, "Towards a Sociology of International Tourism"; Schmidt, "The Guided Tour"; Holloway, "The Guided Tour"; Quiroga, "Characteristics of Package Tours in Europe"; Edensor, *Tourists at the Taj*.

62. The intense border-marking and competition for access to the holy that is often the flip side of communitas was emphasized in Sallnow, "A Trinity of Christs"; Bilu, "The Inner Limits of Communitas," and in many of the articles in Eade and Sallnow, *Contesting the Sacred*.

63. Young, "'The Empty Tomb' as Metaphor"; Kaell, *Walking Where Jesus Walked*; compare Hermkens, Jansen, and Notermans, *Moved by Mary*; Fedele, *Looking for Mary Magdelene*.

64. Todd, "Whither Pilgrimage"; Bowman, "Christian Ideology and the Image of a Holy Land."

65. Ibid.

66. See Ron and Feldman, "From Spots to Themed Sites."

67. Tilley, *A Phenomenology of Landscape*, 33.

68. Coleman, "Mary on the Margins?," 31.

69. Barth, *Political Leadership among the Swat Pathans*.

70. Basu, "Root Metaphors of 'Roots-Tourism' in the Scottish Highland Diaspora," 153.

71. Ibid.

72. Todd, "Whither Pilgrimage"; Nolan and Nolan, *Christian Pilgrimage in Modern Western Europe.*

73. Cohen, "Tourism and Religion," 2.

74. Frey notes that walkers and bikers on the road to Santiago de Compostella referred to themselves as "true pilgrims," as opposed to those travelling by bus, car or plane. The church and municipal authorities have encourages this status distinction by awarding certificates to those who can demonstrate that they have walked or biked at least 100 kilometers. *Pilgrim Stories*, 26.

75. See Beaulieu, "On demande de pélerins, pas des touristes," 360.

76. Margry, "Secular Pilgrimage."

77. Cohen-Hattab, "Zionism, Tourism, and the Battle for Palestine"; Bauman, "From Pilgrim to Tourist"; Badone, "Crossing Boundaries,"185.

78. Graburn, "Tourism"; Adler, "The Holy Man as Traveler and Travel Attraction"; Badone and Roseman, *Intersecting Journeys*, 1–11; Coleman and Eade, "Introduction"; Reader and Walker, *Pilgrimage in Popular Culture*; Chidester and Linenthal, *American Sacred Space;* Hollander, *Political Pilgrims.*

79. Cohen, "Towards a Sociology of International Tourism" and "Pilgrimage and Tourism."

80. See also Olsen, "Pilgrims, Tourists, and Max Weber's 'Ideal Types.'"

81. Morinis, "Introduction," 4.

82. Turner and Turner, *Image and Pilgrimage in Christian Culture*; Hermkens, Jansen, and Notermans, *Moved by Mary.*

83. Written by Pastor Larry Tumbleson (2005); adapted by Pastor Carley Kendrick, Mount of Beatitudes (2006).

84. Friedland and Hecht, "The Powers of Place," 19.

85. de Certeau, *The Practice of Everyday Life*, 125; Nora, "Between Memory and History."

86. There are myriad accounts of the sacred history of Jerusalem in the three mono-theistic religions and among Israelis and Palestinians. For a brief attempt at a parallel presentation of the three religious narratives and a list of their sacred spaces, see Reiter, Eordegian, and Abu Khalaf, "Between Divine and Human," 95–164. For a most recent account of politics and the shaping of sacred (Jewish and Muslim) space in Jerusalem, see Pullan, *The Struggle for Jerusalem's Holy Places.* For an account of the struggles over the Holy Sepulchre, see Bowman, 'In Dubious Battle on the Plains of Heav'n'" and "Viewing the Holy City"; R. Cohen, *Saving the Holy Sepulchre.*

87. Amichai, *The Selected Poetry of Yehuda Amichai*, 136.

88. Jacoby, "The Franciscans, the Jews and the Problem of Mount Zion during the Fifteenth Century"; Friedman and Drory, "Between Warfare and Conflict Resolution."

89. Kapferer, *Legends of People, Myths of State*, xxiv; Marvin and Ingle, *Blood Sacrifice and the Nation.*

90. Schäubele, "How History Takes Place"; Breger, Reiter, and Hammer, *Sacred Space in Israel and Palestine*, 1; Benvenisti, *City of Stome*, 69–105; Friedland and Hecht, "Changing Places"; Alberi, "Conclusion."

91. Ben-Arieh, *The Rediscovery of the Holy Land in the Nineteenth Century.*

92. For Zionism, see Liebman and Don-Yehiya (1983; Handelman and Katz, "State Ceremonies of Israel"; for Palestine, see Aburaya, "Islamism, Nationalism and Western Modernity"; Zilberman, "The Renewal of the Pilgrimage to Nabi Musa."

93. Friedland and Hecht, "Changing Places," 214; Breger, Reiter, and Hammer, *Sacred Space in Israel and Palestine*, 5. Sometimes opposition to a common enemy becomes the cement drawing together pilgrims of different religions, as Bowman documents for Palestinian Moslems and Christians in Beit Sahour (Bowman, "Nationalizing and Denationalizing the Sacred"), while at times the presence of a religious other is needed for authentication of the site, as in the case of Byzantine pilgrim authorities' mobilization of the Jew as reluctant witness to the power of Christ at Golgotha (Limor, "Christian Sacred Space and the Jew").

94. Shapiro, "To the Apple of God's Eye"; Belhassen and Ebel, "Tourism, Faith and Politics in the Holy Land"; Bowman, "Christian Ideology and the Image of a Holy Land."

95 See Kaell, *Walking Where Jesus Walked*.

96. Catholic pilgrims are often received by a member of the Franciscan Order and awarded a certificate of pilgrimage. In his welcome, he often reminds pilgrims of the Franciscans' key role as guardians and custodians of the holy places.

97. Cohen, "Towards a Sociology of International Tourism."

98. Kaell, "Of Gifts and Grandchildren."

99. McDannell, *Material Christianity*.

100. On this, see Hercbergs, "Narrating Instability."

101. Todd, "Whither Pilgrimage"; Bowman, "The Politics of Tour Guiding" and "Christian Ideology and the Image of a Holy Land"; Shapiro, "To the Apple of God's Eye."; Hercbergs, "Narrating Instability"; Young, "'The Empty Tomb' as Metaphor."

102. Clarke, "Self-Presentation in a Contested City"; Noy, "The Political Ends of Tourism"; Menley, "The Accidental Pilgrims."

103. Kaell, *Walking Where Jesus Walked*.

104. Young, "'The Empty Tomb' as Metaphor."

105. Bowman, "Viewing the Holy City," 237.

### 3.Opening their Eyes

1. Jonathan Wynn, in his recent book *The Tour Guide*, assigns a prominent place to such shtick in the repertoire of tour guides of New York walking tours (Wynn 2011, 81–110). In my experience, shtick are important in establishing a guide's authority, humor or seductiveness in tours of short duration or at the opening of tours. As the relationship between guide and group endures, more individualized and less overtly theatrical modes of guiding may play a greater role.

2. Based on Israeli government statistics, in 2009–2010, 54% of Christian visitors were Catholics, 15% Evangelical, 7% mainline, 10% Orthodox, and 14% other. Kaell calculates that in 2011, Evangelicals made up 35% and Catholics 25% of the American Christian market (Kaell, *Walking Where Jesus Walked*, 7, 211, n17). As Pentecostal membership grows worldwide, we should expect an upsurge in the number of Holy Land pilgrims, as has become evident in recent years. The practices here apply to a broader group of Protestants than those discussed by Faydra Shapiro (2008) or in chapter 4 below, who are more interested in modern Israel as fulfillment of prophecy. In Shapiro's words, for them, "it's not so much about where Jesus was, as where Jesus will be" (oral communication). Also, see Wynn (2011).

3. Halbwachs, *La topographie légendaire des Évangiles en Terre sainte*.

4. Calvin, *A Very Profitable Treatise* (1561) in Moore, "The Pilgrimage of Passion in Sidney's Arcadia," 70.

5. Todd, "Whither Pilgrimage," 21.

6. Ben-Arieh, "Perceptions and Images of the Holy Land"; Hummel and Hummel, *Patterns of the Sacred*; Obenzinger, *American Palestine*; Monk, *An Aesthetic Occupation*; Bar and Cohen-Hattab, "A New Kind of Pilgrimage"; Long, *Imagining the Holy Land*.

7. Weber, *On the Road to Armageddon*, 213–220; Shapiro, "To the Apple of God's Eye"; Goldman, *Zeal for Zion*; Kaell, *Walking Where Jesus Walked*.

8. Shapiro, "To the Apple of God's Eye"; Belhassen and Ebel, "Tourism, Faith and Politics in the Holy Land."

9. Coleman, "The Charismatic Gift," 51.

10. Greenberg, *The Holy Land in American Religious Thought 1620–1948*, 106.

11. Itinerary, Religious Group Tours, San Jose, California, mid-1990s.

12. While the Protestants' preferred site of Golgotha, in the Garden Tomb enclosure, is not a lofty panorama, it does offer a view of the Old City walls, thus "confirming" the scripture-inspired view of Jesus' crucifixion outside the walls.

13. Lock, "Bowing Down to Wood and Stone,"112.

14. Collins-Kreiner et al., *Christian Tourism to the Holy Land*, 17.

15. Lock, "Bowing Down to Wood and Stone," 123.

16. Often much staging and narrative work must be invested in order to render such sites natural enough to correspond with the Protestant esthetic. See Monk, *An Aesthetic Occupation,* on the Garden Tomb and Feldman and Ron, "American Holy Land," on Nazareth Village and Yardenit, the Jordan River baptismal site.

17. Hummel and Hummel, *Patterns of the Sacred*, 26.

18. Lock, "Bowing Down to Wood and Stone," 118, 122; see also Todd, "Whither Pilgrimage."

19. cf. Luhrmann, "Metakinesis."

20. Bowman, "Christian Ideology and the Image of a Holy Land."

21. Keane, "'Sincerity', 'Modernity,' and the Protestants."

22 Robinson (1841: xi–xii) in Silberman, "If I Forget Thee, O Jerusalem," 493.

23. Lock, "Bowing Down to Wood and Stone," 112.

24. Ben-Arieh, *The Rediscovery of the Holy Land in the Nineteenth Century.*

25. Long, *Imagining the Holy Land*, 203–208.

26. See Jackson, *The Necessity for Ruins and other Topics*; Abu el-Haj, "Producing (Arti) Facts."

27. Ron and Feldman, "From Spots to Themed Sites"; Feldman and Ron, "American Holy Land."

28. Asad, "Anthropological Conceptions of Religion"; J. Mitchell, "A Moment with Christ"; H. Mitchell, "Postcards from the Edge of History," 134–135; Bowman, "Christian Ideology and the Image of a Holy Land," "Pilgrim Narratives of Jerusalem and the Holy Land."

29. Katz, "The Israeli Teacher-Guide," 69; Katriel, "Touring the Land"; Selwyn, "Landscapes of Liberation and Imprisonment," 119–120.

30. Abu el-Haj, *Facts on the Ground.*

31. Benvenisti, "The Hebrew Map"; Said, *Orientalism.*

32. Bowman, "Christian Ideology and the Image of a Holy Land," 116–120.

33. Bourdieu, *Outline of a Theory of Praxis*, 87. Doxa, according to Pierre Bourdieu (ibid., 164), are the quasi-perfect correspondence between the objective order and the subjective principles of organization that makes the natural and the social world appear self-evident. Bourdieu defines hexis as "a pattern of postures that is both individual and systematic, because linked to a whole system of techniques involving the body and tools, and charged with a host of social meanings and values" (ibid., 87).

34. In the US case, since the nineteenth century, the Holy Land and the vision of biblical Israel projected on it have reflected Americans' self-perception as a chosen nation, a new Israel (Ariel, "In the Shadow of the Millennium"; Greenberg, *The Holy Land in American Religious Thought*; Wagner, "Evangelicals and Israel"; Obenzinger, *American Palestine*; Long, *Imagining the Holy Land*; Feldman and Ron, "American Holy Land").

35. Augé, *Non-lieux, introduction à une anthropologie de la surmodernité*, 100.

36. Edensor, *Tourists at the Taj*, 63.

37. Eliade, *The Sacred and the Profane*.

38. de Certeau, *The Practice of Everyday Life*, 92.

39. Lowe, *A History of Bourgeois Perception*; Urry, *The Tourist Gaze*. See, for example, one of the most influential guide books of the late nineteenth and early twentieth centuries, still in print today: George Adam Smith's *A Historical Geography of the Holy Land*. After a general introduction, in a chapter called "The View from Mount Ebal," Smith (94–97) discusses, through a panoramic view, the land's various regions and their relation to and influence on biblical events.

40. Lock, "Bowing Down to Wood and Stone," 112.

41. Bourdieu, *Outline of a Theory of Praxis*, 33.

42. One of the aims of hiking, as practiced by Zionist settlers (see discussion of "knowledge of the land" hikes above), was to manifest presence in Arab-inhabited or unoccupied areas (Katriel, "Touring the Land"; Almog, *The Sabra*, 160–184). The West Bank and the Lower Galilee are dotted with small Jewish-Israeli mountaintop settlements, one of whose aims is to survey Palestinian Arab building expansion in the villages below (my thanks to Keren- or Schlezinger for this point). The Galilee settlements, first established in the 1980s are called *mitzpim* or outlook points. On the "politics of verticality" in the West Bank, see Weizman, *Hollow Land*; For the Galilee mitzpim, see Renno, "Looking Out for the Arabs."

43. van den Abbeele, "Sightseers," 7–8.

44. Lock, "Bowing Down to Wood and Stone," 118; cf. Todd, "Whither Pilgrimage."

45. cf. MacCannell, *The Tourist*, 44–45.

46. Mitchell, "A Moment with Christ," 89. For more on the materiality of the Bible, see Malley, *How the Bible Works*; Bielo, *The Social Life of Scriptures*.

47. cf. Selwyn, "Landscapes of Liberation and Imprisonment," "Atmospheric Notes from the Fields,"157–158.

48. Fabian, *Time and the Other*.

49. Said, *Orientalism*; Fabian, *Time and the Other*, 28; cf. Pratt, *Imperial Eyes*; Fabian, *Time and the Other*, 26–27.

50. de Certeau, *The Practice of Everyday Life*, 137; Stromberg, M. *Language and Self-Transformation*; Harding, *The Book of Jerry Falwell*; Mitchell, "A Moment with Christ."

51. Katz, "The Israeli Teacher-Guide," 69.

52. Fine and Speer, "Tour Guide Performance as Sight Sacralization"; "The use of the first person plural often signals their self-inclusion in a wider, more encompassing

group of like-minded people" (Katriel, *Performing the Past*, 78). For an in-depth analysis on how the use and shifting of pronouns (you/we/they) in guiding performances creates authority and communality, see ibid., 73–102.

53. de Certeau, *The Practice of Everyday Life*, 118.

54. Harding, *The Book of Jerry Falwell*, 88.

55. cf. Quiroga, "Characteristics of Package Tours in Europe."

56. Security is especially important, given the volatile situation in the Middle East and US and European government warnings against traveling in all or parts of the Middle East. Among the Christian websites and brochures produced over the past five years, almost all I surveyed dedicate a paragraph or more to security arrangements and reassurances. Security is also prominent in the pastor's opening prayer at the airport, above.

57. Augé (1995); Similarly, the Toronto Airport became a significant religious space through the Toronto Blessing (Poloma, *Main Street Mystics*). For other examples of the hallowing of nonplaces, see Miller, *Car Cultures*.

58. This division of authority is confirmed through the materials provided by the guide and pastor, respectively. The guide hands out maps; the pastor (or sometimes, his wife) hands out collections of songs and devotions to be sung or recited along the route.

59. Cohen, "Towards a Sociology of International Tourism."

60. Abu El-Haj, "Translating Truths"; idem.

61. Ibid., 45–59.

62. Thompson, *The Mythic Past*.

63. Lock, "Bowing Down to Wood and Stone," 112; Paz, "Guiding Underground Tourism." On the social practices of biblical texts, see Malley, *How the Bible Works*; Bielo, *The Social Life of Scriptures*.

64. See Raz-Krakotzkin, "The Return to the History of Redemption."

65. Zerubavel, *Recovered Roots*, 31.

66. Raz-Krakotzkin, "The Return to the History of Redemption."

67. cf. Diner (1995); Kimmerling, "Academic History Caught in the Cross-Fire"; Zerubavel, *Recovered Roots*, 31.

68. This chronology was presented in the works of Zionist historians of the pre-state and early state eras, discussed in Ram, "Zionist Historiography and the Invention of Jewish Nationhood," as well as in the history textbook popular through the 1980s, written by Gedalyahu Alon.

69. cf. Katriel, *Performing the Past*; Bruner and Gorfain, "Dialogic Narration and the Paradoxes of Masada." The use of the first person "we" and the present tense to refer to past events is common in Israeli guiding practice (Katz 1985); cf. Haynes, *Reluctant Witnesses*; Limor, "Christian Sacred Space and the Jew," "Christian Sanctity – Jewish Authority."

70. cf. Nederveen-Pieterse, "The History of a Metaphor."

71. As I mention elsewhere, some, though by no means all, Evangelical groups interpret current Israeli history as leading to the apocalyptic events of the end times. See Ariel, "In the Shadow of the Millennium"; Goldman, *Zeal for Zion*; Greenberg, *The Holy Land in American Religious Thought*; Wagner, "Evangelicals and Israel."

72. Haynes, *Reluctant Witnesses*.

73. Limor, ""Christian Sacred Space and the Jew," "Christian Sanctity – Jewish Authority."

74. Haynes, *Reluctant Witnesses*.

75. An example of this is that the well-preserved cellar of the Umayyad palace, though not signposted as such, serves as the theater for the screening of the film on Second Temple pilgrimage. For other examples, see Abu El-Haj, *Facts on the Ground*, "Translating Truths."

76. cf. Abu El-Haj, *Facts on the Ground*, 238. It appears that, with the growing power of El-Ad, the right-wing Jewish settlers' organization active in East Jerusalem, the politicized display of archaeology will only increase (see Greenberg, "Towards an Inclusive Archaeology in Jerusalem"; Paz, "Guiding Underground Jerusalem").

77. Edensor, *Tourists at the Taj*, 333; ibid., 332.

78. de Certeau. *The Practice of Everyday Life*, 91–110.

79. Schmidt, "The Guided Tour"; Quiroga, "Characteristics of Package Tours in Europe"; Pond, *The Professional Guide*.

80. Cohen, "Pilgrimage and Tourism."

81. cf. Urry, *The Tourist Gaze*; Brown, "Genuine Fakes"; Selwyn, "Introduction"; Ritzer and Liska, "'McDisneyization' and 'Post-tourism,'" 107–109); Uriely, Yonay, and Simchai, "Backpacking Experiences"; Selwyn, "Introduction."

82. See Wild, *Waiting for the Presence*, 43–48. Such accusations often reflect the view of monastics and clergy and ignore visitors' desire to be both pilgrims and tourists. They also ignore the importance of shopping for religious souvenirs for family and friends as part of the role of women pilgrims as ritual experts (Kaell, "Of Gifts and Grandchildren").

83. Brown, "Genuine Fakes," 40–41.

84. Bauman, "From Pilgrim to Tourist."

85. Harkin, "Modernist Anthropology and the Tourism of the Authentic," 667; cf. Casey, *Remembering*, 181–215. The ways in which Catholic pilgrims' practices of walking the Holy Land differ from those of Protestants will be explored in a future article.

86. Gow, "Land, People, and Paper in Western Amazonia," 51.

87. As more and more groups use closed-circuit transmitters for guides and pastors, it is easier for pilgrims to keep their ears tuned to the guide, even if their eyes wander elsewhere.

88. Raz-Krakotzkin, "The Return to the History of Redemption"; Khazzoom, "The Great Chain of Orientalism."

89. See Bowman, "Passion, Power and Politics in a Palestinian Tourist Market."

90. Dahles, "The Social Construction of Mokum," 240; cf. Dahles, "The Politics of Tour Guiding."

91. In her recent book, *Walking Where Jesus Walked*, Hillary Kaell illustrates the gap between the private concerns of her aging American female pilgrims and the public narrative of guides and pastors; On one tour, a pilgrim said, "I'm tired of listening to all (guide) Steve's archaeological talk. We don't have time to stay at one place, to be silent and get into the atmosphere."

92. Some guides overestimate their own importance as spiritual facilitators. In the May 2005 issue of the newsletter of the Israel Tour Guides Organization, one veteran guide put it, "When you're on your way to Israel, the Bible is your guide. But in Israel, you need an Israeli tour guide and the Bible serves as evidence of the guide's explanations [*sic*]."

93. de Certeau. *The Practice of Everyday Life*, xix.

94  Ibid., xi–xxiv.

95  Bruner, *Culture on Tour*, 17.

96.  Sizer, "The Ethical Challenges of Managing Pilgrimages to the Holy Land," "Visiting the Living Stones, Pilgrimages to the Un-Holy Land."

97.  Guter and Feldman, "Holy Land Pilgrimage as a Site of Inter-Religious Encounter."

98.  Herzfeld, "Spatial Cleansing," 145.

99.  de Certeau, *The Practice of Everyday Life*, 98.

## 4. Christianizing the Conflict

1.  Said, *Orientalism*, 7.

2.  Halbwachs, *La topographie légendaire des Évangiles en Terre sainte*; Smith, *To Take Place*.

3.  Selwyn, "Introduction."

4.  A nuanced discussion of the Separation Wall and its motivations and effects is beyond the scope of this article. For a discussion that minimizes the security aspect of the Wall and integrates it within broader Israeli aims of control of Palestinian land and resources, see Arieli and Sfard, *Wall and Failure*. For the effects of roadblocks and checkpoints on the Palestinian population, see Havkin, *The Reform of Israeli Checkpoints*, and Handel, "Exclusionary Surveillance and Spatial Uncertainty in the Occupied Palestine."

5.  Sam Bahur, lecture, Van Leer Institute for Advanced Studies, Jerusalem, January 1, 2010.

6.  On the centrality of the semiotics of the attraction in tourism, see MaCannell, *The Tourist*; Culler, "Semiotics of Tourism"; and Urry, *The Tourist Gaze*; on the effects of terrorism on tourist – as both deterrent and attraction, see Sönmez, "Tourism, Terrorism and Political Instability." On borders as tourist attractions, see Gelbman and Timothy, "From Hostile Boundaries to Tourist Attractions." See also Rami K. Isaac's preliminary exploration of the Wall's potential for what he advocates as "justice tourism"(Isaac, "Alternative Tourism: Can the Segregation Wall in Bethlehem be a Tourist Attraction?," 247–254, "Alternative Tourism: New Forms of Tourism in Bethlehem for the Palestinian Tourism Industry").

7.  Cohen-Hattab, "Zionism, Tourism, and the Battle for Palestine," 61–65; see Stein (2008).

8.  Webber, "Religions in the Holy Land"; Bowman, "Unholy Struggle on Holy Land," "Christian Ideology and the Image of a Holy Land," "The Politics of Tour Guiding," and "Pilgrim Narratives of Jerusalem and the Holy Land"; Clarke, "Self-Presentation in a Contested City"; Cohen-Hattab, "Zionism, Tourism, and the Battle for Palestine," 63; Brin, "Politically-Oriented Tourism in Jerusalem"; Hercbergs, "Narrating Instability."

9.  cf. Dahles, "The Social Construction of Mokum."

10.  Friedland and Hecht, "The Powers of Place," 34.

11.  Cardman, "The Rhetoric of Holy Places"; Markus, "How on Earth Could Places Become Holy?"; see Obenzinger, *American Palestine*.

12.  Halbwachs, *La topographie légendaire des Évangiles en Terre sainte*.

13. Wharton, *Selling Jerusalem*.

14. Sizer, "The Ethical Challenges of Managing Pilgrimages to the Holy Land."

15. Reuther, "Western Christianity and Zionism."

16. For a good summary of dispensationalism and the historical context in which it spread in US Evangelicism, see Harding, *The Book of Jerry Falwell*, 228–246. On Evangelical apocalypticism, see Nederveen-Pieterse, "The History of a Metaphor."

17. Shapiro, "To the Apple of God's Eye," 317n5.

18. For surveys of Christian Zionism and their relation to Israel over the past several decades, see Ariel, "In the Shadow of the Millennium"; Wagner, "Evangelicals and Israel"; Weber, *On the Road to Armageddon*; Goldman, *Zeal for Zion*, 289–308, Shapiro, "Thank you Israel for Supporting America."

19. Pilgrim Tours brochure: http://www.pilgrimtours.com/mideast/israel/Info/dear _pilgrim.htm, accessed January 27, 2015.

20. While Living Stones is the registered name of a UK charity, it has been increasingly used to refer to a range of pro-Palestinian Christian tours, under a wide variety of sponsorships.

21. For a brief summary of various Christian church positions toward the State of Israel, see Lowe and Heldt, "Theological Significance of the Rebirth of the State of Israel," 133–145.

22. Sizer (1999, 14–17).

23. In their affirmation of tradition and continuity, we find affinities in conceptions of time and in periodization of history between Catholics and Palestinians, just as the dispensationalist Protestant periodization of contemporary history as a break with the immediate (exilic, Catholic or prior dispensational) past and a return to a pristine biblical past beyond "tradition" is shared by Zionism. For further development of the latter theme, see Raz-Krakotzkin, "The Return to the History of Redemption."

24. Wagner, "Evangelicals and Israel"; Weber, *On the Road to Armageddon*.

25. Kaell, "American Christian Holy Land Pilgrimage in the Post-War Period," 53.

26. Collins-Kreiner et al., *Christian Tourism to the Holy Land*, 93–100. Where Collins-Kreiner refers to "Protestants," it should read "Evangelicals."

27. Sabeel is headed by Pastor Naim Ateek, who promotes a Palestinian liberation theology. The organization, which addresses mainly the Western Christian public, helps organize tours and volunteer programs, published a newsletter, and provides speakers on theological and social justice issues, primarily pertaining to Palestinian Christians.

28. Kaell, *Walking Where Jesus Walked*, 7, 211n17.

29. MacCannell, *The Tourist*, 41–48.

30. See the articles in Selwyn, *The Tourist Image*.

31. Dann, "The People of Tourist Brochures."

32. A prominent example was the Israeli Ministry of Tourism's offer of free graphic frames or "shells" for itineraries, thus saving local agents or churches the costs of graphic design. These "shells" often have hidden ideological content, as in the case of the "Jerusalem 3000" shells, which attribute the foundation of the city to King David and thus bolster the State of Israel's exclusive claims to it. Stephen Sizer, in "The Ethical Challenges of Managing Pilgrimages to the Holy Land," characterizes the decision of church groups as to whether or not to accept the free "Jerusalem 3000" itinerary shells as a moral one (88). In *City of Stone: The Hidden History of Jerusalem*, Meron Benvenisti poignantly summarizes (1–5) the political implications of tourism narratives around Jerusalem 3000:

"The chronicles of Jerusalem are a gigantic quarry from which each side has mined stones for the construction of its myths – and for throwing at each other" (3–4).

33. Michael Hodgson, CEO, Maranatha Tours, Ltd., interview with Amos Ron, October 26, 2008.

34. For more on this seal, see chapter 5.

35. http://www.pilgrimtours.com/mideast/israel/Retail/israelpetra13, accessed 15.12. 2010.

36. For a good analysis of the trope of the child in Holy Land tours, see Kaell, "Age of Innocence."

37. http://www.gtd.org/post/pdfbrochure/070415.pdf, accessed December 15, 2010.

38. http://www.yourisraelconnection.org/israel_tours.htm, accessed October 2, 2010. For more on the pilgrimage/tourism practices of Christian Zionists, especially around the Feast of Tabernacles, see Belhassen and Santos, "An American Evangelical Pilgrimage to Israel"; Shapiro, "to the Apple of God's Eye"; Belhassen, "Fundamentalist Christian Pilgrimages as a Political and Cultural Force."

39. cf. Clarke, "Self-Presentation in a Contested City."

40. Reuther, "Western Christianity and Zionism," 47–50.

41. http://www.calvaryabq.org/pdf/Israel_Tour_2008.pdf, accessed October 2, 2010.

42. Lock, "Bowing Down to Wood and Stone," 112.

43. Bethlehem Bible College is an Evangelical institution run by Palestinians and led by Pastor Bishara Awad. Here, support for the local Palestinian Christian community and opposition to Israeli rule over the West Bank is presented to the visiting public, alongside its mission to witness to the Muslim majority in the West Bank. An analysis of the integration of Palestinian Evangelicals into some Christian Zionist voyages is beyond the scope of this book.

44. Hummel and Hummel, *Patterns of the Sacred.*

45. The expression is that of Jack Hayford, a prominent Evangelical preacher. For other expressions of Christian solidarity with Israel through visiting immigrant absorption centers, hospitals and the like, see Shapiro, "To the Apple of God's Eye"; Belhassen, "Fundamentalist Christian Pilgrimages as a Political and Cultural Force," 138–139.

46. http://www.fosna.org/conferences_and_trips/AlternativeTravelopportunities. html, accessed March 13, 2008 (no longer online).

47. http://www.gtd.org/post/pdfbrochure/070415.pdf, accessed 2.10.2010.

48. http://www.gtd.org/post/pdfbrochure/071107.pdf, accessed 2.10.2010.

49. Handel, "Exclusionary Surveillance and Spatial Uncertainty in the Occupied Palestinian Territories"; Havkin, *The Reform of Israeli Checkpoints.*

50. There is a wealth of publications on Rachel's Tomb. For a recent survey of historical claims of Judaism, Christianity, and Islam to possession as well as current security and access arrangements, see Bowman, "A Weeping on the Road to Bethlehem."

51. Kershner, *Barrier.*

52. For a detailed account of the mechanism of surveillance at crossing points between Palestinian Authority territories and the State of Israel, see Havkin, *The Reform of Israeli Checkpoints.*

53. *What's New in the Holy Land*, Israel Ministry of Tourism, January 2007, http://www.goisrael.com/other/newsletter/eng/1/NewsletterSite.html, accessed October 2, 2010.

54. Peteet, "The Writing on the Wall."

55. Tuqan, "The Rise of Palestinian Graffiti."

56. Moscovitz, *Through the Wall*, 23–29.

57. Banksy, *Wall and Piece*, 172. Not all Palestinians approve of the drawings. One Bany mural, that of a donkey being frisked by Israeli soldiers, was destroyed by local Palestinians, who objected to being depicted as donkeys. Still others object to the murals entirely, feeling it results in an aestheticization of their suffering. As one Bethlehem Palestinian said to Banksy, "We don't want it beautiful here. We hate this wall. Go home" (cited in Moscovitz 2010, 31).

58. See http://www.google.com/imgres?imgurl=http://peoplesgeography.files.word press.com/2007/12/polyp-israeliapartheid-wall.jpg&imgrefurl=http://forum.mpacuk .org/showthread.php%3Ft%3d39210&usg=__Ioq_sXYi-m9jdXuhCifPmHcFbmA=&h =283&w=400&sz=27&hl=iw&start=3&zoom=1&itbs=1&tbnid=lx5h-9IToo2GuM:&tbnh =88&tbnw=124&prev=/images%3Fq%3dpolyp%2B%252B%2Bbethlehem%2B%252B%2B wise%2Bmen%26hl%3diw%26sa%3dG%26gbv%3d2%26tbs%3disch:1, accessed January 4, 2011.

59. The online *Heyoka Magazine*, https://desertpeace.files.wordpress.com/2011/12 /polyp_cartoon_israel_palestine_gaza_bethlehem_wa1111.jpg

60. See Anglican Church of St. John, Pinetown, Ecumenical Accompaniment Programme in Palestine and Israel, http://www.stjohnbaptist.co.za/ecumenical _accompaniment_program1.htm, accessed December 19, 2010.The photo of the chained olive tree trunks is posted on the site.

61. MacCannell, *The Tourist*, 45.

62. Shams, "Bethlehem Walls Transformed in the Presence of the Holy See." For a critical review with a reproduction of the exposed pictures, see Marcus and Zilberdik, "PA Art Exhibit for Pope."

63. I extend the discussion to include some off-site rituals but do not survey the many sermons and pastoral messages condemning the Wall through Christian language and references. One such example is provided in a booklet distributed by Friends of Sabeel Netherlands: "'The wall has been broken down,' Paul (or one of his pupils) writes in the Epistle to the Ephesians (Eph. 2.14). The 'wall of hostility' which separated Jewish people from non-Jewish people has been broken down by Jesus Christ, through God's unconditional and universal love which goes out to all men and women [ . . . ] Time and again such a wall has been rebuilt as in our own days there is once again a high wall of separation in the Holy Land, a wall that divides Israelis from Palestinians and even Palestinians from Palestinians. That wall is a means and a symbol of fear, hostility and violence" (Veldhuis, *The Wall Has Been Broken Down*, 1). Naim Ateek, head of Sabeel opposes Jesus' breaking down of the wall of suspicion and hostility to Jabotinsky's Zionist "iron wall," which he then links to the Separation Wall ("Walls of Separation"). For a scathing Zionist critique of Sabeel's hermeneutic and liturgical interpretations of the Israeli-Palestinian conflict, see Van Zile, "Sabeel Demonizing Liturgy."

64. http://www.maannews.net/eng/ViewDetails.aspx?ID=699742, accessed 23.8.2014. Photo by Ma'an Images/Ramy Abu Diqqa, used by permission.

65. http://www.google.com/imgres?imgurl=http://warc.jalb.de/warcajsp/news_image /483_org.jpg&imgrefurl=http://warc.jalb.de/warcajsp/side.jsp%3Fnews_id%3d483%26 part_id%3d0%26navi%3d5&usg=__dJn-T18AKQIHr7uRGo02wfuhBKE=&h=1368&w =2113&sz=766&hl=iw&start=1&zoom=1&itbs=1&tbnid=wHkcSeCjRn15SM:&tbnh=97&

tbnw=150&prev=/images%3Fq%3dseparation%2Bwall%2B%252B%2Bolive%2Bwood%2
B%252B%2Bprocession%26hl%3diw%26gbv%3d2%26tbs%3disch:1, accessed January 4,
2011.

66. http://www.amostrust.org/downloads/Bethlehempack2010_1.pdf, accessed
December 31, 2010.

67. Travel Experience International, Zola's Holy Land Tours, brochure (n.d., n.p.).

68. See Shapiro, "To the Apple of God's Eye."

69. Kaell, "Age of Innocence."

70. From the outbreak of the second Intifada in 2000 until 2010, the Ministry of
Tourism prohibited Israeli guides from entering Bethlehem. In May 2010, permission
was granted for 50 licensed Israeli guides to enter Bethlehem. This move was opposed by
the Israeli Tour Guides' union, based on security grounds, as well as on their objection
to reciprocity, whereby 50 Palestinian Authority guides could guide within Israel. See
http://www.itga.org.il/ArticleDetails.aspx?Id=175, accessed August 22, 2014. Given the
security situation, most Israeli guides prefer not to enter Bethlehem today (summer
2014).

71. This situation is also in flux, and depends on the security situation (and perceptions of that security situation) on the ground. In quiet times, more Israeli buses enter
Bethlehem. A Palestinian tour guide I interviewed estimated that in 2014, 15% of tourists
disembarked and passed by foot through the checkpoint. "It helps them identify with
the suffering of Palestinians," he added.

72. Conversation with Hani Abu-Dayyeh, CEO Near East Tours, January 2011.

73. Some travel agents, on the other hand, insist on qualified Bethlehem guides for
the two to three hours spent by groups there, and pay them well.

74. Kaell, "Age of Innocence."

75. For a detailed account on how housing practices and municipal regulations
"normalize" the West Bank neighborhood of Gilo as a (West) Jerusalem neighborhood,
see Kallus, "The Political Construct of the 'Everyday.'"

76. de Certeau, *The Practice of Everyday Life*, 92; Lock "Bowing Down to Wood and
Stone," 112.

77. Lefebvre, *The Production of Space*, 280.

78. For travel narratives, see Said, *Orientalism*; Pratt, *Imperial Eyes*. For touring
practices, see Abu El-Haj, *Facts on the Ground*; Cohen-Hattab, "Zionism, Tourism, and
the Battle for Palestine." For the importance of narrated hikes in constructing the new
Jew and laying claim to territory, see Katriel, "Touring the Land"; Almog, *The Sabra*,
150–178.

79. Kaell, *Walking Where Jesus Walked*.

### 5. The Goods of Pilgrimage

1. The Tosefta (Ma'aser Sheni 1:1) expands this prohibition: "He may not weigh gold
dinari against it . . . nor may he give them to a money changer so that he may show off
with them."

2. This corresponds to Victor Turner's understanding of normative communitas, in which ecclesiastic and other authorities will often attempt to limit spontaneous
outbreaks of communitas, by directing them into normative forms ("The Center out

There"). These forms, however, are informed by the "free spirit" of communitas, and are not simply replications of social structure. For a broader analysis of Second Temple pilgrimage in Turnerian terms, see Feldman, "'A City that Makes All Israel Friends.'"

3. Turner, *From Ritual to Theater*, 49.

4. McDannell, *Material Christianity*, 6.

5. Candea and da Col, "The Return to Hospitality."

6. This account does not pretend to be comprehensive. Among the themes not included are the various transmutations of values in the later career of the Holy Land souvenir (Kaell, "Of Gifts and Grandchildren"), and the potentially divisive force of souvenir shopping as a showcase for individuals to display differential economic status otherwise muted by the pre-purchase of the group tour. Also, following McDannell's study of material Christianity (*Material Christianity*), the ties between relics and Holy Land souvenirs should be explored further.

7. Gordon, "The Souvenir," 136.

8. Stewart, *On Longing*, 147.

9. Kaell, "Of Gifts and Grandchildren" and *Walking Where Jesus Walked*, 175–187.

10. On collections of souvenirs, see Stewart, *On Longing*, 161–176. For a preliminary inquiry on how the meanings of souvenirs change with the passage of time, see Collins-Kreiner and Zins, "With the Passing of Time."

11. Morgan, "Introduction."

12. For natural objects, see Kaell, *Walking Where Jesus Walked*, 92–95, 177. Collins-Kreiner and Zins problematize the distinction ("With the Passing of Time," 30). In other religious contexts, we might include saints' relics and brandea (given or stolen), pieces of cloths touched to Christian saints' tombs (Brown, *The Cult of the Saints*) and red strings and cloths and bottles of water, oil or arak which have long been recognized as material objects that convey sanctity or *barake* from sacred sites to worshipper's homes in popular Islam and Judaism (Eickelmann, *Moroccan Islam*; Ben-Ami, *Saint Veneration among the Jews in Morocco*; See also Starrett, "Religious Commodities in Cairo."

13. Stewart, *On Longing*, 134–135.

14. The importance of gift-giving in women's role as ritual experts (Kaell, "Of Gifts and Grandchildren: American Holy Land Souvenirs," 175–182) helps explain why travelers on religious tours to Israel spend significantly more money on souvenirs (25% of the cost of the tour) than those on non-religious voyages (Fleischer 2000, "The Tourist behind the Pilgrim in the Holy Land," 323.

15. McDannell, *Material Christianity*.

16. Zaidman and Lowengart, "The Marketing of Sacred Goods,"14; ibid., 16–17.

17. This is even more obvious in the case of "found" souvenirs, stones, or leaves collected at specific places. Kaell cites two female Evangelical pilgrims, who gathered rocks at many biblical sites except from the towns Jesus cursed – Capernaum, Chorazin, and Bethsaida. "Although Wendy laughed about it, she still felt 'better not take any of that [curse] home with me" (*Walking Where Jesus Walked*, 93).

18. cf. O'Guinn and Belk, "Heaven on Earth,"234.

19. See Feldman and Ron, "American Holy Land."

20. The film shown at the "Jesus Boat" at Nof Ginnosar builds subtly on Christian tropes. Two brothers, both simple fishermen (like Simon Peter and John, the sons of

Zebedee in the New Testament), walk along the lakeside, where they discover what seems to be rotten wood in the mud. Eventually, they overcome their skepticism and inform archaeologists who dramatically "rescue" the boat from the mud. Painstakingly preserved, reconstructed, and displayed, it becomes the "Jesus Boat," one just like the one in which the Savior might have sailed.

21. For a broader account, see Reuven Efraim Schmalz and Raymond Robert Fischer, *The Messianic Seal of the Jerusalem Church*. In http://www.olimpublications.com/Mes sianicSeal.html, accessed 10.9.2012.

22. See also Kaell, "Evangelical Ketuba, Messianic Mezuzah."

23. http://www.thejerusalemgiftshop.com/, accessed 28.8.2012.

24. Kaell, *Walking Where Jesus Walked*, 146. A striking example is the massive adoption of Jewish symbols and pseudo-Jewish rituals by the Brazilian Igreja Universal do Reino de Deus, based in São Paulo, which recently constructed a massive "Temple of Solomon" there, and conduct rites in Hebrew accopanied by Israeli folk songs, while wearing Jewish prayer shawls and skullcaps. This church directs Holy Land pilgrims to shops it owns in the Holy Land, where they also purchase items like flour, wine, and oil. A study of the church's Holy Land pilgrimages (*caravanas*) is currently being done by Matan Shapiro. For an informative recent discussion of Evangelical adoption of Jewish ritual, see Dulin, "Reversing Rupture: Evangelicals Practice of Jewish Ritual."

25. Hillary Kaell provides an example of an American pilgrim who purchased bottles of olive oil she had no intention to use, simply in order to support the Palestinian Christian community. When she could not successfully give them away, she left them at her hotel. (*Walking Where Jesus Walked*,127).

26. See the site of the Holy Land Cooperative, Bet Sahour at http://www.holyland -handicraft.org/index.php?option=com_content&task=view&id=5&Itemid=26, accessed 29.8.2012. Occasionally, religious souvenirs make overt use of politics – as in the Separa-tion Wall nativity set sold by Amos Trust and in the Christmas liturgies designed to use them. In that creche, the separation wall separates the three wise men of the East from the infant Jesus. See chapter 4.

27. For an illustration of the plate, see http://www.bethlehembiblecollege.edu/gifts hop/items/lords-prayer-arabic-plate-xl, accessed 29.8.2012.

28 Kaell, *Walking Where Jesus Walked*, 146.

29. Ibid., 159.

30. Bird-David and Darr, "Mass-Gift," 304.

31. Bird-David and Darr, "Commodity, Gift and Mass-Gift."

32. Stewart, *On Longing*,136–139.

33. Cited in Pritchard, "Remembering Jesus at the Garden Tomb."

34. Keane, "Sincerity, 'Modernity,' and the Protestants."

35. Bruner, *Culture on Tour.*

36. Zaidman and Lowengart, "The Marketing of Sacred Goods," 22.

37. Bird-David and Darr, "Commodity, Gift and Mass-Gift," 304. Further studies might compare this case with the use of religion, tradition and handcrafting as markers of authenticity in other contexts. Shelly Shenhav-Keller's study ("The Israeli Souvenir," especially pages 138–140) of the purchase of Israeli souvenirs at Maskit provides fertile ground for such work.

38. McDannell, *Material Christianity*, 6.

39. Kopytoff, "The Cultural Biography of Things"; in the case of many Orthodox and Catholics, we should add, their subsequent blessing or physical contact with the sacred site.

40. Stewart, *On Longing*, 138.

41. Ibid., 134–135.

42. Smith, *To Take Place*, 54–55.

43. Suetonius, *The Twelve Caesars*, 285; Bloch, "The Symbolism of Money in Imerina," 165–174; Parry and Bloch, *Money and the Morality of Exchange*, 1–32; Maurer, "The Anthropology of Money."

44. Peebles, "Filth and Lucre."

45. Zelizer, *The Social Meaning of Money* and "Fine Tuning the Zelizer View."

46. See summary chart in Zelizer, *The Social Meaning of Money*, 26.

47. Zelizer, "Fine Tuning the Zelizer View," 386.

48. Parry and Bloch, *Money and the Morality of Exchance*; Maurer, "The Anthropology of Money."

49. Carsten, "Cooking Money."

50. Kosansky, "Tourism, Charity and Profit."

51. In Moroccan *hilulot*, Moroccan organizers, French Jewish businessmen, local beggars, and commercial travel agents all take part in the negotiation of the moral values of purchases and exchange. Through purchase of expensive candles at public auctions conducted at the tomb by the rabbinic authorities responsible for the maintenance of saints' tombs and his festival, charitable gifts to saints become returnable as entrepreneurial profits; through the performed discourse of *mitzvah*, even travel expenses can be classified as *charité*, meritorious expenditures worthy of divine recompense, rather than *dépenses*, self-indulgent vacation monies. Cheap candles purchased offsite from vendors nearby, however, are not *charité* (Kosansky, "Tourism, Charity and Profit").

52. Dahles, "The Politics of Tour Guiding," 784.

53. Lynn, "National Character and Tipping Customs."

54. In more prestigious positions, a large amount of "informal" money is paid out as perks, premiums, benefits, bonuses, Christmas gifts, stock options, etc. Nevertheless, the fact that they are not referred to as "tips" (or paid out as informally as are tips) distinguishes the moral status of such monies from plebian "tips." For a fascinating look at the shifting and culturally specific values attached to clean and dirty money, see Peebles, "Filth and Lucre."

55. Furthermore, Palestinian drivers are unlikely to join a union or seek redress for poor or unfair working conditions from the courts or from Israeli labor enforcement agencies.

56. Since the mid-1990s, diamond factories declare commissions paid out to drivers and guides and deduct income tax at the source from the commissions paid. The Palestinian economy (Bethlehem) is far more informal.

57. Hochschild, *The Managed Heart*.

58. Lynn, "National Character and Tipping Customs," (2000a, 2000b).

59. Foster, "The Anatomy of Envy," 166–167.

60. Ibid., 167.

61. Shamir, "Between Gratitude and Gratuity," 66.

62. Shamir, "Between Gratitude and Gratuity," 62; see also Shamir, "Reply to Holloway." The similarities between Shamir's description of hospitality and Mauss's characterization of the gift (*The Gift*) are evident. This is expressed in a recent collection of theoretizations of hospitality, which begins with: "Imagine what anthropology might look like today if Marcel Mauss had chosen hospitality rather than the gift as the subject of his 1924 treatise. . ." (Candea and da Col, "The Return to Hospitality," S1).

63. One veteran tour guide told us: "I will never open the tip envelope before they leave at the airport, so that if I'm not content, it won't affect my guiding. (G. J., interview, 2003).

64. See Butler and Skipper, "Working for Tips," 16.

65. In some cases, group leaders have not collected the tip in advance, and it requires diplomatic skill on the part of the guide to get him to do so before the pilgrims have spent all their money. A particular problem arises when the group leader pockets part of the collected tip or loses the money before giving it to the guide or driver.

66. On national culture and tipping, see Lynn, "National Character and Tipping Customs," (2000a, 2000b).

67. Holloway, "Between Gratitude and Gratuity," 240.

68. Shamir, "Reply to Holloway," 242.

69. "Greens," *akhdar* in Arabic or *yerukim* in Hebrew, is the common word used by guides and drivers to refer to dollars, especially when conversing within earshot of pilgrims.

70. Although a similar expression exists in Hebrew, *hakol mishamayim* – all is from heaven – Hebrew-speaking Jewish drivers and guides will frequently use the Arabic words.

71. Butler and Skipper, "Working for Tips," 15.

72. Likewise, if guides or drivers conceal their commission revenues or refuse to divide them with their counterparts, an environment of distrust will develop between them and spread through the tourism grapevine.

73. Relations and gestures of trust play out in particular ways in multi-bus tours – where a large group travels with several buses and is led by a number of guides. The willingness to manifest trust in fellow drivers and invest in a common lot – by splitting all commissions among all drivers and guides – demands a level of trust, as many smaller commissions may be concealed. Often, drivers agree to pool their commission monies, even if they suspect that it is not in their financial interest, as an investment in the mutual relations among drivers and in the expectation that such confidence may express greater trust in God and bring more income "from Allah." Guides are less likely to pool commission monies, as their relations with other guides are far less ongoing and intense, and they often tend to see commission revenues as their private due recompense and as an evaluation of their guiding (and sometimes, salesmanship) performances.

74. This is especially true since the second Intifada in 2000, as most Jewish-Israeli guides may not and do not enter Bethlehem. While travel agents may intervene in the case of disputes between drivers and guides over commissions, they tend to do so only in the most flagrant cases.

75. On the *stiftach*, the initial sale of the day as a portent of blessing for the business in the Middle East, see Ben-Amos and Ben-Yehuda, *Milon Olami le-Ivrit Meduberet*, 161.

76. cf. Kosansky, "Tourism, Charity and Profit"; Coleman, "The Charismatic Gift."

77. Kosansky, "Tourism, Charity and Profit." On love offerings in charismatic congregations as a way of breaking down distinctions between persons and objects, see Coleman, "The Charismatic Gift."

78. The wrapping of money in envelopes, like the wrapping of presents in gift paper, is a way of shifting attention away from the market/commodity value of the object/money and highlighting its nature as a gift (Cheal, "'Showing Them You Love Them,'" 158–159; see also Hendry, *Wrapping Culture.*

79. This positive moral evaluation may distinguish the commission discourse from "wolf pack" thefts of longshoremen and others described in Mars, *Cheats at Work.*

80. G. Feldman, "Understanding Others," 290; cf. Dzenovska, "Reply to Comments."

81. These vendors' performances, in turn, are foreseen and countered by guides, sometimes through religious language. See chapter 3.

82. Maurer, "The Anthropology of Money," 16.

83. Carsten, "Cooking Money."

84. Appadurai, *The Social Life of Things*; Kopytoff, "The Cultural Biography of Things"; Parry and Bloch, *Money and the Morality of Exchange*; Bird-David and Darr, "Commodity, Gift and Mass-Gift" and "Mass-Gift"; Selwyn, "An Anthropology of Hospitailty"; Candea and da Col, "The Return to Hospitality."

### 6. The Seductions of Guiding Christians

1. Noel Salazar calls this "seducation" – "the trade of tourist enticement." The Northern Tanzanian guides he studies are "formally schooled and informally trained in the art of narrating and performing seducing tourist tales" (Salazar, "Seducation," 111).

2. For a more sustained argument on the relevance of "seduction" for an understanding of Christian pilgrimage, see Di Giovine and Picard (2015).

3. Baudrillard, *Seduction*, 1.

4. Ibid., 153.

5. Bauman, "From Pilgrim to Tourist," 23.

6. di Giovine, "The Imaginaire Dialectic and the Refashionig of Pietrelcina," 151; Leite, "Locating Imaginaries in the Anthropology of Tourism," 264.

7. Bajc, "Creating Ritual through Narrative, Place and Performance in Evangelical Protestant Pilgrimage in the Holy Land."

8. Dahles, "The Politics of Tour Guiding."

9. Baudrillard, *Seduction*, 54.

10. Stromberg, *Caught in Play.*

11. As pilgrim groups travel on Saturday and visit churches, the number of "religious" (Orthodox) Jewish guides working with Christian groups is small.

12. My interviews with Palestinian guides indicate that Muslim guides, more than all others, most frequently conceal their religious identity, passing as Christians (cf. Kaell, *Walking Where Jesus Walked*, 48–49.

13. Kaell, *Walking Where Jesus Walked*, 49.

14. Keane, "Sincerity, 'Modernity,' and the Protestants."

15. On impression management and face work, see Goffman, *Interaction Ritual*; Hochschild, *The Managed Heart.*

16. Boissevain, "Ritual, tourism and cultural commoditization in Malta"; Greenwood, "Culture by the Pound"; Urry, *The Tourist Gaze*; Bruner, "Transformation of Self

in Tourism" and "The Ethnographer/Tourist in Indonesia"; Edensor, *Tourists at the Taj*; Black, "Negotiating the Tourist Gaze"; Ness, *Where Asia Smiles*; Salazar, *Envisioning Eden.*

17. Crang, "Performing the Tourist Product," 152.

18. Hochschild, *The Managed Heart.*

19. Compare this with New York City guides' account of their career choices and trajectories in Wynn, *The Tour Guide*, 35–80.

20. Exceptions are sometimes made for Yom Kippur, when travel agents will make efforts to replace Jewish guides who observe the holiday with non-Jewish guides or shift the program to move the group's free day to Yom Kippur.

21. For similar observations on air hostesses, see Hochschild, *The Managed Heart*; Wouters, "The Sociology of Emotions and Flight Attendants," 118–119.

22. Geva and Goldman, "Satisfaction Measurement in Guided Tours."

23. Cohen, "The Tourist Guide." These roles were first explored in the pilgrimage context in Guter and Feldman, "Holy Land Pilgrimage as Site of Inter-Religious Encounter."

24. Guter and Feldman, ibid. "Holy Land Pilgrimage as Site of Inter-Religious Encounter."

25. Fine and Speer, "Tour Guide Performance."

26. Modlin, Alderman, and Gentry, "Tour Guides as Creators of Empathy."

27. Katz, "The Israeli Teacher-Guide," 69.

28. Haynes, *Reluctant Witnesses*; Limor, "Christian Sacred Space and the Jew."

29. Harding, *The Book of Jerry Falwell.*

30. Wuthnow, *After Heaven*, 1–18.

31. The ceremony has numerous variations, but adheres to the basic structure I describe.

32. Medieval custom required the rending of clothes and other practices of mourning for the destruction of the Temple, rather than celebration. The current form seems to have begun sometime after the capture of East Jerusalem in the Six-Day War in 1967. The ceremony has become such a standard part of Jewish tour groups' itineraries, that, in Jewish tour itineraries, it has acquired a generic name name, as in the announcement: "we will arrive in Jerusalem for a *shehecheyanu.*"

33. The increasingly popular adoption of Jewish ritual by Evangelicals has been recently discussed in Dulin, "Reversing Rupture: Evangelicals' Practice of Jewish Rituals."

34. This rite of purification will be discussed further below.

35. Katz, "The Israeli as Teacher-Guide," 62–63.

36. Compare Mitchell, "A Moment with Christ."

37. Messianic Judaism insists on the synthesis of Christian faith and Jewish belonging. To quote one Messianic publication, "Messianic Jews challenge the received Christian and Jewish consensus that when Jews come to faith in Jesus they cease to be Jews and become Christians instead. They claim the same status in the Church that the first generation of Jewish believers in Jesus enjoyed, who expressed their faith precisely as Jews and whose faith in Yeshua in no way denied or compromised their status as part of the chosen people." (Justen and Hocken, *The Messianic Jewish Movement*, 6). Most Jewish-Israelis, as well as the Israeli Supreme Court, strongly reject these claims.

38. Kobi strengthens the "good soldier" motif by announcing that any profits received from shopping (commissions) will be contributed to LIBI – an organization providing food packages and comforts for Israeli soldiers.

39. While Kobi openly proclaimed himself as a Messianic believer on Evangelical websites, book blurbs, speaking tours, and in guiding Evangelical groups, in the interview with us, he was quite reticent to speak of his faith in Christ. This may have to do with the stigmatization of Messianic Jews in Israeli society.

40. A Mormon tour operator agent, in response to our query, responded: "I have one guide that was proud that she was learning the scriptures we used at sites and then wanted to do them instead of the director. I had a hard time convincing her that that wasn't what we wanted. . . . I always tried to impress on the guide and the director that it was the director's tour. He planned the itinerary and recruited the group. Thus why would a guide think he could come in and take it over and treat it as his tour?" (-. M., May 1, 2002; thanks to Yael Guter for sharing this e-mail).

41. Geertz, *The Interpretations of Cultures.*

42. Of course, such logic assumes that if one is a *tzabar*, a native Israeli, one cannot believe in Jesus.

43. Kaell, *Walking Where Jesus Walked*, 158.

44. This practice will rarely solicit comment, as the turning over of marked passages in the Bible for the pastor to read in public is understood as the guide's recognition of the pastor's authority; it can only improve pastor-guide relations.

45. A similar impulse underlies my reticence to tell my daughter New Testament bedtime stories.

46. In another article, we argue that Yardenit, the Jordan River baptismal site, is constructed in ways that both reflect and increase the theatrality of Evangelical megachurch baptisms (Feldman and Ron, "American Holy Land," 159–163).

47. It is possible that he could have found another way out by asking the pastor of another group at the site if he would be willing to baptize "his" pilgrims.

48. Koepping, "The Ludic as Creative Disorder," 20.

49. Schechner, *The Future of Ritual*, 26–27.

50. Bado-Fralick and Norris, *Toying with God*, 151.

51. Kathryn McClymond, "That Can't Be Ritual – They're Having Fun!" AAR panel response, Washington, DC, November 19, 2006, in Bado-Fralick and Norris, *Toying with God*, 202 n50.

52. Gila refers to her participation in a Mormon communion in almost identical words.

53. Douglas, *In the Wilderness* and *Purity and Danger.*

54. Adler, "Travel as Performed Art," 1385.

55. Quiroga, "Characteristics of Package Tours in Europe."

56. Schieffelin, "Problematizing Performance," 195.

57. Hochschild, *The Managed Heart*, "Reply to Cas Wouters's Review Essay on *The Managed Heart*," and *The Commercialization of Intimate Life*; Crang, "Performing the Tourist Product," 152.

58. Stromberg, *Caught in Play.*

59. Schieffelin, "Problematizing Performance," 197.

60. In response to Wouters's critique ("The Sociology of Emotions and Flight Attendants") of Hochschild's *The Managed Heart* and her subsequent response, "Reply to Cas Wouters's Review Essay on *The Managed Heart*," I substitute "public" and "private" selves for "false" and "true" selves.

61. Hochschild, *The Managed Heart*, 213.

62. For similar observations on air hostesses, see Hochschild, *The Managed Heart* (1983); Wouters, "The Sociology of Emotions and Flight Attendants," 118–119.

63. Hochschild, *The Managed Heart*, "Reply to Cas Wouters's Review Essay on *The Managed Heart*," and *The Commercialization of Intimate Life*.

64. MacCannell, *The Tourist*.

65. My thanks to Michael diGiovine who insisted on an answer to this question, and to David Satran, Meirav Mack, and Adoram Schneidleder who helped me think this through.

66. E-mail correspondence with the author, August 20, 2012.

67. Gager, *The Origins of Anti-Semitism*, 3–13.

68. cf. Douglas, *Purity and Danger* and *In the Wilderness*.

69. Based on participant-observation of one of Steve's groups in 2005.

70. Based on an interview held with J.L., an American leader of one of Steve's groups in 2005.

## 7. Conclusion

1. See the literature survey and discussion on tourism and transformation in Sampaio, Simoni, and Isnart, "Tourism and transformation."

2. cf. Basu, "Root Metaphors of 'Roots-Tourism' in the Scottish Highland Diaspora,"167–172. Feldman, "Les voyages scolaire israeliens," 229–235.

3. Feldman, "Israeli Youth Voyages to Holocaust Poland."

4. Orsi, "When 2+2=5," 225.

5. cf. Ben-Yehuda, *The Masada Myth*; Zerubavel, *Recovered Roots*.

6. Nora, "Between Memory and History."

7. Cohen, "The Tourist Guide."

8. Cf. Wynn, *The Tour Guide*.

9. Among these are the marshaling of only the supporting facts as "evidences" for the truth of a Biblical text, and the obscuring of contradictory archaeological-historical facts by advancing spiritualizing explanations that ignore contradictions, while purporting to transcend them; Fine and Speer, "Tour Guide Performances as Sight Sacralization."

10. cf. Kaell, *Walking Where Jesus Walked*, 157–158.

11. Rothenberg, "Willful Overlooking."

12. This is a common problem in the field for anthropologists of religion at least since Levy-Bruhl and Evans-Pritchard (see, for example, van Dijk and Pels, "Contested Authorities and the Politics of Perception"), but the guiding situation imposes additional pressures and constraints. "They" may not read what "we" write, but as pilgrims, they usually hear what we say. For contextualization of sincere speech as a historically embedded Protestant value (rather than a universal moral one), see Keane, "Sincerity, 'Modernity,' and the Protestants."

13. Harding, *The Book of Jerry Falwell*, 59–60.

14. Geertz, *Works and Lives*, 92.

15. MacCannell, *The Tourist*.

16. Geertz, *Works and Lives*, 93.

17. This is another case of the constraint posed by the expectations of many Christian groups that the guide display Orthodox Jewish practice in order to be authentically

Jewish in their eyes. In this case, I projected these expectations onto the assistant bishop and acted accordingly.

18. After the Ayyubid conquest, Salah-ed-Din turned it into a *madrasa*, a school of Islamic learning. Later, under the Mamelukes, it became a stable, and in the nineteenth century, was given by Muhammad Ali to Louis Napoleon and the French government. They, in turn, had the White Fathers of Africa administer the site.

19. Turner, *The Ritual Process*, 30.

20. Bado-Fralick and Norris, *Toying with God*, 166–167.

21. Ibid., 130, 202n50.

22. Feldman, "Israeli Youth Voyages to Holocaust Poland."

23. Turner, "The Center out There."

24. Wheeler, "Models of Pilgrimage," 36.

25. Chidester and Linenthal, *American Sacred Space*, 17.

26. Lanfant, "International Tourism, Internationalization, and the Challenge to Identity," 36.

27. Bado-Fralick and Norris, *Toying with God*, 154–155.

# REFERENCES

*The Fathers According to Rabbi Nathan.* Translated by Judah Goldin. New Haven, CT: Yale University Press, 1990.

Abu El-Haj, Nadia. "Translating Truths: Nationalism, the Practice of Archaeology and the Remaking of Past and Present in Contemporary Jerusalem." *American Ethnologist* 25, no. 2 (1998): 166–188.

———. *Facts on the Ground: Archaeological Practice and Territorial Self-Fashioning in Israeli Society.* Chicago: University of Chicago Press, 2001.

———. "Producing (Arti) Facts: Archaeology and Power during the British Mandate of Palestine." *Israel Studies* 8 (2002): 33–61.

Aburaya, Issam. "Islamism, Nationalism and Western Modernity: The Case of Iran and Palestine." *International Journal of Politics, Culture and Society* 22, no. 1 (2009): 57–68.

Adler, Judith. "The Holy Man as Traveler and Travel Attraction: Early Christian Asceticism and the Moral Problematic of Modernity." In *From Medieval Pilgrimage to Religious Tourism: The Social and Cultural Economics of Piety*, edited by William H. Swatos Jr. and Luigi Tomasi, 25–50. Westport, CO: Praeger, 2002.

———. "Travel as Performed Art." *American Journal of Sociology* 94, no 6 (1989): 1366–1391.

Alberi, Dionigi. "Conclusion: Crossing the Frontiers between the Monotheistic Religions, an Anthropological Approach." In *Sharing Sacred Space in the Mediterranean: Christians, Muslims, and Jews at Shrines and Sanctuaries*, edited by Dionigi Alberi and Mari Coroucli, 219–244. Bloomington: Indiana University Press, 2012.

Almog, Oz. *The Sabra: The Creation of the New Jew.* Berkeley: University of California Press, 2000.

Amichai, Yehuda. *The Selected Poetry of Yehuda Amichai.* Edited and translated by Chana Bloch and Stephen Mitchell. Berkeley: University of California Press, 1996.

———. *Open, Closed, Open.* Jerusalem: Schocken Press (Hebrew), 1998.

Amir, Yehoshua. "Pilgrimage According to Philo." In *Pilgrimage: Jews, Christians, Muslims*, edited by Ora Limor and Elchanan Reiner, 110–121. Ra'anana: Open University (Hebrew), 2005.

Appadurai, Arjun, ed. *The Social Life of Things: Commodities in Cultural Perspective.* New York: Cambridge University Press, 1986.

Ariel, Yaakov. "In the Shadow of the Millennium: American Fundamentalism and the Jewish People." In *Studies in Church History* 29 (1992): 435–450.

Arieli, Shaul, and Michael Sfard. *Wall and Failure: Security or Greed?* Tel Aviv: Yediot Aharonot (Hebrew), 2008.

Asad, Talal. "Anthropological Conceptions of Religion: Reflections on Geertz." *Man* (n.s.) 18, no. 2 (1983): 237–259.

Ateek, Naim. "Walls of Separation." *Cornerstone* 29 (2003). http://www.sabeel.org /documents/cs29.pdf.

Augé, Mark. *Non-lieux, introduction à une anthropologie de la surmodernité.* La Librairie du XX$^e$ siècle, Paris: Seuil, 1995.

Bado-Fralick, Niki, and Rebecca Sachs Norris, eds. *Toying with God: The World of Religious Games and Dolls.* Waco, Texas: Baylor University Press, 2010

Badone, Ellen. "Crossing Boundaries: Exploring the Borderlands of Ethnography, Tourism and Pilgrimage." In *Intersecting Journeys: The Anthropology of Pilgrimage and Tourism,* edited by Ellen Badone and Sharon Roseman, 180–189. Urbana: University of Illinois, 2004.

Badone, Ellen, and Sharon Roseman, eds. *Intersecting Journeys: The Anthropology of Pilgrimage and Tourism.* Urbana: University of Illinois, 2004.

Bajc, Vida. "Creating Ritual through Narrative, Place and Performance in Evangelical Protestant Pilgrimage in the Holy Land." *Mobiliites* 2, no. 3 (2007): 395–412.

Banksy. *Wall and Piece.* London: Random House, 2006.

Bar, Doron, and Kobi Cohen-Hattab. "A New Kind of Pilgrimage: The Modern Tourist Pilgrim of 19th-Century and Early 20th-Century Palestine." *Middle East Studies* 39, no. 2 (2003): 131–148.

Barth, Fredrik. *Political Leadership among the Swat Pathans.* 1965. Oxford and New York: Berg, 2004.

Basu, Paul. *Highland Homecomings: Genealogy and Heritage Tourism in the Scottish Diaspora.* New York: Routledge, 2007.

———. "Root Metaphors of 'Roots-Tourism' in the Scottish Highland Diaspora." In *Reframing Pilgrimage: Cultures in Motion,* edited by Simon Coleman and John Eade, 150–174. New York: Routledge, 2004.

Baudrillard, Jean. *Seduction.* 1979. New York: New World Perspectives, 1990.

Bauman, Zygmunt. "From Pilgrim to Tourist – or a Short History of Identity." In *Questions of Cultural Identity,* edited by Stuart Hall and Paul du Gay, 18–16. London: Sage, 1996.

Bax, Mart. "Female Suffering, Local Power Relations, and Religious Tourism: A Case Study from Yugoslavia." *Medical Anthropology Quarterly, New Series* 6, no. 2 (1992): 114–127.

Beaulieu, Mary-Anne. "On demande de pélerins, pas des touristes." *La Terre Sainte* 616 (2011): 360.

Belhassen, Yaniv. "Fundamentalist Christian Pilgrimages as a Political and Cultural Force." *Journal of Heritage Tourism* 4, no. 2 (2009): 131–144.

Belhassen, Yaniv, and C. A. Santos. "An American Evangelical Pilgrimage to Israel: A Case Study on Politics and Triangulation." *Journal of Travel Research* 44, no. 4 (2006): 431–441.

Belhassen, Yaniv, and Jonathan Ebel. "Tourism, Faith and Politics in the Holy Land: An Ideological Analysis of Evangelical Pilgrimage." *Current Issues in Tourism* 12, no. 4 (2009): 359–378.

Ben-Ami, Issachar. *Saint Veneration among the Jews in Morocco.* 1984. Detroit: Wayne State University Press, 1998.

Ben-Amos, Dahn, and Netivah Ben-Yehuda. World Dictionary of Spoken Hebrew. Jerusalem: A. Levin-Epstein (Hebrew), 1972.

Ben-Arieh, Yehoshua. *The Rediscovery of the Holy Land in the Nineteenth Century.* Jerusalem: Magnes Press, Detroit: Wayne State University Press, 1979.

———. "Perceptions and Images of the Holy Land." In *The Land that Became Israel*, edited by Ruth Kark, 37–53. Berkeley: University of California Press, 1989.

Benvenisti, Meron. *City of Stone: The Hidden History of Jerusalem*. Berkeley: University of California Press, 1996.

———. "The Hebrew Map." *Theory and Criticism* 11: 7–29 (Hebrew), 1997.

Ben-Yehuda, Nachman. *The Masada Myth: Collective Memory and Mythmaking in Israel*. Madison: University of Wisconsin Press, 1995.

Bielo, James, ed. *The Social Life of Scriptures: Cross-Cultural Perspectives on Biblicism*. New Brunswick, NJ: Rutgers University Press, 2009.

Bilu, Yoram. "The Inner Limits of Communitas." *Ethos* 16, no. 3 (1988): 227–352.

Bird-David, Nurit, and Asaf Darr. "Commodity, Gift and Mass-Gift: On Gift-Commodity Hybrids in Advanced Mass Consumption Cultures." *Economy and Society* 38, no. 2 (2009): 304–325.

———. "Mass-Gift: On Market Giving in Advanced Capitalist Societies." In *Economic Persuasions*, edited by Stephen Gudeman, 118–135. New York: Berghahn, 2009.

Bishara, Amahl. "Covering the Barrier in Bethlehem: The Production of Sympathy and the Reproduction of Difference." In *The Anthropology of News and Journalism: Global Perspectives*, edited by Elizabeth Bird, 54–70. Bloomington: Indiana University Press, 2009.

Black, Annabel. "Negotiating the Tourist Gaze: The Example of Malta." In *Coping with Tourists: European Reactions to Mass Tourism*, edited by Jeremy Boissevain, 112–140. Oxford: Berghahn Books, 2000.

Blau, Peter. *Exchange and Power in Social Life*. New York: Transaction, 1964.

Bloch, Maurice. "The Symbolism of Money in Imerina." In *Money and the Morality of Exchange*, edited by Maurice Bloch and Jonathan Parry, 165–190. New York: Cambridge University Press, 1989.

Boissevain, Jeremy. "Ritual, tourism and cultural commoditization in Malta: Culture by the Pound." In *The Tourist Image: Myths and Myth Making in Tourism*, edited by Tom Selwyn, 105–120. Chichester: Wiley, 1996.

Bourdieu, Pierre. *Outline of a Theory of Praxis*. Cambridge: Cambridge University Press, 1977.

Bowman, Glenn. "Unholy Struggle on Holy Ground: Conflict and Interpretation in Jerusalem." *Anthropology Today* 2, no. 3 (1986): 14–17.

———. "The Politics of Tour Guiding: Israeli and Palestinian Guides in Israel and the Occupied Territories." In *Tourism and the Less-Developed Countries*, edited by David Harrison, 121–134. London: Belhaven, 1992.

———. "Pilgrim Narratives of Jerusalem and the Holy Land: A Study in Ideological Distortion." In *Sacred Journeys: The Anthropology of Pilgrimage*, edited by E. Alan Morinis, 149–168. Westport, CT: Greenwood, 1992.

———. "Nationalizing and Denationalizing the Sacred: Shrines and Shifting Identities in the Israeli-Occupied Territories." *Man: The Journal of the Royal Anthropological Institute* 28, no. 3 (1993): 431–460.

———. "Passion, Power and Politics in a Palestinian Tourist Market." In *The Tourist Image: Myths and Myth Making in Tourism*, edited by Tom Selwyn, 83–103. Chichester, UK: Wiley, 1996.

———. "Christian Ideology and the Image of a Holy Land: The Place of Jerusalem Pilgrimage in the Various Christianities." 1991. In *Contesting the Sacred: The Anthro-*

*pology of Christian Pilgrimage*, edited by John Eade and Michael Sallnow, 98–121. Urbana: Illinois University Press, 2000.

———. "Viewing the Holy City: An Anthropological Perspectivalism." *Jerusalem Quarterly* 31 (2007): 27–39.

———. "In Dubious Battle on the Plains of Heav'n': The Politics of Possession in Jerusalem's Holy Sepulchre." *History and Anthropology* 22, no. 3 (2011): 371–399.

———. "Nationalizing and Denationalizing the Sacred: Shrines and Shifting Identities in the Israeli-Occupied Territories." In *Sacred Space in Israel and Palestine: Religion and Politics*, edited by Yitzhak Reiter, Marshall Breger and Leonard Hammer, 195–227. London and New York: Routledge, 2012.

———. "A Weeping on the Road to Bethlehem: Contestation over the Uses of Rachel's Tomb." *Religion Compass* 7, no.3 (2013): 79–92.

Box, George, ed. and trans. *Philonis Alexandrini in Flaccu.* London: Oxford University Press, 1939.

Breger, Marshall, Yitchak Reiter, and Leonard Hammer, eds. *Sacred Space in Israel and Palestine: Religion and Politics.* New York: Routledge, 2012.

Brin, Eldad. "Politically-Oriented Tourism in Jerusalem." *Tourist Studies* 6, no. 3 (2006): 215–243.

Brown, David. "Genuine Fakes." In *The Tourist Image: Myths and Myth Making in Tourism*, edited by Tom Selwyn, 33–47. Chichester, UK: Wiley, 1996.

Brown, Peter. *The Cult of the Saints: Its Rise and Function in Latin Christianity.* Chicago: University of Chicago Press, 1982.

Bruner, Edward. "Transformation of Self in Tourism." *Annals of Tourism Research* 18 (1991): 238–250.

———. "The Ethnographer/Tourist in Indonesia." In *International Tourism: Identity and Change*, edited by Marie Francoise Lanfant, John B. Allcock and Edward M. Bruner, 224–241. Thousand Oaks, California: Sage, 1995.

———. *Culture on Tour: Ethnographies of Travel.* Chicago: University of Chicago Press, 2005.

Bruner, Edward, with Phyllis Gorfain. "Dialogic Narration and the Paradoxes of Masada." In *Culture on Tour: Ethnographies of Travel*, 169–188. Chicago: University of Chicago Press, 2005.

Butler, Suellen, and James K. Skipper Jr. "Working for Tips: An Examination of Trust and Reciprocity in A Secondary Relationship of the Restaurant Organization." *The Sociological Quarterly* 22 (1981): 15–27.

Candea, Matei, and Giovanni da Col. "The Return to Hospitality." *Journal of the Royal Anthropological Institute* (n.s.) (2012): S1–S19.

Cardman, Francis. "The Rhetoric of Holy Places: Palestine in the Fourth Century." *Studia Patristica* 17 (1982): 18–25.

Carsten, Janet. "Cooking Money: Gender and the Symbolic Transformation of Means of Exchange in a Malay Fishing community." In *Money and the Morality of Exchange*, edited by Jonathan Parry and Maurice Bloch, 117–141. Cambridge: Cambridge University Press, 1989.

Casey, Edward. *Remembering: A Phenomenological Study.* Bloomington: Indiana University Press, 1987.

Cheal, David. "Showing Them You Love Them': Gift Giving and the Dialectic of Intimacy." *Sociological Review* 35 (2011): 150–169.

Chidester, David, and Edward T. Linethal, eds. *American Sacred Space*. Bloomington and Indianapolis: Indiana University Press, 1995.

Clarke, Richard. "Self-Presentation in a Contested City: Palestinian and Israeli Political Tourism in Hebron." *Anthropology Today* 16, no. 5 (2000): 12–18.

Cohen, Erik. "Towards a Sociology of International Tourism." *Social Research* 39, no. 1 (1972): 164–182.

———. "A Phenomenology of Tourist Experiences." *Sociology* 13, no. 2 (1979): 179–201.

———. "The Tourist Guide – The Origins, Structure and Dynamics of a Role." *Annals of Tourism Research* 12, no. 1 (1985): 5–29.

———. "Pilgrimage and Tourism: Convergence and Divergence." In *Sacred Journeys: The Anthropology of Pilgrimage*, edited by Alan Morinis, 47–61. Westport: Greenwood, 1992.

———. "Tourism and Religion: A Comparative Perspective." *Pacific Tourism Review* 2 (1998): 1–10.

Cohen, Raymond. *Saving the Holy Sepulchre: How Rival Christians Came Together to Rescue their Holiest Shrine*. New York: Oxford University Press, 2008.

Cohen-Hattab, Kobi. "Zionism, Tourism, and the Battle for Palestine: Tourism as a Political-Propaganda Tool." *Israel Studies* 9, no. 1 (2004): 61–85.

Coleman, Simon. "Mary on the Margins? The Modulation of Marian Imagery in Place, Memory, and Performance." In *Moved by Mary: The Power of Pilgrimage in the Modern World*, edited by Anna-Karina Hermkens, Willy Jansen, and Catrien Notermans, 17–32. Farnham: Ashgate, 2009.

———. "The Charismatic Gift." *Journal of the Royal Anthropological Institute* (n.s.) 10 (2004): 421–442.

———. "Do You Believe in Pilgrimage? Communitas, Contestation and Beyond." *Anthropological Theory* 2, no. 3 (2002): 355–368.

Coleman, Simon, and John Eade. "Introduction: Reframing Pilgrimage." In *Reframing Pilgrimage: Cultures in Motion*, 1–25. New York: Routledge, 2004.

Collins-Kreiner, Noga, and Yael Zins. "With the Passing of Time: The Changing Meaning of Souvenirs." In *Tourism and Souvenirs: Glocal Perspectives from the Margins*, edited by Jenny Cave, Lee Jolliffe, and T. Baum, 29–39. Bristol: Channel View, 2013.

Collins-Kreiner, Noga, N. Kliot, Y. Mansfeld, and K. Sagi. *Christian Tourism to the Holy Land: Pilgrimage during Security Crisis*. Aldershot: Ashgate, 2006.

Crang, Philip. "Performing the Tourist Product." In *Touring Cultures: Transformations of Travel and Theory*, edited by Chris Rojek, and John Urry, 137–154. New York: Routledge, 1997.

Culler, J. "Semiotics of Tourism." *American Journal of Semiotics* 1 (1981): 127–40.

Dahles, Heidi. "The Social Construction of Mokum: Tourism and the Quest for Local Identity in Amsterdam." In *Coping with Tourists: European Reactions to Mass Tourism*, edited by Jeremy Boissevain, 227–246. Oxford: Berghahn, 1996.

———. "The Politics of Tour Guiding – Image Management in Indonesia." *Annals of Tourism Research* 29, no. 3 (2002): 783–800.

Dann, Graham. "The People of Tourist Brochures." In *The Tourist Image: Myths and Myth Making in Tourism*, edited by Tom Selwyn, 61–82. Chichester: Wiley, 1996.

de Certeau, Michel. *The Practice of Everyday Life*. Berkeley: University of California Press, 1984.

Di Giovine, Michael. "The Imaginaire Dialectic and the Refashionig of Pietrelcina." In *Tourism imaginaries: Anthroplogical Approaches,* edited by Noel B. Salazar and Nelson H. H. Graburn, 147–171. New York and Oxford: Berghahn, 2014.

Di Giovine, Michael A., and David Picard. "Introduction." In *Astray: The Seductions of Pilgrimage,* Aldershott: Ashgate, 2015.

Diner, Dan. "Cumulative Contingency: Historicizing Legitimacy in Israeli Discourse." *History and Memory* 7 (1995): 147–170.

Douglas, Mary. *Purity and Danger: An Analysis of the Concepts of Pollution and Taboo.* 1966. London: Ark, 1984.

———. *In the Wilderness: The Doctrine of Defilement in the Book of Numbers.* Oxford: Oxford University Press, 2001.

Dulin, John. "Reversing Rupture: Evangelicals' Practice of Jewish Rituals and Processes of Protestant Inclusion." *Anthropological Quarterly,* 88, no. 3 (2015): 601–634.

Dzenovska, Dace. "Reply to Comments." *Social Anthropology* 22, no. 3 (2014): 300–305.

Eade, John, and Michael Sallnow, eds. *Contesting the Sacred: The Anthropology of Christian Pilgrimage* (second edition). Urbana: University of Illinois, 2000.

Edensor, Tim. *Tourists at the Taj: Performance and Meaning at a Symbolic Site.* London and New York: Routledge, 1998.

———. "Staging Tourism: Tourists as Performers." *Annals of Tourism Research* 27, no. 2 (2000): 322–344.

Eickelmann, Dale. *Moroccan Islam.* Dallas: University of Texas Press, 1976.

Eliade, Mircea. *The Sacred and the Profane: The Nature of Religion.* New York, Houghton Mifflin Harcourt, 1959.

Fabian, Johannes. *Time and the Other: How Anthropology Makes Its Object.* New York: Columbia University Press, 1983.

Fedele, Anna. *Looking for Mary Magdalene: Alternative Pilgrimage and Ritual Creativity at Catholic Shrines in France.* New York: Oxford University Press, 2013.

Feldman, Gregory. "Understanding Others: Agency and Articulation in a Historical Perspective." *Social Anthropology* 22, no. 3 (2014): 288–292.

Feldman, Jackie. "'A City that Makes All Israel Friends': Normative Communitas and the Struggle for Religious Legitimacy in Pilgrimages to the Second Temple." In *A Holy People: Jewish and Christian Perspectives on Religious and Communal Identity,* edited by Marcel Poorthuis and Joshua Schwartz, 109–126. Leiden: Brill, 2006.

———. "Israeli Youth Voyages to Holocaust Poland: Through the Prism of Pilgrimage." In *Redefining Pilgrimage: New Perspectives on Historical and Contemporary Pilgrimages,* edited by Antón M. Pazos, 87–101. Farnham, Surrey, UK: Ashgate, 2014.

———. "Contested Narratives of Storied Places – The Holy Lands." *Religion and Society: Advances in Research* 5 (2014): 106–127.

Feldman, Jackie, and Amos Ron. "American Holy Land: Orientalism, Disneyization, and the Evangelical Gaze." In *Orient – Orientalistik – Orientalismus: Geschichte und Aktualität einer Debatte,* edited by Burkhard Schnepel, Gunnar Brands, and Hanne Schönig, 151–176. Bielefeld: Transcript, 2011.

Fernandez, James. "Emergence and Convergence in some African Sacred Places." In *Anthropology of Space and Place: Locating Culture,* edited by Setha Low and Denise Lawrence-Zúñiga, 187–203. Malden, MA: Blackwell, 2003.

Festinger, Leon, Henry W. Riecken, and Stanley Schachter. *When Prophecy Fails: A Social and Psychological Study of a Modern Group That Predicted the End of the World.* Minneapolis: University of Minnesota Press, 1956.

Fine, Elizabeth C., and Jean Haskell Speer. "Tour Guide Performances as Sight Sacralization." *Annals of Tourism Research* 12 (1985): 73–95.

Fleischer, Aliza. "The Tourist behind the Pilgrim in the Holy Land." *Hospitality Management* 19 (2000): 311–314.

Foster, George M. "The Anatomy of Envy: A Study of Symbolic Behavior." *Current Anthropology* 13 (1972): 165–186.

Frey, Nancy Louise. *Pilgrim Stories: On and Off the Road to Compostella.* Berkeley: University of California Press, 1998.

Friedland, Roger, and Richard Hecht. "The Powers of Place." In *Religion, Violence, Memory and Place*, edited by J. Shawn Landres and Oren Baruch Stier, 18–36. Bloomington: Indiana University Press, 2006.

———. "Changing Places: Jerusalem's Holy Places in Comparative Perspective." *Israel Affairs* 5, no. 2/3 (1999): 200–225.

Friedman, Yvonne. "Francescinus of Pontremoli: A Pilgrim's Path to Pardon." *Franciscan Studies* 43 (1986): 279–297.

Friedman Yvonne, and Zeev Drori. "Between Warfare and Conflict Resolution: Pilgrimage and Politics in the Holy Land." In *Pilgrims and Politics: Rediscovering the Power of Pilgrimage*, edited by Antón Pazos, 55–68. Aldershot: Ashgate, 2014.

Gager, Paul. *The Origins of Anti-Semitism: Attitudes towards Judaism in Pagan and Christian Antiquity.* New York: Oxford University Press, 1985.

Geertz, Clifford. *The Interpretation of Cultures.* New York: Basic, 1973.

———. *Works and Lives: The Anthropologist as Author.* Stanford, CA: Stanford University Press, 1988.

Gelbman, Alon, and Dallen J. Timothy. "From Hostile Boundaries to Tourist Attractions." *Current Issues in Tourism* 13, no. 3 (2010): 239–259.

Geva, Aviva, and Arieh Goldman. "Satisfaction Measurement in Guided Tours." *Annals of Tourism Research* 18, no. 2 (1991): 177–185.

Goffman, Erving. *Interaction Ritual: Essays in Face-to-Face Behavior.* 1967. New York: Random House, 2005.

Goldman, Shalom. *Zeal for Zion: Christians, Jews, and the Idea of the Promised Land.* Chapel Hill: University of North Carolina Press, 2009.

Gordon, Beverly. "The Souvenir: Messenger of the Extraordinary." *Journal of Popular Culture* 20, no. 3 (1986): 135–146.

Gow, Peter. "Land, People, and Paper in Western Amazonia." In *The Anthropology of Landscape: Perspectives on Place and Space*, edited by Eric Hirsch and Michael O'Hanlon, 43–62. Oxford: Clarendon, 1995.

Graburn, Nelson. "Tourism: The Sacred Journey." In *Hosts and Guests: The Anthropology of Tourism*, edited by Valene Smith, 21–36. Philadelphia: University of Pennsylvania Press, 1989.

Greenberg, Gershon. *The Holy Land in American Religious Thought 1620–1948.* Lanham, MD: University Press of America, 1993.

Greenberg, Rafi. "Towards an Inclusive Archaeology in Jerusalem: The Case of Silwan/the City of David." *Public Archaeology* 8, no. 1 (2009): 35–50.

Greenwood, Davydd. "Culture by the Pound: An Anthropological Perspective on Tourism as Cultural Commoditization." In *Hosts and Guests: The Anthropology of Tourism*, edited by Valene L. Smith, 171–182. Philadelphia: University of Pennsylvania, 1989.

Gurevitch, Zali. "The Double Site of Israel." In *Grasping Land: Space and Place in Contemporary Israeli Discourse and Experience*, edited by Eyal Ben-Ari and Yoram Bilu, 203–216. Albany: SUNY Press, 1997.

Guter, Yael, and Jackie Feldman. "Holy Land Pilgrimage as a Site of Inter-Religious Encounter." *Studia Hebraica* 6 (2006): 87–93.

Halbwachs, Maurice. *La topographie légendaire des Évangiles en Terre sainte: Étude de mémoire collective*. Paris: Presses Universitaires de Paris, 1941.

———. "The Sacred Topography of the Gospels." 1941. In *On Collective Memory*, 193–235. Chicago: University of Chicago Press, 1992.

Halevi, Masha. "An Italian Nationalist and a Religious Artist: Antonio Berluzzi and his Activities for the Promotion of Italian Interests in the Holy Land." *Kathedra* 144 (2012): 75–106 (Hebrew).

Handel, Ariel. "Exclusionary Surveillance and Spatial Uncertainty in the Occupied Palestinian Territories." In *Surveillance and Control in Israel/Palestine; Population, Territory and Power*, edited by Elia Zureik, David Lyon, and Yasmeen Abu-Laban, 259–275. New York: Routledge, 2011.

Handelman, Don. "Introduction: Why Ritual in Its Own Right? How So?" *Social Analysis* 48, no. 2 (2004): 1–32.

———. *Models and Mirrors: Toward an Anthropology of Public Events*. 1990. New York and Oxford: Berghahn, 1998.

Handelman, Don, and Elihu Katz. "State Ceremonies of Israel – Remembrance Day and Independence Day." 1990. In *Models and Mirrors: Toward an Anthropology of Public Events*, edited by Don Handelman, 190–233. New York and Oxford: Berghahn, 1998.

Harding, Susan Friend. *The Book of Jerry Falwell: Fundamentalist Language and Politics*. Princeton, NJ: Princeton University Press, 2000.

Harkin, Michael. "Modernist Anthropology and the Tourism of the Authentic." *Annals of Tourism Research* 22, no. 3 (1996): 650–670.

Havkin, Shira. *The Reform of Israeli Checkpoints: Outsourcing, Commodification, and Redeployment of the State*. Les Etudes du CERI – n° 174 bis (2011): 3–37.

Haynes, Stephen R. *Reluctant Witnesses: Jews and the Christian Imagination*. Louisville, KY: Westminster John Knox, 1995.

Hendry, Joy. *Wrapping Culture: Politeness, Presentation, and Power in Japan and Other Societies*. Gloucestershire: Clarendon, 1995.

Hercbergs, Dana. "Narrating Instability: Political Detouring in Jerusalem." *Mobilities* 12 (2012): 1–24.

Hermkens, Anna-Karina, Willy Jansen, and Catrien Notermans, eds. *Moved by Mary: The Power of Pilgrimage in the Modern World*. Farnham UK: Ashgate, 2009.

Herzfeld, Michael. "Spatial Cleansing: Monumental Vacuity and the Idea of the West." *Journal of Material Culture* 11, nos. 1–2 (2006): 127–149.

Hochschild, Arlie Russell. *The Managed Heart: Commercialization of Human Feeling*. Berkeley: University of California Press, 1983.

———. "Reply to Cas Wouters's Review Essay on T*the Managed Heart*." *Theory, Culture and Society* 6 (1989): 439–445.

———. *The Commercialization of Intimate Life: Notes from Home and Work.* Berkeley: University of California Press, 2003.

Hollander, Paul. *Political Pilgrims: Western Intellectuals in Search of the Good Society.* Piscataway, NJ: Transaction, 1997.

Holloway, John Christopher. "Between Gratitude and Gratuity: Commentary on Shamir." *Annals of Tourism Research* 12 (1985): 239–242.

———. "The Guided Tour – A Sociological Approach." *Annals of Tourism Research* 8, no. 3 (1981): 377–402.

Hummel, Ruth, and Thomas Hummel. *Patterns of the Sacred: English Protestant and Russian Orthodox Pilgrims of the Nineteenth Century.* London: Scorpion Cavendish (with the Swedish Christian Study Center, Jerusalem), 1995.

Hunt, Edward David. *Holy Land Pilgrimage in the Later Roman Empire: AD 312–460.* Oxford: Oxford University Press, 1984.

Isaac, Rami Khalil. "Alternative Tourism: Can the Segregation Wall in Bethlehem be a Tourist Attraction?" *Tourism and Hospitality Planning & Development* 6, no. 3 (2009): 247–254.

———. "Alternative Tourism: New Forms of Tourism in Bethlehem for the Palestinian Tourism Industry." *Current Issues in Tourism* 13, no. 1 (2010): 21–36.

Israel, Ministry of Tourism website. Accessed August 28, 2015. http://www.tourism.gov.il/GOVheb/Ministry%20of%20Tourism/MoreyDerech/Pages/default.aspx.

Jackson, John B. *The Necessity for Ruins and other Topics.* Amherst: University of Massachusetts Press, 1980.

Jacoby, David. "The Franciscans, the Jews and the Problem of Mount Zion during the Fifteenth Century: A Reappraisal." *Cathedra* 39 (1986): 51–70. (Hebrew).

Jeremias, Joachim. *Heiligen Gräber im Jesu Umwelt: Eine Untersuch ung zur Volksreligion der Zeit Jesu.* Göttingen: Vanderhoeck und Ruprecht, 1958.

Justen, David, and Peter Hocken. *The Messianic Jewish Movement: An Introduction.* Toward Jerusalem Council 2 (2004): (n.p.).

Kaell, Hillary. "American Christian Holy Land Pilgrimage in the Post-war Period." Ph.D. diss., Harvard University, 2010.

———. "Of Gifts and Grandchildren: American Holy Land Souvenirs." *Journal of Material Culture* 17, no. 2 (2012): 133–151.

———. "Evangelical Ketubah, Messianic Mezuzah: Judaica for Christians." Religion and Politics, March 12, 2013. http://religionandpolitics.org/2013/03/12/evangelical-ketubah-messianic-mezuzah-judaica-for-christians/.

———. *Walking Where Jesus Walked: American Christians and Holy Land Pilgrimage.* New York: New York University Press, 2014.

———. "Age of Innocence: The Symbolic Child and Political Conflict on American Holy Land Pilgrimage." *Religion and Society* 5 (2014): 157–172.

Kallus, Rachel. "The Political Construct of the 'Everyday': The Role of Home in Making Place and Identity." In *Constructing a Sense of Place: Architecture and the Zionist Discourse*, edited by Haim Yacobi, 136–161. Aldershot: Ashgate, (2004).

Kapferer, Bruce. *Legends of People, Myths of State: Violence, Intolerance and Political Change in Sri Lanka and Australia*, 1988. Washington, DC: Smithsonian Institution, 2000.

Katriel, Tamar. "Touring the Land: Trips and Hiking as Secular Pilgrimages in Israeli Culture." *Jewish Ethnology and Folklore Review* 17, nos. 1–2 (1995): 6–13.

———. *Performing the Past: A Study of Israeli Settlement Museums*. Mahwah, New Jersey: Lawrence Erlbaum, 1997.

Katz, Shaul. "The Israeli Teacher-Guide: The Emergence and Perpetuation of a Role." *Annals of Tourism Research* 12, no. 1 (1985.): 49–72.

Keane, Webb. "Sincerity, 'Modernity,' and the Protestants." *Cultural Anthropology* 17, no. 1 (2002): 65–92.

Kellner, Douglas. "Jean Baudrillard." In *The Blackwell Companion to Major Contemporary Social Theorists*, edited by George Ritzer, 310–332. New York: Wiley-Blackwell, 2003.

Kelner, Shaul. *Tours that Bind: Diaspora, Pilgrimage, and Israeli Birthright Tourism*. New York: New York University Press, 2010.

Kershner, Isabel. *Barrier: The Seam of the Israeli-Palestinian Conflict*. New York: Palgrave Macmillan, 2005.

Khazzoom, Aziza. "The Great Chain of Orientalism: Jewish Identity, Stigma Management, and Ethnic Exclusion in Israel." *American Sociological Review* 68, no. 4 (2003): 481–510.

Kimmerling, Baruch."Academic History Caught in the Cross-Fire: The Case of Israeli-Jewish Historiography." *History and Memory* 7, no. 1 (1995): 41–65.

Knott, Kim. "Religion, Space, and Place: The Spatial Turn in Research on Religion." *Religion and Society* 1 (2010): 29–43.

Koepping, Klaus-Peter, ed. "The Ludic as Creative Disorder: Framing, de-Framing and Boundary Crossing." In *The Games of God and Man*, 1–39. Hamburg: LIT, 1997.

Kopytoff, Igor. "The Cultural Biography of Things: Commoditization as Process." In *The Social Life of Things: Commodities in Cultural Perspective*, edited by Arjun Appadurai, 64–91. New York: Cambridge University Press, 1986.

Kosansky, Oren. "Tourism, Charity and Profit: The Movement of Money in Moroccan Jewish Pilgrimage." *Cultural Anthropology* 17, no. 3 (2002): 359–400.

Lanfant, Mary Francoise. "International Tourism, Internationalization, and the Challenge to Identity." In *International Tourism: Identity and Change*, edited by Marie Francoise Lanfant, John B. Allcock and Edward M. Bruner. Thousand Oaks, CA: Sage; *Studies in International Sociology* 47 (1995): 24–43.

Lefebvre, Henri. *The Production of Space*. Oxford, UK, and Cambridge, MA: Basil Blackwell, 1991.

Leite, Naomi. "Locating Imaginaries in the Anthropology of Tourism." In *Tourism Imaginaries: Anthropological Approaches*, 260–278. Oxford: Berghahn, 2014.

Liebman, Charles and Eliezer Don-Yehiya. *Civil Religion in Israel,* University of California Press, Berkeley, 1983

Limor, Ora. "Christian Sacred Space and the Jew." In *Witness to Witchcraft: Jews and Judaism in Medieval Christian Thought*, edited by Jeremy Cohen. Wiesbaden: Otto Harrassowitz; *Wolfenbutteler Mittelalter-Studien* 11 (1996): 55–77.

———. "Christian Sanctity – Jewish Authority." *Kathedra* 80 (1996): 31–62. (Hebrew).

Lock, Charles. "Bowing Down to Wood and Stone: One Way to Be a Pilgrim." In *Pilgrim Voices: Authorizing Christian Pilgrimage*, edited by Simon Coleman and John Elsner, 110–132. New York: Berghahn, 2003.

Long, Burke O. *Imagining the Holy Land: Maps, Models and Fantasy Travel*. Bloomington: Indiana University Press, 2003.

Lowe, Donald. *A History of Bourgeois Perception*. Brighton, UK: Harvester, 1982.

Lowe, Malcolm, and Petra Heldt. "Theological Significance of the Rebirth of the State of Israel: Different Christian Attitudes." *Immanuel* 22–23 (1989): 133–145.

Luhrmann, Tanya. "Metakinesis: How God Becomes Intimate in Contemporary U.S. Christianity." *American Anthropologist* 106, no. 3 (2004): 518–528.

Lynn, Michael. "National Character and Tipping Customs: The Needs for Achievement, Affiliation, and Power as Predictors of the Prevalence of Tipping." *International Journal of Hospitality Management* 19 (2000): 205–210.

———. "National Personality and Tipping Customs." *Personality and Individual Differences* 28 (2000): 395–404.

MacCannell, Dean. *The Tourist: A New Theory of the Leisure Class.* New York: Schocken, 1976.

Malley, Brian. *How the Bible Works: An Anthropological Study of Evangelical Biblicism.* Walnut Creek, CA: Alta Mira, 2004.

Margry, Peter Jan, ed. "Secular Pilgrimage: A Contradiction in Terms?" In *Shrines and Pilgrimage in the Modern World: New Itineraries into the Sacred*, 13–46. Amsterdam: Amsterdam University Press, 2008.

Marcus, Itamar, and Nan Jacques Zilberdik. "PA art exhibit for Pope presents Palestinians as Jesus." *Palestine Media Watch.* Accessed August 29, 2015. http://palwatch.org/main.aspx?fi=157&doc_id=11523.

Markus, Robert. "How on Earth Could Places Become Holy? Origins of the Christian Idea of Holy Places." *Journal of Early Christian Studies* 2, no. 3 (1994): 257–271.

Mars, Gerald. *Cheats at Work: An Anthropology of Workplace Crime.* London: George Allen and Unwin, 1982.

Marvin, Carolyn, and David W. Ingle. *Blood Sacrifice and the Nation: Totem Rituals and the American Flag.* Cambridge, UK: Camridge University Press, 1999.

Maurer, Bill. "The Anthropology of Money." *Annual Review of Anthropology* 35 (2006): 15–36.

Mauss, Marcel. *The Gift: Forms and Functions of Exchange in Archaic Society*, translated by Ian Cunnison. New York: Norton, 1967.

McDannell, Colleen. *Material Christianity: Religion and Popular Culture in America.* New Haven and London: Yale University Press, 1995.

Menley, Anne. "The Accidental Pilgrims: Olive Pickers in Palestine." *Religion and Society* 5 (2014): 186–199.

Miller, Daniel. *Car Cultures: Materializing Culture.* London: Bloomsbury Academic, 2001.

Mitchell, Hildi J. "Postcards from the Edge of History: Narrative and the Sacralization of Mormon Historical Sites." In *Pilgrim Voices: Authorizing Christian Pilgrimage*, edited by Simon Coleman and John Elsner, 133–157. New York: Berghahn, 2003.

———. "'Being There': British Mormons and the History Trail." In *Reframing Pilgrimage: Cultures in Motion*, edited by John Eade and Simon Coleman, 26–43. New York: Routledge, 2005.

Mitchell, Jon P. "A Moment with Christ: The Importance of Feelings in the Analysis of Belief." *Journal of the Royal Anthropological Institute* (n.s.) 3, no. 1 (1997): 79–94.

Mitchell, Timothy. "The World as Exhibition." *Comparative Studies in Society and History* 31 (1989): 217–36.

Modlin, E. Arnold, Jr., Derek -. Alderman, and Glenn W. Gentry. "Tour Guides as Creators of Empathy: The Role of Affective Inequality in Marginalizing the Enslaved at Plantation House Museums." *Tourist Studies* 11 (2011): 3–19.

Monk, Daniel Bertrand. *An Aesthetic Occupation: The Immediacy of Architecture and the Palestine Conflict.* Durham, London: Duke University Press, 2002.

Moore, Helen. "The Pilgrimage of Passion in Sidney's Arcadia." In *Pilgrim Voices: Authorizing Christian Pilgrimage*, edited by Simon Coleman and John Elsner, 61–83. New York: Berghahn, 2003.

Morgan, David A., ed. "Introduction: The Matter of Belief." In *Religion and Material Culture: The Matter of Belief.* New York and London: Routledge, 2010.

Morinis, E. Allan, ed. "Introduction: The Territory of the Anthropology of Pilgrimage." In *Sacred Journeys, the Anthropology of Pilgrimage*, 1–27. Westport, CT: Greenwood, 1992.

Moscovitz, Talia. *Through the Wall – The West Bank Wall as Global Canvas.* Honors Junior/Senior Project, Northeastern University, 2010. Accessed January 1, 2010. http://ins.lib.neu.edu/honors-projects/54.

Nederveen-Pieterse, Jan. "The History of a Metaphor: Christian Zionism and the Politics of Apocalypse." *Archives de Sciences Sociales des Religions* 36 (1991): 75–103.

Ness, Sally Ann. *Where Asia Smiles: An Ethnography of Philippine Tourism.* Philadelphia: University of Pennsylvania Press, 2003.

Nolan, Mary Lee, and Sidney Nolan. *Christian Pilgrimage in Modern Western Europe.* Chapel Hill: University of North Carolina, 1989.

Nora, Pierre. "Between Memory and History: Les Lieux de Memoire." *Representations* 26 (1989): 7–25.

Noy, Chaim. "The Political Ends of Tourism: Voices and Narratives of Silwan/The City of David in East Jerusalem." In *The Critical Turn in Tourism Studies* (Routledge Advances in Tourism), edited by Irena Ateljevic, Annette Pritchard and Nigel Morgan, 27–41. New York: Routledge, 2007.

O'Guinn, Thomas, and Russell W. Belk. "Heaven on Earth: Consumption at Heritage Village, USA." *Journal of Consumer Research* 16 (1989): 227–238.

Obenzinger, Hilton. *American Palestine: Melville, Twain and the Holy Land Mania.* Princeton, NJ: Princeton University Press, 1999.

Olsen, Daniel. "Pilgrims, Tourists, and Max Weber's 'Ideal Types.'" *Annals of Tourism Research* 37, no. 3 (2010): 848–851.

Orsi, Robert. "When 2+2=5." *The American Scholar* (Spring 2007). Accessed January 26, 2014. http://theamericanscholar.org/when-2-25-/#.UuUABNL8Kt8.

———. "Abundant History: Marian Apparitions as Alternative Modernity." In *Moved by Mary: The Power of Pilgrimage in the Modern* World, edited by Anna-Karina Hermkens, Willy Jansen and Catrien Notermans, 215–225. Farnham, Surrey, UK: Ashgate, 2009.

Parry, Jonathan, and Maurice Bloch, eds. *Money and the Morality of Exchange.* New York: Cambridge University Press, 1989.

Paz, Alejandro. "Guiding Underground Jerusalem: The Voices of History in East Jerusalem Settler Tours." *Religion and Society* 5 (2014): 128–142.

Peebles, Gustav. "Filth and Lucre: The Dirty Money Complex as a Taxation Regime." *Anthropological Quarterly* 85, no. 4 (2012): 1229–1255.

Peteet, Julie. "The Writing on the Wall: The Graffiti of the Intifada." *Cultural Anthropology* 11, no. 2 (1996): 139–153.

Poloma, Margaret. *Main Street Mystics: The Toronto Blessing and Reviving Pentecostalism.* Lanham, MD: Alta Mira, 2003.

Pond, Kathleen. *The Professional Guide: Dynamics of Tour Guiding.* New York: Van Nostrand Reinhold, 1993.

Pratt, Mary Louise. *Imperial Eyes: Travel Writing and Transculturation.* New York: Routledge, 1996.

Preston, Robert. "Spiritual Magnetism: An Organizing Principle for the Study of Pilgrimage." In *Sacred Journeys: The Anthropology of Pilgrimage*, edited by E. Alan Morinis. Westport, CT: Greenwood, 1992.

Pritchard, Ray. "Remembering Jesus at the Garden Tomb." *Keep Believing* (blog), October 26, 2009. http://www.keepbelieving.com/2009/10/26/remembering-jesus-at-the-garden-tomb.

Pullan, Wendy. *The Struggle for Jerusalem's Holy Places.* New York: Routledge, 2013.

Quiroga, Isabel. "Characteristics of Package Tours in Europe." *Annals of Tourism Research* 17 (1990): 185–207.

Ram, Uri. "Zionist Historiography and the Invention of Jewish Nationhood: The Case of Ben Zion Dinur." *History and Memory* 7, no. 1 (1995): 91–124.

Raz-Krakotzkin, Amnon. "The Return to the History of Redemption (Or, What is the 'History' to which the 'Return' in the Phrase 'The Jewish Return to History' Refers)." In *Zionism and the Return to History*, edited by S. N. Eisenstadt and M. Lissak, 249–279. Jerusalem: Yad Ben-Zvi Press, 1998. (Hebrew).

Reader, Ian, and Tony Walter. *Pilgrimage in Popular Culture.* Basingstone: McMillan, 1993.

Reiter, Yithak, Marlen Eordegian, and Marwan Abu Khalaf. "Between Divine and Human: The Complexity of Holy Places in Jerusalem." In *Jerusalem: Points of Friction and Beyond*, edited by Moshe Maoz and Sari Nusseibeh, 95–164. The Hague: Kluwer Law International, 2000.

Renno, Pierre. "Looking Out for the Arabs: Mobilization in Favor of the Israeli-Arab Sector in the Galilean *Mitzpim* Hilltop Settlements." In *Civil Organizations and Protest Movements in Israel: Mobilization Around the Israel-Palestinian Conflict*, edited by Elisabeth Marteu, 145–162. New York: Palgrave McMillan, 2009.

Reuther, Rosemary Radford. "Western Christianity and Zionism." In *Faith and the Intifada: Palestinian Christian Voices*, edited by Naim Ateek, Marc Ellis and Rosemary Radford Reuther, 147–157. Mayknoll, New York: Orbis, 1992.

Richardson, Miles. "Being-in-the-Market versus Being-in-the-Plaza: Material Culture and the Construction of Social Reality in Spanish America." In *The Anthropology of Space and Place: Locating Culture*, edited by Setha M. Low and Denise Lawrence-Zúñiga, 74–91. Malden, MA: Blackwell, 2003.

Ritzer, George, and Allan Liska. "'McDisneyization' and 'Post-tourism': Complementary Perspectives on Modern Tourism." In *Touring Cultures: Transformations of Travel and Theory*, edited by Chris Rojek and John Urry, 96–109. New York: Routledge, 1997.

Robinson, Edward, and G. Smith. *Biblical Researches in Palestine, Mt. Sinai and Arabia Petrea: A Journal of Travels in the Year 1838.* Vol. 1–3. Boston: Crocker and Brewster, 1841.

Rodman, Margaret C. "Empowering Place: Multilocality and Multivocality." In *The Anthropology of Space and Place*, edited by Setha M. Low and Denise Lawrence-Zúñiga 204–223. Malden, MA: Blackwell, 2003.

Ron, Amos, and Jackie Feldman. "From Spots to Themed Sites – The Evolution of the Protestant Holy Land." *Journal of Heritage Tourism* 4, no. 3 (2009): 201–216.

Rothenberg, Celia E. "Willful Overlooking: Stories from the Islamic Diaspora and the Palestinian West Bank." *Anthropology and Humanism* 35, no. 1 (2010): 101–111.

Safrai, Shmuel. *Pilgrimage in the Second Temple Period*. Jerusalem: Akademon/Am Hasefer (Hebrew), 1965.

Said, Edward. *Orientalism*. New York: Random House, 1979.

———. *Culture and Imperialism*. New York: Vintage, 1994.

Salazar, Noel. *Envisioning Eden: Mobilizing Imaginaries in Tourism and Beyond*. New York and Oxford: Berghahn, 2010.

———. "Seducation: Learning the Trade of Tourist Enticement." In *Tourism and the Power of Otherness: Seductions of Difference*, edited by David Picard and Michael A. Di Giovine, 110–123. Bristol: Channel View, 2014.

Salazar, Noel, and Nelson Graburn, eds. *Tourism Imaginaries: Anthropological Approaches*. Oxford: Berghahn, 2014.

———. "Introduction: Toward an Anthropology of Tourism Imaginaries." In *Tourism Imaginaries: Anthropological Approaches*, 1–28. Oxford: Berghahn, 2014.

Sallnow, Michael J. "A Trinity of Christs: Cultic Processes in Andean Catholicism." *American Ethnologist* 9, no. 4 (1982): 730–749.

Sampaio, Sofia, Valerio Simoni, and Cyril Isnart. "Tourism and transformation: negotiating metaphors, experiencing change." *Journal of Tourism and Cultural Change* 12, no. 2 (2014): 93–101.

Satran, David. *Biblical Prophets in Byzantine Palestine: Reassessing the Lives of the Prophets*. Studia in Veteris Testamenti Pseudepigrapha, vol. 11, Leiden: Brill, 1995.

Schäubele, Michaela. "How History Takes Place: Sacralized Landscapes in the Croatian-Bosnian Border Region." *History and Memory* 23, no. 1 (2011): 23–61.

Schechner, Richard. *The Future of Ritual: Writings on Culture and Performance*. London and New York: Routledge, 1993.

Schieffelin, Edward L. "Problematizing Performance." In *Ritual, Performance, Media*, edited by Felicia Hughes-Freeland, 194–208. London and New York: Routledge, 1998.

Schmalz, Reuven Efraim, and Raymond Robert Fischer. *The Messianic Seal of the Jerusalem Church*. (n.d.). Accessed September 10, 2012. http://www.olimpublications.com/MessianicSeal.html.

Schmidt, Caroline. "The Guided Tour: Insulated Adventure." *Urban Life* 7, no. 4 (1979): 441–467.

Selwyn, Tom. "Landscapes of Liberation and Imprisonment: Towards an Anthropology of the Israeli Landscape." In *The Anthropology of Landscape: Perspectives on Place and Space*, edited by Eric Hirsch and Michael O'Hanlon, 114–134. Oxford: Clarendon, 1995.

———, ed. *The Tourist Image: Myths and Myth Making in Tourism*. Chichester, UK: Wiley, 1996.

———, ed. "Introduction." In *The Tourist Image: Myths and Myth Making in Tourism*, 1–32. Chichester, UK: Wiley, 1996.

———, ed. "Atmospheric Notes from the Fields: Reflections on Myth-Collecting Tours." In *The Tourist Image: Myths and Myth Making in Tourism*, 147–161. Chichester, UK: Wiley, 1996.

———. "An Anthropology of Hospitality." In *In Search of Hospitality*, edited by C. Lashley and A. Morrison, 18–37. Oxford: Butterworth-Heinemann, 2000.

Shamir, Boas. 1984. "Between Gratitude and Gratuity: An Analysis of Tipping." *Annals of Tourism Research* 11: 59–78.

———. 1985. "Reply to Holloway" *Annals of Tourism Research* 12: 242–245.

Shams, Alex. 2014. "Bethlehem Walls Transformed in The Presence of The Holy See." *Ma'an News Agency*, published Saturday 24.5.2014 (updated) 29.5.2014. Accessed August 8, 2014. http://www.maannews.com/eng/ViewDetails.aspx?ID=699704.

Shapiro, Faydra. "To the Apple of God's Eye: Christian Zionist Travel to Israel." *Journal of Contemporary Religion* 23, no. 3 (2008): 307–320.

——— "'Thank you Israel, for Supporting America': The Transnational Flow of Christian Zionist Resources." *Identities: Global Studies in Culture and Power* 19, no. 5 (2012): 616–631.

Shenhav-Keller, Shelly. "The Israeli Souvenir: Its Text and Context." *Annals of Tourism Research* 20, no. 1 (1993): 182–196.

Silberman, Neil Asher. "If I Forget Thee, O Jerusalem: Archaeology, Religious Commemoration and Nationalism in a Disputed City, 1801–2001." *Nations and Nationalism* 7, no. 4 (2001): 487–501.

Sizer, Stephen. 1994. "Visiting the Living Stones, Pilgrimages to the Un-Holy Land. An Investigation of the Perceptions of British and Palestinian Christians on the Subject of Pilgrimages to the Holy Land, with Particular Reference to their Impact on the Indigenous Anglican Church in Israel and the Occupied Territories." Submitted in part-fulfilment of the requirements of the degree of MTh in Applied Theology, University of Oxford.

———. "The Ethical Challenges of Managing Pilgrimages to The Holy Land." *International Journal of Contemporary Hospitality Management* 11, no. 2/3 (1999): 85–90.

Smith, George Adam. *The Historical Geography of the Holy Land*. 1894. Jerusalem: Ariel, 1966.

Smith, Jonathan Z. *To Take Place: Toward Theory in Ritual*. 1987. Chicago: University of Chicago Press, 1992.

Sönmez, Sevil F. "Tourism, Terrorism and Political Instability." *Annals of Tourism Research* 25, no. 2 (1998): 416–456.

Starrett, Gregory. "Religious Commodities in Cairo." *American Anthropologist* 97, no. 1 (1995): 51–68.

Stein, Rebecca. *Itineraries in Conflict: Israelis, Palestinians and the Political Lives of Tourism*. Durham and London: Duke University Press, 2008.

Stewart, Susan. *On Longing: Narratives of the Miniature, The Gigantic, The Souvenir, The Collection*. Durham and London: Duke University Press, 1993.

Stromberg, Peter G. *Language and Self-Transformation: A Study of the Christian Conversion Narrative*. Cambridge: Cambridge University Press, 1993.

———. *Caught in Play: How Entertainment Works on You*. Stanford: Stanford University Press, 2009.

Suetonius, Gaius. *The Twelve Caesars*, translated by Robert Graves. Harmondsworth: Penguin, 1957.

Taysom, Stephen. 2012. "Abundant Events or Narrative Abundance: Robert Orsi and the Academic Study of Mormonism " In *Dialogue: A Journal of Mormon Thought* 45, no. 4 2012): 1–26. Accessed January 1, 2014. https://www.dialoguejournal.com/archive/dialogue-premium-content/winter-2012/.

Thomas, Julian. "'The Politics of Vision' in Landscape: Politics and Perspectives." In *Landscape: Politics and Perspectives*, edited by Barbara Bender, 19–48. Providence and London: Berg, 1993.

Thompson, Thomas. *The Mythic Past: Archaeology and the Myth of Israel*. New York: Basic, 1999.

Tilley, Christopher. *A Phenomenology of Landscape*. Oxford: Berg, 1994.

Todd, Jane R. 1984. "Whither Pilgrimage: A Consideration of Holy Land Pilgrimage Today." In *Annales de la Commission des Pelerinages Chretiens*, 20–54. Jerusalem: Notre Dame Center.

Tuqan, Salim. 2009. "The Rise of Palestinian Graffiti." An Extract from *The Politics of Graffiti and Calligraphy of War, Art Dubai Journal*, January-February. Accessed January 29, 2010. http://www.artdubai.ae/journal/2009/february/Palestinian_Graffiti.html.

Turner, Edith. "Pilgrimage: An Overview." In *Encyclopedia of Religion*, Lindsay Jones, editor in chief, vol. 10, 7145–7148. Farmington Hills, MI: McMillan Reference–, 2005.

Turner, Victor. *The Ritual Process*. Chicago: Aldine, 1969.

———. "The Center out There: The Pilgrim's Goal." *History of Religions* 12 (1973): 191–230

———. *From Ritual to Theatre: The Human Seriousness of Play*. 1982. Cambridge, MA: PAJ, 2001.

Turner, Victor, and Edith Turner. *Image and Pilgrimage in Christian Culture*. Oxford: Oxford University Press, 1978.

Uriely, Natan, Y. Yonay, and D. Simchai. 2002. "Backpacking Experiences: A Type and Form Analysis." *Annals of Tourism Research* 29, no. 2 (2002): 520–538.

Urry, John. *The Tourist Gaze: Leisure and Travel in Contemporary Societies*. 1990. Reprinted with new appendixes. London: Sage, 2002.

———. *Consuming Places*. London: Sage, 1995.

van den Abbeele, Georges. "Sightseers: The Tourist as Theorist." In *Diacritics: A Review of Contemporary Criticism* 10, no. 4 (1980): 3–14.

van Dijk, Rijk A., and Peter Pels. "Contested Authorities and the Politics of Perception: Deconstructing the Study of Religion in Africa." In *Postcolonial Identities in Africa*, edited by Richard Werbner and Terrence Ranger, 245–270. London: Zed, 1996.

Van Zile, Dexter. 2007. "Sabeel's Demonizing Liturgy." Accessed August 24, 2014. http://www.camera.org/index.asp?x_context=2&x_outlet=118&x_article=1409.

Veldhuis, Henri. *The Wall Has Been Broken Down: The Israeli-Palestinian Conflict in the Light of Christian Faith and International Law*. Holland: Kairos Palestine Netherlands/Friends of Sabeel Netherlands, 2012. Accessed August 24, 2014. http://www.henriveldhuis.nl/LocalFiles/Israel_Palestijnen/Muur_afgebroken/The_Wall_has_been_broken_down.pdf.

Vessey, Mark, Sharon V. Betcher, Robert A. Daum, and Harry O. Maier, eds. *The Calling of the Nations: Exegesis, Ethnography, and Empire in a Biblical-Historic Present*. Toronto: University of Toronto Press, 2011.

Wagner, Donald. "Evangelicals and Israel: Theological Roots of a Political Alliance." *Christian Century*, November 4 (1998): 1020–1029.

Webber, Jonathan. 1985. "Religions in the Holy Land: Conflicts and Interpretations." *Anthropology Today* 1, no. 2 (1985): 3–10.

Weber. Timothy. *On the Road to Armageddon: How Evangelicals Became Israel's Best Friend*. Grand Rapids, MI: Baker, 2004.

Weizmann, Eyal. *Hollow Land: Israel's Architecture of Occupation.* London: Verso, 2007.

Wharton, Anabel Jane. *Selling Jerusalem: Relics, Replicas. Theme Parks*, Chicago: University of Chicago Press, 2006.

Wheeler, Bonnie. "Models of Pilgrimage: From Communitas to Confluence." *Journal of Ritual Studies* 13, no. 2 (1999): 26–41.

Wild, Robert. *Waiting for the Presence: Spirituality of Pilgrimage to the Holy Land.* Jerusalem: Franciscan Press, 1988.

Wouters, Cas "The Sociology of Emotions and Flight Attendants: Hochschild's *Managed Heart*." *Theory, Culture and Society* 3 (1989): 1–18.

Wuthnow, Robert. *After Heaven: Spirituality in America Since the 1950s.* Berkeley: University of California, 1998.

Wynn, Jonathan R. *The Tour Guide: Walking and Talking New York.* Chicago: University of Chicago Press, 2011.

Young, Donna. "'*The Empty Tomb*' as Metaphor: Finding Comfort in Nothingness." *Religion and Society* 5 (2014): 173–185.

Zaidman, Nurit, and Oded Lowengart. "The Marketing of Sacred Goods: Interaction of Consumers and Retailers." *Journal of International Consumer Marketing* 13, no. 1 (2001): 5–25.

Zelizer, Viviana. *The Social Meaning of Money.* Princeton: Princeton University Press, 1997.

———. "Fine Tuning the Zelizer View." *Economy and Society* 29 (2000): 383–389.

Zerubavel, Yael. *Recovered Roots: Collective Memory and the Making of Israeli National Tradition.* Chicago: University of Chicago Press, 1995.

Zilberman, Ifrah. "The Renewal of the Pilgrimage to Nabi Musa." In *Sacred Space in Israel and Palestine: Religion and Politics*, edited by Marshall Breger, Yitchak Reiter, and Leonard Hammer, 103–115. London and New York: Routledge, 2012.

Zimmerli, Walther. *A Commentary on the Book of the Prophet Ezekiel, Chapters 25–48*, translated by James D. Martin. Philadelphia: Fortress, 1983.

Zipperstein, Steven. "Ahad Ha'am and the Politics of Assimilation." In *Assimilation and Community: The Jews in Nineteenth-Century Europe*, 344–365. Cambridge: Cambridge University Press, 1992.

# INDEX

Abraham, 37, 68, 72–73, 123, 125–126, 148

Adler, Judith, 137

Ahad Ha'am, x, 9, 10

airport, 44, 53, 107, 113, 121, 136; security measures at, 11, 76, 163n64; Toronto Airport, 163n66. *See also* Ben Gurion Airport

*aliya* (immigration to Israel), 1, 9, 10

allochronicity, allochronism, 50, 57

Amichai, Yehuda, 24, 31–32

Amos Trust, 80, 83, 171n27

anti-Judaism, 127, 139

anti-Semitism, 3, 126–127, 139

apartheid wall. *See* Separation Wall

Arab market, 58–61, 107

Aramaic, 3, 99

archaeology, archaeologists, 56, 72, 145, 146, 148, 164n87, 171n21, 191n9; Israeli, 43, 55, 57; as "proof" of truth, 55, 56; Protestant, 41, 56, 57; replicas, 94; revealed, 38; sites, 14, 24, 28, 55, 69, 73; and tour guide course, 11, 25; Zionist projects, 56

Ateek, Naim, 167n30, 169n66

authenticity, 9, 146, 172n38; existential, 140, 142; and messianics, 97; and pilgrims, 3, 73, 98, 104, 119, 148

autoethnography, ix

Bado-Fralick, Niki, 153, 154

Badone, Ellen, 29

Bajc, Vida, 174n7

Banksy, 79, *79*, 168n60

Baptism, 133–135, *135*, 137, 176n49; Catholic, 123; sites, 24, 94, 133, 176n48

Barluzzi, Antonio, 24

Basu, Paul, 29

Baudrillard, Jean, 116

Bauman, Zygmunt, 116

BDS (boycott, disinvestment, sanctions movement), 69

Beit Sahour, 73, 74, 85, 87, 98, 160n117

Ben Gurion Airport, 37, 51, 54, 163n64, 173n66

Benvenisti, Meron, 167n35

Bethlehem, 12, 64–90, 111, 169n74, 179n53; in brochures and itineraries, 72–75; and buying souvenirs in, 98–103, 107; Christmas eve in, *78*; and commissions from purchases in, 106; and guides, 65–66, 67, 86, 169n73, 169n78, 174n77; pilgrimage economic impact, 34; and nativity sets, 94, 107. *See also* Separation Wall

Bible, 4, 19, 25, 165n107; attachment to, 16, 113, 153; authoritative text for groups, 53; Christian, 6, 146; conduit for direct contact with God, 49; education, 112; as embodied text, reading of, 62; group reading of, 4, 27, 54; and guides, 8, 20, 54, 62, 132; Hebrew, 8, 116, 124, 127, 132, 141; naming places through, 53; pastor reading from, *50*, 55, 176n46; and Protestants, 40, 44, 52; read as embodied text, 62; return to the, 56; stories, 8

Bible Land, 17, 19, 69, 90, 149; and Christian discourse, 28; guides, 37–39; Israel as, 63; itineraries for, 64; Judeo-Christian encounter in, 124, 140, 142; and pilgrim voyages, 19; shared Protestant-Israeli, 37–63. *See also* Holy Land

JACKIE FELDMAN is a senior lecturer in the Department of Sociology and Anthropology at Ben-Gurion University of the Negev. He is author of *Above the Death Pits, Beneath the Flag: Youth Voyages to Poland and the Performance of Israeli National Identity* and has published many articles on pilgrimage, Holocaust museums, and collective memory. A resident of Jerusalem, he has been a licensed tour guide in Israel for more than three decades.